BACKGROUND PAPERS FOR SOCIAL STUDIES TEACHERS

Leonard S. Kenworthy
Brooklyn College

Wadsworth Publishing Company, Inc.
Belmont, California

L. C. Cat. Card No.: 66-23797
Printed in the United States of America

Have you ever wished that you could quickly find a summary of the problems of today's urbanization or a resumé of the background of Scandinavia? Have you ever quizzed your colleagues about new devices for teaching the functions of federal government or probed for new ways to motivate student interest in geography? Have you ever searched for a brief, current list of biographies about the leaders of the new nations—and finally given up the futile search?

If you answer "yes" to any of these questions, you should find this book of Background Papers for Social Studies Teachers helpful. The title describes, in shorthand style, what the book is intended to provide. It was written to give ideas, background material, interpretations, methodology, and resources to pre- and in-service teachers.

In some instances, you may find all the information you need in the two pages devoted to a subject; in other cases, you will want to follow the leads those pages provide for further ideas, background, and source materials on the subject.

The papers contained in this volume are not lesson plans. I firmly believe that lesson plans should be tailored to meet the needs of a particular class. But the book does contain suggestions for social studies teachers to follow in planning lessons.

These Background Papers were originally prepared to assist student teachers in the social studies at Brooklyn College. Many of them needed an immediate source of data that they did not have and could not find quickly. Soon after I began to compile these sheets, cooperating teachers and other social studies teachers asked for copies, and I realized that they served a larger purpose than I had intended. For this reason, it seemed desirable to make them available in book form for teachers. Possibly, librarians will find the reading lists helpful in selecting books for both school and public libraries.

There are hundreds, even thousands of subjects on which background papers could be written. The ones I have selected for this volume represent subjects on which my student teachers have needed help or in which I have been especially interested. A few topics were included because of the lack of information about them elsewhere: for example, the biographical information about Dorothea Dix and Mary McLeod Bethune.

Six of the papers are general in nature; they form the first section of the book. Twenty-five papers on world history, 25 on world geography and world cultures, and 25 on United States history follow. Each of these major subjects forms a separate section. Finally, there are 14 papers on economics, 12 on government or civics, and 15 on contemporary affairs and problems. This arrangement roughly follows the courses that ordinarily appear in high school social studies curricula.

Teachers will find, however, that many of the Background Papers serve more than one course. For example, some of the material found under economics could have been grouped with United States history or contemporary problems. Some of the topics found in the contemporary affairs section could have been included with world geography. Teachers should, therefore, develop their own indexes and filing systems for these papers. The sheets are printed with perforated edges so that they can be removed from the book and filed in appropriate folders.

This book may be considered a companion volume to the writer's Guide to Social Studies Teaching in Secondary Schools (Wadsworth). In a sense, it is an amplification of that book. A few items appear in both books, but duplication is limited.

Some of the material in this volume is taken from other writings by the author. The sections on the United Nations, for example, are condensations of material that appeared in Telling the U.N. Story: New Approaches to Teaching about the U.N. and Its Related Agencies (Oceana

Press). Some of the data on Africa, the Middle East, and South America appeared first in the <u>World Study Guides</u> on those areas, published by the Teachers College Press of Teachers College, Columbia University.

Scores of people have helped in the preparation of this book. Special acknowledgment is made first to the student teachers in my classes of recent months and to their cooperating teachers. Professor Helen Storen and Professor Robert Edgar of Queens College suggested several volumes on Negroes that have proved of interest to junior high school readers. Professor Margaret Cormack and Professor Melvin Levison prepared the original materials on Hinduism and Judaism. Professors Campbell, Levison, and Watkins of Brooklyn College have helped me from time to time with suggestions on a number of these papers as well as serving as stimulating colleagues.

The American Education Press, the Civic Education Service, Scholastic Publications, the <u>Nation's Business</u>, the <u>New York Times</u>, <u>U.S. News & World Report,</u> and the Tennessee Valley Authority have all granted permission to use charts, maps, or other pictorial material in this volume.

To these, and others not mentioned, I owe a deep debt of gratitude. The final responsibility for anything that appears in printed form, however, rests with me alone.

I welcome comments and criticism on this volume. Should teachers want to submit Background Papers similar to those printed here, I would be delighted, and I assure them that any of their material used in future editions will be credited to them.

Leonard S. Kenworthy

Brooklyn College

Contents

World Geography and World Cultures

United States History

Economics

Government and Civics

Contemporary Affairs and World Problems

Addresses of Publishers and Organizations 245

Ferment in the Social Studies

There is more ferment in the social studies today than there has been for at least 25 years or, perhaps, during the entire life-span of public education in the United States. The reasons for this upheaval are varied and interrelated. Here are some of them.

1. The fear inspired by Sputnik and other Russian accomplishments.
2. The "explosion of knowledge" in many fields, including the social sciences (particularly the behavioral sciences).
3. New data on the learning process.
4. A renewed interest in the "structure" of the various social science disciplines.
5. A realization that we are living in a different kind of United States—urban, suburban, industrial, with more leisure time.
6. The increasingly large percentage of high school students going on to colleges and junior colleges.
7. The effects of curriculum changes in other fields, especially science and mathematics.
8. An awareness of the ineffective teaching in certain areas of social studies, such as geography and economics.
9. A realization that, although we are now living in an international community, the non-Western world has been woefully neglected in social studies courses.
10. The effects of automation.
11. A revived concern on the part of some learned societies and college professors with secondary school teaching.
12. The present-day social upheavals resulting from racial problems.

As a result of these and other factors, new programs are being suggested and tried, new research is being undertaken, and new pressures are being placed on the persons in charge of social studies curricula. Some of these changes are being introduced by national organizations in learned societies. Others are being brought about by the Project Social Studies of the U.S. Office of Education under the National Defense Act. Still others are being sponsored by local, county, state, and intersystem groups of schools.

Some innovations involve methodology. Examples:

1. Team teaching.
2. Programmed learning.
3. Role playing.
4. Use of source materials.
5. Use of "gaming."

Other changes affect curricula. Here are a few of the projects listed in the November 1963 issue of the N.E.A. Journal, with additions and corrections to bring the information up to date.

SOCIAL STUDIES

Greater Cleveland Social Science Program. Ethel K. Howard and George H. Baird. Rockefeller Building, Cleveland 13, Ohio.

Project Social Studies. Gerald R. Smith. Cooperative Research Program, U.S. Office of Education, Washington 25, D.C. (Research projects and curriculum improvement projects.)

ANTHROPOLOGY

Anthropology Curriculum Study Project. Malcolm Collier, Director. 5632 Kimbark Avenue, Chicago 37, Ill.

CIVICS

The Joint Committees on Civic Education. 11 West 42nd Street, New York, N.Y. 10036.

ECONOMICS

Economic Education Committee of the Southern States Work Conference. Marvin Lee, Chairman. College of Education, West Virginia University, Morgantown, W. Va.

Elkhart, Indiana Experiment in Economic Education. Lawrence Senash, Director. Department of Economics, Purdue University, West Lafayette, Ind.

GEOGRAPHY

Curriculum Guide Committee. Wilhelmina Hill, Chairman. National Council for Geographic Education, U.S. Office of Education, Washington 25, D.C.

High School Geography Project. Gilbert F. White, Director. 1201 16th Street, N.W., Washington 6, D.C.

HISTORY

Service Center for Teachers of History. Walter Rundell, Jr., Director. 400 A Street, S.E., Washington, D.C.

Seventeenth and Eighteenth Century Backgrounds of American History. Franklin Patterson, Junior High School Project Director. Social Studies and Humanities Project, Education Services, Inc., 12 Gordon Street, Cambridge, Mass.

World History Project. L. S. Stavrianos, Director, Department of History, Northwestern University, Evanston, Ill.

WORLD LAW

World Law Fund High School Materials and Teacher Education Project. Betty Reardon, Director. 11 West 42nd Street, New York, N.Y. 10036.

History All Around Us

To most students, history means something far away in time and space. Yet it should not mean only that—and should include recent events and nearby places.

Perhaps it would pay at the beginning of a history course to stop and think about the history contained in your classroom, in your school, in your neighborhood or community. In fact, you might want to do this at any time during the course. This is an ideal one-day lesson for substitute teachers who find no prescheduled assignment.

No matter how this approach is handled, the key question might be: "What history can you find in this room, in this building, in this community?" Or it could be phrased another way: "If you were writing the history of this room, what would you include?" The key question could be followed with questions about the building and the community.

The answers may come quickly. If not, you can suggest one or two, then ask for other examples. You can either list them quickly and then discuss them or discuss each topic briefly as it is suggested. Here are some "leads" for a discussion.

OUR   CLASSROOM   AND   SCHOOL

1. Where did the idea of writing paper and books originate?
2. What was window glass like in colonial days? How were changes made?
3. When was electricity harnessed? By whom? With what effects?
4. What is the history of the steel in our building? Who discovered the process which we now use? What effects?
5. What is the reason for the podiums in our classrooms? (They resemble pulpits in churches; the early schools were run by churches.)
6. What kind of heat do we use? Why? When was it developed? What effects has this kind of heat had on houses and factories?
7. What did people use before the invention of chalkboards or blackboards?
8. What is the importance of the name of our school? Why was it chosen? When?
9. What changes in thinking does the globe or world map in our room represent?
10. Why do we sit on chairs rather than on the floor as people do in some parts of the world? (Probably because of the climate rather than for comfort.)
11. In what style is our school building built? Why? Where did this style originate?
12. What is the history of the clothing we wear today?

13.

14.

15.

OUR SCHOOL PREMISES AND THE COMMUNITY

1. How old are the trees on our school grounds? What was going on in the United States when they were first planted?
2. Who lived on this land 100 years ago? 200 years ago? 500 years ago? What do we know about those people?
3. What flags are flying on our school building or on the school grounds? (These may include a city flag and/or a state flag as well as the United States flag, and possibly a United Nations flag.) What is the history of these flags?
4. What is the historic meaning of the name of our town?
5. How many streets in our city are named after Presidents? After other famous Americans? Do you know why our state is named as it is?
6. What schools are named for Presidents? For other famous Americans?
7. How many buildings can you name whose architecture originated in some other part of the world?
8. How many different religions are represented in our community? Where did those religions originate? Who were their leaders?
9. When did the idea of public libraries originate in our country? With what persons is this movement associated?
10. Where were the first houses in our community? Why were they built in that particular spot?
11. In which direction did the community first grow? Why?
12. From what countries have most of the inhabitants of this community come? Why did they come to this particular place?
13. What means of transportation were used 200 years ago in this community? 100 years ago? 50 years ago?
14. What are the two or three biggest changes in this community in the last 25 years? In the last 10 years? Why?

15.

16.

17.

18.

Once a class begins on a project like this, it will dream up many more topics than are listed here, if you are patient and allow the students time to glance around the room and think about the community.

The major aim is to show pupils or help them to discover for themselves that history is all around us. But there may be other results from such a lesson. For example, it might stimulate students to find out more about their school and community.

Importance of "Little People" in History

While reading some of the writings of Boris Pasternak, I came across the following brief but provocative quotation:

> No single man makes history. History cannot be seen, just as one cannot see grass growing.

Later I read this statement in Gustavson's <u>Preface to History</u>:

> ...the history that is reported to later generations is the extraordinary rather than the ordinary.

Certainly the same statement could be made about the people of history. History records the extraordinary individuals rather than the ordinary ones, the conspicuous rather than the inconspicuous.

However, it seems to me highly important for teachers in the social studies to examine from time to time the role of the "little people" and their contributions to civilization. Who are they? Here are a few random examples.

1. The men who constructed those giant monuments – the pyramids – in Mexico, in Egypt, and elsewhere.
2. The men who did the really hard work in erecting the Parthenon in Athens.
3. The men who worked on the magnificent cathedrals of Europe.
4. The men who accompanied the famous explorers on their voyages of discovery.
5. The immigrants to the United States who played with fate by crossing the ocean and settling here.
6. The men and women who defied the federal law and transported Negro slaves north in the "underground railroad."
7. The millions of Jews who died in concentration camps or in furnaces during the Hitler regime in Germany.
8. The million Arab refugees now living outside their homelands in refugee camps throughout the Middle East.

Of course, you could make a list many times this length. Possibly it would be a good idea to do so with your students at some point.

You might also collect pictures of monuments to some of the "nameless" people of history. Such pictures might include:

1. The monument along the National Road in the United States depicting a pioneer mother with her children huddled around the folds of her dress.

2. The Tomb of the Unknown Soldier in the Arlington National Cemetery in Arlington, Virginia, as well as similar monuments in other parts of the world.

5

You could develop a list of novels that portray some of these "little" or inconspicuous people of history. The five following volumes might serve as samples:

1. Pearl Buck's The Good Earth, for its descriptions of the common people of China, sympathetically and vividly told. Valuable even though times have changed in China.

2. Alan Paton's Cry the Beloved Country, for its poignant story of a Negro minister in South Africa, his son, and the white man that his son killed.

3. Erich Remarque's All Quiet on the Western Front, one of the best novels that has ever been written on war, depicting the life of common soldiers.

4. Ole E. Rolvaag's Giants in the Earth, for its story of the restless, rugged pioneer father and his stay-at-home wife, who wanted to remain in the settled country but joined in the western trek with her husband.

5. John Steinbeck's Grapes of Wrath, for its graphic presentation of the Okies in the migrant labor camps of California in the 1930s.

Don't be limited to this list. Scores of other novels can add an important and often neglected dimension to your teaching of history.

There are possibilities for using these techniques in any history course, whatever the place and time. The ideas apply equally well to the men and women of today who work in the local community, in the nation, and in the world—from the night watchmen, policemen, and firemen to the soldiers in the United Nations Emergency Force. Why not consider how you can include this vast multitude of the "nameless" of history in your course this term?

Problem Solving
or the Discovery Method

What are the key words in teaching—informing, inquiring, telling, and/or discovering? Confronted with such a question, most teachers can "get" the "right answer." Of course, teaching is encouraging pupils to inquire, to discover, to think.

But, in practice, far too many teachers proceed upon the assumption that teaching is telling or informing or imparting. Even many of the teachers who would like to stimulate thinking fall back upon the methods they have observed and experienced, especially in college classrooms.

In a typical lesson of the traditional type, the teacher writes the aim on the chalkboard. If the lesson is on imperialism, the class opens with the question "Who can define imperialism?" Or if the lesson is on Canada, the pupils are asked, "Why are we interested in Canada?" In truth, their interest hasn't been aroused and probably never will be. They will learn the names of places, products, and a few famous people, but they will gain little or no understanding of Canada.

Using this approach, a teacher merely scratches the surface, then plants a few seeds. Some of these may take root, especially in the minds of the brighter or more verbal students. But when harvest time (known as exam time) comes, such teachers are appalled at how little knowledge has flourished.

Good teachers plow up the soil a great deal deeper. They plant fewer seeds, but most of these take root. The immediate harvest is much more likely to be bountiful, the power to think in later life much more possible.

Almost any lesson can be planned as a problem-solving exercise. Whole units can be organized around a series of questions that the pupils raise. Even courses can be based upon the discovery method or problem solving (see Background Paper No. 59, Important Decisions in United States History). A world history course can focus on the various concepts people have had of "the good society" in different times and in different places. In economics, pupils can wrestle with a variety of problems based upon the central concept of unlimited wants versus limited resources, or on ways to increase and preserve available and potential resources.

Your first step in approaching the discovery method is to take tomorrow's lesson (or a whole unit) and work out ways in which pupils can be encouraged to think. The results may not show immediately if your pupils have been taught for years to memorize what is in the book and hand it back. But persist; try different methods; encourage your pupils; experiment. Then you will begin to teach.

There are many approaches that can help teachers to encourage inductive thinking, problem solving, or discovery. Here are some examples.

1. You are farmers in New England in the colonial period. Your farms are not yielding the crops you want. Ask why, then, "To what other occupations might you turn?" In the process of solving this question, you will have to examine a good many factors, such as the supply of trees, the possibilities of trade, the potentialities of fishing.

2. You bring a cartoon to class and show it through an opaque projector or have a student make a large copy of it in advance so that every pupil can see it. Perhaps it is Mauldin's famous cartoon of President Lincoln crying. You ask the class "What does this picture tell you?" From this, you can move in several directions: into a discussion of President Kennedy's assassination or of the civil-rights movement.

3. You come into class and pose as one of the Presidents or as some other person in history. You have a problem, and the pupils are your advisers. You discuss together how the problem can be solved, debating the merits of various proposals. This method can be used in many lessons. One variation is to serve as Secretary of State and ask for suggestions on a problem in foreign policy. Another is to ask the class to advise you (or an able student) in the role of the Secretary-general of the United Nations.

4. Ask students to bring to class various newspaper accounts of a particular event. The discussion would center about why each newspaper reported the event as it did. Similarly, you could compare different textbooks or several books covering the same subject.

5. You bring to class slips of paper bearing figures, such as $500 or $5000. Pass them to the students, then ask how they will invest their money. In this way, you will be more likely to discuss the stock market or other forms of investment realistically than you would in a straight question-answer lesson.

6. You place on the board a house marked "democracy" and discuss, in a day or over a period of several days, the most important foundation stones of a truly democratic society.

7. You draw a long line or a horseshoe-shaped line on the board to represent a continuum. On it, you place the different positions of political parties or organizations in any period or country you are studying. No—you get the pupils to place them!

8. You bring in two contradictory quotations on a man, a period, a problem, an issue, or a country. You get the pupils to line up the arguments for each of the two quotations and then decide between them—or reserve judgment for insufficient evidence!

9. You are studying the Mediterranean area but have not yet assigned reading on any particular country. You bring in pictures (perhaps from a National Geographic), on which the students spend a good part of the period figuring out the country.

10. You propose a Hall of Heroes for a period of history or a country and encourage the pupils to discuss who should be included—and why.

What examples can you add of methods you are now using—or could use—to encourage problem solving, discovery, thinking?

Scales as a Teaching Device

There are a few visual devices that can be used to advantage to foster learning in many social studies courses. The time-line is one of these. The volcano, pictured with gases as causes of the eruption, is another. The path of democracy and the process by which it became a wider road is a third. Although such devices should not be overused, they can be presented more than once in any given course, especially in world history or in United States history.

A set of scales is still another teaching device that lends itself to several uses and to several courses.

Any teacher can draw simple scales or a balance with a few strokes of chalk. Or he can ask a pupil who likes to draw to sketch a set of scales as his contribution to the class discussion. Some teachers might ask a person with construction ability to build scales for class use.

At the beginning of the period, you can ask the class how the scales should be drawn—and why. With slower students, actual weights can be placed in the pans or shown in the drawing to demonstrate the balance of power in a given place, at a given time, or in a given movement.

The discussion can then show how the balance changed in any particular movement or between two nations or alliances. A second drawing should describe the new balances.

This is a motivating and visualizing device that can be used throughout a period, or in two or three periods of class discussion, with the pupils telling the teacher what to do with the scales.

In slow classes, the teacher may want to stop the discussion after a short time so that each pupil can draw in his notebook what the class has developed on the chalkboard. There will be wider participation if the pupils in such classes do not write until after the discussion is complete. In other classes, students can either complete notebook drawings while the discussion proceeds or do it as homework.

Here are a few of the ways in which scales can be used.

1. In discussing the alliances in ancient Greece: Athens and Thebes versus Sparta in 377 B.C.; Thebes versus Athens and Sparta in 369 B.C.

2. In discussing the shifts in Europe from 1806 to 1815: France and Spain versus England, Russia, Prussia, and Austria in 1806; the balance achieved by the Congress of Vienna in 1815.

3. In examining the alliances during the periods before World Wars I and II and the shifts in those alliances: how were the various nations persuaded to join one side or the other?

4. In understanding the relative power of various nations in today's world: U.S.S.R. versus the United States; India versus China.

5. In analyzing the relative power of labor and management at different times in the United States and the shifts in their power over long periods of time.

6. In determining the balance between agriculture and industry in any given nation—for example, the relatively balanced economy of France.

7. In inquiring as to the public and private sectors of the economy of any nation.

8. In determining the relative strength of the colonists and the British at the opening of the Revolutionary War and at some point near its close; a valuable discussion can be encouraged as to what factors threw the weight of the war in favor of the colonists. Was the shift caused by the aid of European nations, the leadership of the colonial cause, the dedication of the colonists to their cause, the fact that the colonists were fighting on their own soil, England's involvement in other parts of the world, or other factors?

9. In discovering the relationship between the various states of the United States and the federal government at different periods in our history.

10. In analyzing the strengths of the North and the South at the beginning of the Civil War: what factors threw the balance in favor of the North eventually?

11. In investigating the balance of power between political parties in the United States and deciding what issues or personalities tipped the scales in crucial periods: for example, why could Franklin Roosevelt swing most of the minority groups over to the side of the Decmocrats in 1932? By what means and issues did he accomplish this shift in power?

Probably you can think of other instances where scales or a balance can be used effectively. Why not jot them down here for future use?

12.

13.

14.

Cartoons as a Teaching Device

How often do you use cartoons in your social studies teaching? If you use them from time to time, fine. If not, perhaps this is a method you will want to add to your repertoire.

The best sources for cartoons are the daily and Sunday newspapers and the current events magazines. Some review books, such as those published by the Oxford Book Company, utilize them too.

Although some cartoons are fairly simple and can be used with almost any group of students, many are sophisticated; therefore, you should select classroom cartoons carefully.

Here are a few situations in which they can be used to promote good learning.

1. A chalkboard drawing of a cartoon by you or a student at the beginning of, or before, class.
2. A cartoon enlarged in the opaque projector at the start of a lesson or a unit.
3. A series of cartoons used as review, either shown in the opaque projector or reproduced for each student.
4. In an examination, providing either the same cartoon for every student, or a different one for each.
5. Original cartoons suggested by the class and drawn by one of its artists.

Here is a famous cartoon by Mauldin, published at the time of the assassination of President Kennedy. It can be used as a device for stimulating thinking by asking ''What is President Lincoln disturbed about?''

Copyright©1963, by Bill Mauldin. Reprinted courtesy of the Chicago Sun-Times.

11

Sometimes you may want to use historical cartoons, including the telling sketches of Tom Nast. Occasionally you may select a humorous cartoon, such as one that appeared in the Saturday Review (April 10, 1965) with the caption "Elephants? In the Alps mountains? Marius, you've been at the wine stores again!" And sometimes you will use current ones, along the lines of this cartoon on the Supreme Court ruling on reapportionment.

Berryman, Washington, D.C., Star. By permission.

For motivation or review in either a contemporary problems class or any current events lesson, this cartoon might be stimulating.

Reprinted courtesy of the Albany Knickerbocker News.

There are no better books of cartoon collections than Herblock's Here and Now, Herblock's Book, Herblock's Special for Today, and Straight Herblock, all published by Simon and Schuster.

12

Time Chart of World History

		FAR EASTERN SOCIETY	INDIA AND SOUTHEAST ASIA	THE MIDDLE EAST AND MOSLEM SOCIETY
B.C.	3000			Early Egyptian civilization Sumerian cities
	1200	Shang city-state Earliest written records	Indus Valley cities Aryan migrations begin	Babylonia—laws of Hammurabi Assyrian Empire established Hittite-Egyptian conflicts Hebrews migrate to Canaan
	300	Feudalism: Chou Dynasty Confucius and Lao-tzu Legendary founding of Japanese imperial rule	Vedic age Gautama Buddha Mahavira—Jainism Invasions from the West	Phoenicians in Mediterranean Persian empire, Mesopotamia to Egypt Alexander the Great
A.D.	1	Chinese Empire established Han Dynasty Korea tributary to China	Maurya Dynasty Reign of Asoka Andhra rule in central India Trade with Southeast Asia	Hellenistic age Extension of Roman rule into the Middle East
	400	Development of Chinese civil service Buddhism spreads to China	Kushan Empire Gupta Dynasty—the "Golden Age" of Indian culture Southeast Asian kingdoms	Beginning and growth of Christianity New Persian empire Constantinople founded
	800	Spread of Chinese culture to Korea and Japan	Rajputs settle in India—become feudal nobility	Founding and growth of Islam Ommiads at Damascus Abbasside Caliphate, Baghdad Byzantium resists Moslems
	1200	Art, literature, inventions, and trade flourish in China Koryo Kingdom unites Korea Fujiwara rule in Japan	Cambodia, Burma, Siam, and Malaya take shape Moslem conquests in India and Southeast Asia begin	Harun al-Rashid Age of Moslem learning Seljuks take over caliphate Crusades to Holy Land start
	1400	Mongols rule China and Korea; fail to conquer Japan Kyoto the political and cultural capital of Japan	Mongolian attacks on India and Java repulsed Reign of slave dynasties Majapahit empire, East Indies	Mongolian conquests and rule Tamerlane Rise of Ottoman Turks
	1600	Ming Dynasty Japanese invasion of Korea Jesuit missionaries in the Far East	Portuguese in India Spanish in the Philippines Mogul Dynasty established Islam in Southeast Asia	Ottomans rule most Moslem areas and much European land Mamelukes govern Egypt within the Ottoman Empire
	1800	Manchus rule China under the Ching Dynasty Tokugawa Shogunate rules Japan from Edo (Tokyo)	Reign of Akbar British India established Dutch control East Indies trade; start political rule	Turks turned back at Vienna Hungary freed from Turks Turkish wars with Russia—some land on Black Sea lost
	1900	Forced opening of China to Western trade Imperial restoration and industrial growth of Japan	British, Dutch, French empires spread in Southeast Asia U.S. wins the Philippines Indian nationalism develops	Wahabi uprising in Arabia Turks lose Balkan territory Egypt autonomous Suez Canal built and opened
	1914	Chinese Republic set up Japan rules Korea and expands power	Nationalist movements grow Indian Councils Act passed by British Parliament East Indian *Volksraad* set up	Reforms of Young Turks British-Russian agreement suspends rivalry over Persia Italy wins war with Turkey
	1920	World War I—fought in all parts of the world; peace treaties		
	1939	Kuomintang overcomes war lords and unites China Japan takes Manchuria and invades China	Philippine Commonwealth set up British and Indians prepare for Indian self-government *Volksraad* asks independence	Ataturk rebuilds Turkey Egypt fully independent Saudi Arabia formed Unrest in Palestine Mandate
	1945	World War II—fought in all parts of the world; no general		
Since	1945	Communists take China War in Korea Japanese peace treaty signed	New nations established throughout the area Vietnam split; Communists control North Vietnam	Emergence of new nations Arab-Israeli conflict Iran nationalizes oil Egypt seizes Suez Canal

13

SLAVIC SOCIETY	WESTERN EUROPEAN SOCIETY	ANGLO-AMERICAN SOCIETY	LATIN AMERICAN SOCIETY
	New Stone Age	Migrations and settlement of Indian tribes	Migrations and settlement of Indian tribes
	Aegean civilization, centered in Crete		
Slavs appear in Carpathian region	Homeric age—Mycenae Greek city-states flourish and colonize Mediterranean Classical culture develops		
	Rome conquers Mediterranean world Roman Republic transformed Caesar Augustus "Imperator"		
Slavs migrate eastward and to west and south	Pax Romana reigns, but decline of Rome commences Christianity adopted Barbarians gain strength		Development of civilizations of Mexican plateau, Yucatan, and Andes
Khazar in Volga area Vikings develop Dnepr trade	Barbarians invade the Empire Byzantine empire grows Justinian codifies Roman law Roman Popes extend authority		
Growth of Kiev and Novgorod Russians adopt Eastern Orthodox Christianity	Reign of Charlemagne Feudalism established Holy Roman Empire founded Conflict of church and state	Discoveries and settlements by Leif Ericson and other Norsemen—not permanent	Mayan culture at highest point
Mongolian conquest and rule Moscow grows up on frontier Novgorod remains free	Magna Carta signed Cities and kingdoms develop Universities flourish		Aztec Empire in Mexico Inca Empire in Peru
Moscow expands rule Ivan III becomes czar Serfdom begins	Discovery of new routes to the east and land to the west Splits in Christian church Elizabethan age in England	Voyages of the Cabots Cartier on the St. Lawrence Search for Northwest Passage Roanoke—"the lost colony"	Exploration and conquest follow voyages of Columbus Spanish and Portuguese empires founded in New World
Russia expands to Pacific Peter the Great turns west Wars with Sweden and Turkey Partition of Poland	Wars for land and power Limited monarchy in England Industrial Revolution starts French Revolution	Development of New France English settle Atlantic area British win Canada United States established	Decline of Spanish power Brazilians defeat the Dutch Revolts in Paraguay, Peru, and Colombia suppressed
Russia helps defeat Napoleon Reforms partly successful Russification forced Industrialization starts	Napoleonic era Liberalism and nationalism Spread of industry Africa explored and divided	U.S. expands across continent Civil War confirms Union Dominion of Canada founded American business grows fast	Winning of independence Growth of A B C countries Juarez and Mexican reforms Foreign debts cause problems
Russia defeated by Japan Parliamentary reform starts Russia claims leadership of all Slavic peoples	Welfare and democracy spread Disarmament efforts fail Rivalry over Balkans backed by alliances makes tension	Introduction of assembly-line methods in manufacturing Federal income-tax law Federal Reserve Board	Panama Canal built by U.S. Mexican Revolution breaks out Nations seek social welfare and political stability
made at Paris; League of Nations established			
U.S.S.R. under Communist dictatorship Alliance with Nazi Germany heralds World War II	Locarno agreements Economic depression Fascism wins Italy, Germany Hitler's Germany expands	Depression and unemployment New Deal recovery measures Neutrality legislation Good Neighbor policy adopted	Gran Chaco War U.S. Good Neighbor policy welcomed Regional organizations grow
peace treaty made; United Nations established			
Satellite system develops "Iron Curtain" isolates people "De-Stalinization" adopted Unrest among satellites	"Cold war" slows peace treaties Marshall Plan aids recovery Western Europe seeks greater unity	Continuing atomic research Involvement in "cold war" U.S. gives economic aid Leadership for world peace	OAS founded, with regional peace and development aims Perón dictatorship ends

This time chart is reprinted from Ethel Ewing's Our Widening World, by permission of the publisher, Rand McNally.

14

Studying Early Man

Articles on archaeological finds from current or recent newspapers and magazines are an excellent way of introducing pupils to the study of early man and arousing their interest in this aspect of history. Once you begin to look for them, you will find many more of these stories than you might expect.

Clip the articles and file them for future use. They can be mounted on paper or cardboard and passed out for the class to read at the beginning of a period or shown in an opaque projector. They can also be displayed on the bulletin board. In that case, you may want to read the headlines aloud or write them on the chalkboard.

Here are excerpts from a few clippings, collected in just a few weeks in 1964.

> Experts Unearth New Viking Data — the discovery of a stone wheel in Newfoundland, believed to have been used by Norse explorers.
>
> India Unearths Old Civilization — the unearthing of a settlement from the year 3000 B.C.
>
> New Excavations in Cyprus Reveal Interesting Finds — dating from the 7th century B.C.
>
> Metal Tools Believed 9000 Years Old Discovered — copper tools by a University of Chicago archaeologist in Turkey.
>
> Longer Ancestry of Man Suggested — a Yale anthropologist believes recent finds push the date of human origins back about 15 million years.
>
> Breakthrough into the Past — the linking of ancient Greek and Hebrew civilizations, based on the flow of Phoenician culture — a theory that could well revolutionize classical studies.

From these clippings, a teacher can move in any one of several directions, according to his wishes or the questions raised by the class. Among the possibilities you might explore are the following:

1. The ways in which archaeologists work.
2. The financing of expeditions.
3. Some unsolved mysteries about early man (including the Stonehenge remains in England, the writing of the Etruscans—which has not yet been deciphered—and the meaning of the huge stones found in the jungles of Mexico).
4. Carbon 14 and its contribution to archaeology.
5. Some famous archaeologists and their discoveries.
6. Milestones in archaeology.
7. How early men lived.
8. The earliest inventions of man.

These and related topics are nicely adapted to individual and committee reports. Some background reading materials are listed on the next page.

1. Baumann, Hans. The Caves of the Great Hunters. New York:Pantheon, 1962. 183 pp.
2. Baldwin, Gordon C. The World of Prehistory: The Story of Man's Beginnings. New York: Putnam, 1963. 192 pp.
3. Braidwood, Robert J. Archaeologists and What They Do. New York: Watts, 1960. 180 pp. Too detailed for average students but good for faster pupils.
4. Braymer, Marjorie. The Walls of Windy Troy: A Biography of Heinrich Schliemann. New York: Harcourt, 1960. 189 pp.
5. Cottrell, Leonard. Digs and Diggers: A Book of World Archaeology. Cleveland: World, 1964. 288 pp.
6. Cram, C. W. Gods, Graves and Scholars. New York: Knopf, 1959. 428 pp. For good readers only.
7. Daugherty, Charles M. The Great Archaeologists. New York: Crowell, 1962. 140 pp. A book of lives, with a humorous touch.
8. De Borhegyi, Suzanne. Ships, Shoals, and Amphoras: The Story of Under-water Archaeology. New York: Holt, 1961. 176 pp. The use of the "aqualung" in research on Greek, Roman, and Mayan civilizations.
9. Editors of Look, and Lincoln Barnett. The Epic of Man. New York: Golden Press, 1962. 176 pp. Beautiful, colored illustrations of early life in various parts of the world.
10. Falls, C. B. The First 3000 Years: Ancient Civilizations of the Tigris, Euphrates, and Nile River Valleys. New York: Viking, 1961. 220 pp.
11. Fortiner, Virginia J. Archaeology as a Hobby. Maplewood, N.J.: Hammond, 1962. 45 pp.
12. Hogben, Lancelot. How the First Men Lived. New York: Chanticleer, 1950. 36 pp.
13. Lisitzsky, Genevieve H. Four Ways of Being Human: An Introduction to Anthropology. New York: Viking, 1956. 303 pp.
14. Longsworth, Polly. Exploring Caves. New York: Crowell, 1959. 175 pp.
15. Mead, Margaret. People and Places. Cleveland: World, 1959. 318 pp. An introductory statement on anthropology, followed by studies of the Ashanti, Balinese, Eskimo, Minoan, and Plains Indians. Striking drawings and photographs.
16. Pfeiffer, John E. The Search for Early Man. New York: Heritage, 1963. 153 pp. Includes much material on the recent finds in Tanganyika by the Leakeys.
17. Quennell, Marjorie and C. H. B. Everyday Life in Prehistoric Times. New York: Putnam, 1959. 225 pp.
18. Poole, Lynn and Gray. Carbon-14; and Other Science Methods That Date the Past. New York: McGraw-Hill, 1961. 160 pp. Newer methods in dating historical materials.
19. Rogers, Frances. Painted Rock to Printed Page. Philadelphia: Lippincott, 1960. 175 pp.
20. Samachson, Dorothy and Joseph. Good Digging: The Story of Archaeology. New York: Rand McNally, 1960. 224 pp.
21. Silverberg, Robert. Sunken History: The Story of Underwater Archaeology. Philadelphia: Chilton, 1963. 177 pp.
22. Shippen, Katherine B. Portals to the Past: The Story of Archaeology. New York: Viking, 1963. 242 pp. Sections on early archaeology, on the methods of archaeology today, and recent finds. Lively style.
23. White, Anne Terry. The First Men in the World. New York: Random House, 1953. 178 pp. A Landmark book.
24. Winer, Bart. Life in the Ancient World. New York: Random House, 1961. 215 pp. 3000 B.C. to the time of Christ.

16

Our Debt to Other Peoples in the Past

It is often difficult for pupils to see the relevance of history to their daily lives. They think of history as events of the past—long past, and best ignored. Thus, from time to time, history teachers need to remind pupils of the debt they owe to people in the past. One method would be to read aloud the material given below and let the class discuss it, probably during the first week of a course in world history or United States history.

The following excerpt is taken from The Study of Man by Ralph Linton. Copyright, 1936, by D. Appleton-Century Company, Inc. Reprinted by permission of Appleton-Century-Crofts.

Our solid American citizen awakens in a bed built on a pattern which originated In the Near East but which was modified in Northern Europe before it was transmitted to America. He throws back covers made from cotton, domesticated in India, or linen, domesticated in the Near East, or wool from sheep, also domesticated in the Near East, or silk, the use of which was discovered in China. All of these materials have been spun and woven by processes invented in the Near East. He slips into his moccasins, invented by Indians of the eastern woodlands, and goes into the bathroom, whose fixtures are a mixture of European and American inventions, both of recent date. He takes off his pajamas, a garment invented in India, and washes with soap invented by the ancient Gauls. He then shaves, a masochistic rite which seems to have been derived from Sumer or ancient Egypt.

Returning to the bedroom, he removes his clothes from a chair of Southern European style and proceeds to dress. He puts on garments whose form originally derived from the skin clothing of the nomads of the Asiatic steppes, puts on shoes made from skins tanned by a process invented in ancient Egypt and cut to a pattern derived from the classical civilizations of the Mediterranean, and ties around his neck a strip of bright-colored cloth which is a vestigial survival of the shoulder shawls worn by the seventeenth-century Croatians. Before going out to breakfast he glances through the window, made of glass invented in Egypt, and if it is raining, puts on overshoes discovered by the Central American Indians, and takes an umbrella, invented in southeastern Asia. Upon his head he puts a hat made of felt, a material invented in the Asiatic steppes.

On his way to breakfast he stops to buy a paper, paying for it with coins, an ancient Lydian invention. At the restaurant a whole series of borrowed elements confronts him. His plate is made of a form of pottery invented in China. His knife is of steel, an alloy first made in southern India, his fork a medieval Italian invention, and his spoon a derivative of a Roman original. He begins breakfast with an orange, from the eastern Mediterranean, a cantaloupe from Persia, or perhaps a piece of African watermelon. With this he has coffee, an Abyssinian plant, with cream and sugar. Both the domestication of cows and the idea of milking them originated in the Near East, while sugar was first made in India. After his fruit and first coffee, he goes on to waffles, cakes made in a Scandinavian technique from wheat domesticated in Asia Minor. Over these he pours maple syrup, invented by the Indians of the eastern woodlands. As a side dish he may have the egg of a species of bird domesticated in Indo-China, or thin strips of the flesh of an animal domesticated in Eastern Asia which have been salted and smoked by a process developed in modern Europe.

When our friend has finished eating, he settles back to smoke, an American Indian habit, consuming a plant domesticated in Brazil, in either a pipe, derived from the Indians of Virginia, or a cigarette, derived from Mexico. If he is hardy enough, he may attempt a cigar, transmitted to us from the Antilles by way of Spain. While smoking, he reads the news of the day, imprinted in characters invented by the ancient Semites upon a material invented in China by a process invented in Germany. As he absorbs the accounts of foreign troubles, he will, if he is a good conservative citizen, thank a Hebrew deity in an Indo-European language, that he is 100% American.

*Periods of Hegemony of Europe
and the Middle East*

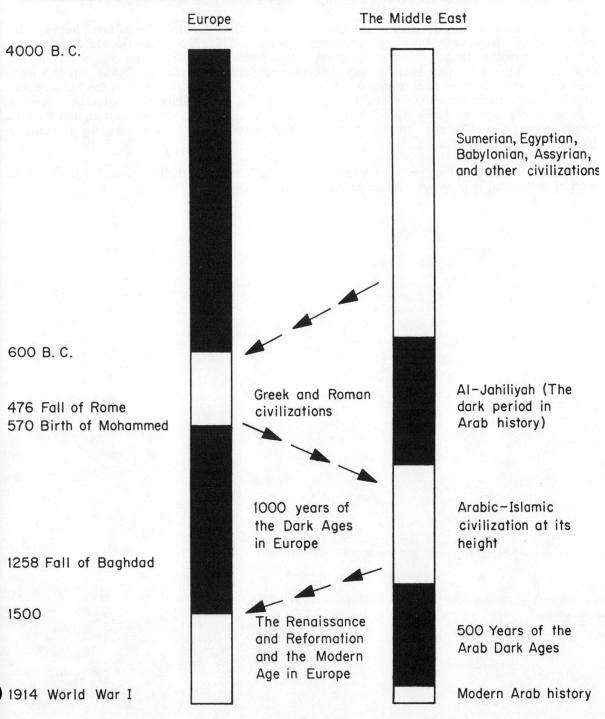

Europe

The Middle East

4000 B.C.

Sumerian, Egyptian,
Babylonian, Assyrian,
and other civilizations

600 B.C.

Greek and Roman
civilizations

Al-Jahiliyah (The
dark period in
Arab history)

476 Fall of Rome
570 Birth of Mohammed

1000 years of
the Dark Ages
in Europe

Arabic-Islamic
civilization at its
height

1258 Fall of Baghdad

1500

The Renaissance
and Reformation
and the Modern
Age in Europe

500 Years of the
Arab Dark Ages

1914 World War I

Modern Arab history

19

The chart on the previous page is adapted by permission from a similar chart in Mohammad Mehdi's A Nation of Lions, Chained (San Francisco: New World Press, 1962. 177 pp.).

You could make a large copy of the chart to post in any world history classroom and refer to it from time to time. Pupils could look at it when their minds wandered from the lesson. They could also make notebook copies for frequent reference.

The chart shows vividly the alternative periods of Middle Eastern and European leadership and/or hegemony since the beginnings of recorded history.

It also shows the long pre-Greek and pre-Roman period, which tends to be shortened in the minds of most people because of the limited space most textbooks devote to it.

Its great value, however, lies in its graphic portrayal of the shifts in cultural (and for the most part political and military) leadership back and forth between the Middle East and Europe over the long period of history. Thus, while the Middle East was producing the Sumerian, Egyptian, Babylonian, and Assyrian civilizations, Europe was still in a dark period. When Greece and Rome were the centers of the Western world, the Semetic and Middle East culture was in decline. During the period of Arabic-Islamic civilization, Europe was going through the Dark Ages. And when the Renaissance, the Reformation, and modern times emerged in Europe, the Middle East and North Africa were undergoing a period of dark ages.

Commentators might disagree on whether World War I marks a turning point for the Islamic part of the world; it is worth discussing and debating.

The Renaissance

One of the responsibilities of social studies teachers is to help pupils understand that history is constantly being reinterpreted in the light of new findings and current interests. The Renaissance is one of the periods in our past that is being examined continuously by scores of scholars whose evaluations of it differ radically from each other and from the interpretations of earlier writers.

Here are some of the points on which there is relatively "new" thinking.

1. ITS ECONOMIC BASE. For a long time, the Renaissance was described as a period of prosperity and economic expansion. But economic historians, working over that period with the aid of statistical analyses and studies of businesses, are not as certain now as people once were of its strong economic base. Many of them now interpret the Renaissance as a period of depression and stagnation or of three major stages—depression, economic stabilization, then prosperity. Some historians point out that when businessmen could not make profits in industry and commerce, they turned to the arts for their profits.

2. ITS EGALITARIAN BASE. The Renaissance has long been described as a period in which society was increasingly egalitarian. But some scholars today say that it was not especially egalitarian. They hold that the merchant capitalists moved from an early stage of democratic tendencies through a period of increasing conservatism to an alliance with the aristocratic, courtly society of their day.

3. ITS RELIGIOUS BASE. Most historians in the past have spoken and written about the Renaissance as a period of secularism. That view is now being challenged. Some writers maintain that Italian humanism, at least, was deeply religious in a broad sense of the term. Roland Bainton, for example, finds that Christianity in the Renaissance was influenced by Hellenic rather than Judaic forces, whereas the Reformation was Judaic in its interpretations.

4. ITS CREATIVITY. In the past, people have averred that the Renaissance was the example, par excellence, of creativity. Today some writers say that the 12th and 13th centuries were at least as creative as the Renaissance, possibly more.

5. ITS SCIENTIFIC CONTRIBUTIONS. The idea that modern science began in the Renaissance went unchallenged for a long time. Now some historians say that the 15th century did not differ enough from preceding periods to merit recognition as the beginning of the scientific age. There were changes, of course, but they were not outstanding enough to warrant the claims previously made for the Renaissance era.

6. ITS RELATION TO THE MODERN WORLD. The idea has likewise been presented that the Renaissance ushered in the modern period in Western history. Today some historians say that the modern era did not really begin until the 17th or 18th centuries.

You, and some of your students, may want to pursue these and other interpretations in depth.

21

Working from your own experience, or with the help of your students, you can develop a list of ideas about the Renaissance that you want to stress. These suggestions may help you organize your thoughts.

1. The causes of the Renaissance in such events as the accounts of Marco Polo, the Crusades, the expansion of trade and the building of ships, and the development of city-states.

2. The deep interest of many individuals in antiquity—particularly that of Greece and Rome.

3. The development of independent cities or city-states (especially Florence, Milan, Rome, and Venice) and their influence on this period.

4. Some of the outstanding personalities of the period, including:
   Michelangelo, Raphael, Rembrandt, da Vinci, Holbein, Fra Angelico, Fra Lippi, Dürer, Titian.
   Shakespeare, Chaucer, Cervantes, Dante, Boccaccio, Rabelais, Montaigne, Erasmus.
   Galileo, Copernicus, Harvey, Newton, Kepler, Vesalius, Fra Luca Pacioli, Girolamo Fracastoro, Sir Francis Bacon.

5. The relation of the church to the developments of this period.

6. The relation of the Germanic Emperor to events of this period.

7. The development of diplomacy in the Renaissance.

8. The growth of Renaissance art and architecture.

9. The development of science.

10. The spread of the Renaissance to some parts of Europe but not to others.

11. The relation of Asia and Europe as a part of the Renaissance.

12. The more sordid aspects of the period—violence, wars, and disease as outstanding characteristics.

What other items would you want to add?

13.

14.

15.

Teaching about the Renaissance

There are many imaginative ways in which you can help students to understand and enjoy the Renaissance period and see its relevance to their lives today. Here are some teaching techniques to consider in dealing with this period.

1. Show a film giving students an overview of the period or some important aspect of it. See, for example, Coronet's "The Renaissance" (11 minutes). This may either serve to introduce the era or come later in your study of it.

2. Use a filmstrip, such as Life's "Michelangelo" (60 frames) or Coronet's "Boy of the Renaissance," to introduce the period.

3. Develop a series of pictures to be used in the opaque projector showing some of the outstanding products in Renaissance art and architecture. At the close of the display, ask why these advances were made.

4. Invite the art teacher to work with your class on an aspect of Renaissance art in which he is particularly interested.

5. After your students have done some background reading, take a trip to a nearby museum that has Renaissance materials. Try to have a guide talk about the pictures and displays.

6. Arrange for several individual reports on leading personalities of the period, urging pupils with an interest in art to choose artists, pupils interested in science to choose scientists, etc.

7. Divide the class into committees on art, architecture, science, literature, politics, and diplomacy. Have them prepare lessons on what they learn.

8. After an introductory study of the period, divide the students into groups by countries. Have them report on the Renaissance in their particular areas.

9. Assign individual or committee reports on the cities of Renaissance Italy.

10. Let several students present their summary of the period in the form of a mural, with different students assigned to different parts of the mural.

11. Develop a Hall of Fame of the Renaissance, with illustrations and brief biographies of the persons nominated. These could be mimeographed with a copy for each pupil. Some students may do the drawings, others write the biographical sketches.

12. Discuss the statement "Renaissance men looked backward and forward."

PAPERBACKS ON THE RENAISSANCE
(For teachers and good high school readers)

1. Brucker, Gene A. Renaissance Italy. New York: Rinehart, 1958. 56 pp. An introduction and source materials. In the Source Problems of World Civilization series.
2. Burckhardt, Jacob. The Civilization of the Renaissance in Italy. New York: Harper, 1958. 278 pp. A translation from the German of a classic account written in the mid-19th century. Some of its interpretations are now under attack.
3. Dannenfeldt, Karl H., ed. The Renaissance: Medieval or Modern? Boston: Heath, 1959. 115 pp. Various interpretations outlined by 14 writers. Includes an extensive bibliography. In the Problems of European Civilization series.
4. Facets of the Renaissance. New York: Harper, 1959. 130 pp. Essays by five experts—on reinterpreting the period, changing attitudes towards the state, Machiavelli's Prince and More's Utopia, Renaissance conception of the lessons of history and Platonism.
5. Helton, Tindsley, ed. The Renaissance: A Reconsideration of the Theories and Interpretations of the Age. Madison, Wisc.: University of Wisconsin Press, 1964. 160 pp. Papers prepared for a conference on the Renaissance.
6. Pater, Walter. The Renaissance. New York: Mentor, 1959. 159 pp.
7. Plumb, J. H. The Italian Renaissance: Concise Survey of Its History and Culture. New York: Harper, 1961. 164 pp.
8. Plumb, J. H., ed. Renaissance Profiles. New York: Harper, 1961. 161 pp. Profiles of Petrarch, Machiavelli, the young Michelangelo, Lorenzo de Medici, Leonardo da Vinci, Pope Pius II, Doge Francesco Foscari, Frederigo de Montefeltro, and Beatrice and Isabella d'Este.
9. Ross, James B., ed. The Portable Reader. New York: Viking, 1963. 756 pp. A tremendous compendium of writings.
10. Schevill, Ferdinand. The Medici. New York: Harper, 1949. 240 pp.
11. Schevill, Ferdinand. Medieval and Renaissance Florence. Vol. I, II. New York: Harper, 1961.

OTHER BOOKS
(For slower readers)

1. Crandall, Elizabeth L. Leonardo da Vinci. Evanston: Row, 1951. 36 pp. Grades 5-8.
2. Hahn, Emily. Leonardo da Vinci. New York: Random House, 1956. 181 pp. Grades 7-9.
3. Price, Christine. Made in the Renaissance: Arts and Crafts of the Age of Exploration. New York: Dutton, 1963. 120 pp. Grades 7-10. Chapters on such topics as clothes and textiles, armor, sports and games, ships and navigation, musical instruments.
4. Ripley, Elizabeth. Raphael: A Biography. Philadelphia: Lippincott, 1961. 68 pp. Grades 7-10.
5. Shapiro, Irwin. The Golden Book of the Renaissance. New York: Golden Book, 1961. 168 pp. Beautifully illustrated. Text not too simple. Can be used by many students for a variety of purposes.
6. Stone, Irving. The Great Adventure of Michelangelo. New York: Doubleday, 1964. 297 pp. Grades 5-8.

The Reformation

Studying the Reformation with your students may be very difficult for it is highly controversial. Some of your students may have definite opinions on the topics you discuss, although their knowledge may be limited. You may be more personally involved in the controversy than you realize and have deeply imbedded attitudes of which you are not aware. Before you teach about this period, you would do well to examine your feelings as well as your background in facts. Then you should be able to handle the topic objectively.

In spite of its difficulties, teaching about the Reformation should be very worthwhile. Many of our present-day institutions stem from it. Some of our current problems have their origins at least that far back in history. The relevance of the Reformation to the lives of your pupils is therefore high. You could start a discussion of the Reformation by reference to the divisions between Catholics and Protestants in your own classroom, school, and community or refer to the current "dialogue" between officials in Catholic and Protestant groups and their recent moves towards reconciliation and unity.

Most pupils, even in high school, will be confused about the divisions of Christianity. The writer has had Protestant students who thought they were Catholics because of the phrase in The Apostles' Creed "we believe in the holy catholic church . . . . " A diagram or drawing of a tree (showing the trunk as a united Christendom with branches for the Anglican, Lutheran, and other groups) should clarify the divisions.

The key question of the classroom discussion that follows might be "How does it happen that Christianity is split?" From the discussion, the students should learn that it is difficult for any large institution to maintain its vitality and unity. Almost all human groups—whether religious organizations or political parties—split at some time.

As background, you may want to read summaries of recent interpretations about the Reformation, for this is a period of history on which many scholars are still working. George L. Mosse maintains that "there is hardly another area of modern scholarship in which there has been so general a reevaluation." Perhaps the best brief summary is to be found in Chapter 10 of the 34th Yearbook of the National Council for the Social Studies, New Perspectives in World History (Shirley Engle, ed., 1964. 677 pp.). The author, Robert M. Kingdom, suggests four main areas of reinterpretation. These are (1) the religious psychology of the Reformation, (2) the social impact of the Reformation, (3) the relations between religious groups created by the Reformation, and (4) the exotic or "radical" developments on the fringes of the Reformation.

Roland H. Bainton, a well-known scholar of this period, has another brief account of the "Interpretations of the Reformation" in the introductory chapter of Lewis W. Spitz's pamphlet The Reformation: Material or Spiritual? in the D. C. Heath series on Problems in European Civilization.

As you think through the major points to stress in any study of the Reformation, you may want to consider the following:

1. The way in which human groups and institutions divide because of the difficulty of maintaining unity and vitality; the Reformation as a "civil war."

2. The numerous criticisms and challenges within the church prior to the Reformation and some of the leaders of open revolts, such as Peter Waldo, John Wycliffe, John Huss, and John Wessel.

3. The undeniable fact that the causes of the Reformation are complex and difficult to determine.

4. The general awareness that, even though there were other factors at work, the Reformation was essentially a religious movement.

5. The extent of the church's control and influence in political as well as religious affairs at the time of the Reformation.

6. The criticisms of church practices: (a) the corrupt practices of the papal court, (b) the sale of indulgences, (c) the sale of offices (simony).

7. The importance of political factors: (a) the position of the Elector of Saxony—Luther's home area, (b) the position of the newly crowned Charles V, (c) the rise of city-states, (d) the rise of nationalism, (e) political events in such places as France and England, and (f) the weakening of the political power of the Pope.

8. The importance of the new printing presses and the related question of translating the Bible into languages other than Latin by Wycliffe and Luther.

9. The role of religious or doctrinal issues, such as the number of sacraments and the infallibility of the Pope.

10. Economic factors: (a) the financial demands of the church upon the peasants, (b) the criticisms of the wealth of the church, and (c) the rising economic power of the middle-class merchants and the princes.

11. The reasons why so many people supported Luther and other leaders.

12. The place of individuals, with special emphasis upon Luther and Calvin.

13. The fact that the revolt was not intended to bring about separation of the the church but reform within the church.

14. The importance of the Counter-Reformation within the Catholic church.

15. The long and often bloody wars of religion and the resulting antagonisms that developed between the two parts of Christianity.

Studying the Reformation

Considerable time could be spent profitably on the Reformation. But, in most history courses, you will have only five or six days for this complex and interesting topic. Here is a suggestion as to the use of those days.

First day: Film or filmstrip on the Reformation.
Second day: The Catholic church in the 16th century.
Third day: Martin Luther and the Reformation in Germany.
Fourth day: The Protestant Reformation outside Germany.
Fifth day: The Catholic Counter-Reformation.
Sixth day: Review.

During your study of the Reformation period, you may want to use a few of the following techniques:

1. Have a student or small group of students prepare a large time-line of the main events of the Reformation. Hang it in a very prominent place to refer to frequently.

2. Have other students prepare a map of the Protestant world and the Catholic world today, possibly in two colors, to make the divisions stand out.

3. Encourage students to bring in textbooks used in parochial schools, especially Catholic and Lutheran, and compare their accounts with the textbook you use.

4. Ask a few students to read about the leaders of the Reformation and Counter-Reformation. You need not have formal reports on this reading; the information can be used in class discussions.

5. Make a list of the possible causes of the Reformation, then discuss whether there might have been a revolution without each of the factors. Your discussion will probably be more important than any conclusions you may reach.

6. Develop a word list. Post it where students can refer to it in their discussions of the Reformation.

7. Outside of class or during your discussions of this period, develop a tree of Christianity with the various branches that have appeared. You may want to indicate the roots in Judaism and in Greek philosophy as well as in the person of Jesus Christ.

8. Arrange a panel discussion by students who have done special reading; avoid debates on topics as controversial as this one.

9. If you teach in a private school, you may want to invite a Lutheran or Catholic to speak to the class; in most public schools this will not be possible.

PAPERBACKS ON THE REFORMATION
(For teachers and good high school readers)

1. Bainton, Roland H. The Age of the Reformation. Princeton, N.J.: Van Nostrand, 1956. 191 pp. An introductory account, followed by excerpts from source materials.
2. Bainton, Roland H. The Reformation of the Sixteenth Century. Boston: Beacon Press, 1963. 278 pp.
3. Belloc, Hilaire. How the Reformation Happened. New York: Dodd, 1928 (original edition). 290 pp. A strong, pro-Catholic interpretation.
4. Engle, Shirley. New Perspectives in World History. Washington: National Council for the Social Studies, 1964. 667 pp. Chapter 10 by Robert M. Kingdom on "The Renaissance and Reformation: 1300 - 1848."
5. Erikson, Erik H. Young Martin Luther: A Study in Psychoanalysis and History. New York: Norton, 1962. 288 pp. A facinating study but heavy for most students.
6. Greene, V. H. H. Luther and the Reformation. New York: Capricorn, 1964. 192 pp.
7. Gustavson, Carl G. A Preface to History. New York: McGraw-Hill, 1955. 222 pp. (See pages 56 - 64 on the Reformation.) Suggestions primarily on how to teach it, suggested emphases or interpretations.
8. Huizinga, Johan. Erasmus and the Age of Reformation. New York: Harper, 1957. 266 pp.
9. Mossem, George L. Calvinism. New York: Holt. 1959. 29 pp. In the Source Problems in World Civilization series.
10. Mosse, George L. The Reformation. New York: Holt, 1963. 136 pp.
11. Rupp, Gordon. Luther's Progress to the Diet of Worms. New York: Harper, 1964. 108 pp.
12. Smith, Preserved. The Social Background of the Reformation. New York: Collier, 1962. 320 pp.
13. Spitz, Lewis W., ed. The Reformation: Material or Spiritual? Boston: Heath, 1962. 104 pp. In the Problems in European Civilization series.

OTHER VOLUMES
(Primarily for younger readers)

1. Bainton, Roland H. Here I Stand. Nashville: Abingdon. A biography of Luther.
2. Belloc, Hilaire. Characters of the Reformation. New York: Doubleday, 1958. 200 pp.
3. Fosdick, Harry Emerson. Luther. New York: Random House.
4, NcNeer, May Y., and Lynd Ward. Martin Luther. Nashville: Abingdon, 1952. 96 pp. Grades 6 - 8.
5. Thomas, Henry, and Dana Lee. Living Biographies of Religious Leaders. Garden City: Garden City Books, 1959. 298 pp. Brief chapters on Huss, Luther, Loyola, and Calvin.

The Industrial Revolution

Certainly no social studies teacher doubts the centrality of the Industrial Revolution in teaching history. Deep and far-reaching changes have occurred as the result of a cluster of events that are grouped together under the misleading but generally accepted phrase—the Industrial Revolution. In fact, this may well be the most important movement of modern times.

In teaching about the Industrial Revolution, teachers must guard against oversimplification. Too much teaching about this movement is confined to a list of inventors and inventions, generalizations about the factory system, and a few references to the living conditions of the workers. Certainly these are important aspects of the Industrial Revolution, but they are only parts of that movement, and those simple statements may be only partial truths. Students need to see the interrelationships between various inventions and the "moving dynamic" that prompted them as well as the fact that "systematic thought lay behind most of the innovations in industrial practice." They need to examine the question of whether the poor living conditions were a result of the factory system or were, in reality, a part of the movement to cities as a result of changing land practices in England.

The most important aim in teaching about the causes of the Industrial Revolution is to show that it came as a result of a complex of factors. T. S. Ashton summarizes those factors cogently and concisely in his small book on The Industrial Revolution: 1760 - 1830:

> The conjuncture of growing supplies of land, labour, and capital made possible the expansion of industry; coal and steam provided the fuel and power for large-scale manufacture; low rates of interest, rising prices, and high expectations of profit offered the incentive. But far behind and beyond these material and economic factors lay something more. Trade with foreign parts had widened men's views of the world, and science their conception of the universe; the industrial revolution was also a revolution of ideas.

Teachers should stress the fact that the Industrial Revolution was a movement extending over a long period of time in many places in the world, rather than being limited to a brief period of time in England.

They should also emphasize the radical changes in life that came about as a result of the Industrial Revolution—changes in politics, in economics, in ways of living, in philosophy, and in religion.

Covering the topic in this way is time-consuming. For that reason, perhaps the Industrial Revolution should be treated as a small unit in a course in world history, even though some of its later events would be taken out of their usual time sequence to be included.

There are many ways of developing the Industrial Revolution either as a unit or in various lessons. Here are some suggestions for your consideration.

1. As an initial activity, take a trip to a modern factory.
2. Show a film or filmstrip on the Industrial Revolution to introduce the topic.
3. Assign able students one or two basic questions for outside reading. After two or three days, organize your class work around these base questions: Why did the Industrial Revolution occur first in England? Why did the Industrial Revolution really start in the middle of the 18th century?
4. Assign inventors to individual students and have them report, in the first person, on "What I Invented." Let them summarize their reports on the chalkboard in this fashion:

Who I Am	What I Invented	The Importance of My Invention

5. Develop a time-line of the Industrial Revolution.
6. Start your unit or series of lessons on the Industrial Revolution with a discussion of how some product is made today. (The production of cloth or of nails is a good illustration.) Discuss how an individual would have produced that product in 1750. Then, point out the changes, called the Industrial Revolution, between these two dates. In broad outline, your chalkboard summary might look like this:

The Industrial Revolution

The Product as Produced – 1750	Changes That Have Taken Place	The Product as Produced Today
A Local Furnace		A Modern Factory
a. A few nails	a.	a. Thousands of nails
b. From local materials	b.	b. Assembly line
c. Produced by one or two men	c.	c. Raw materials from near and far
d. Sold locally, etc.	d.	d. Sold locally and at a distance, etc.
	e.	
	f.	
	etc.	

REFERENCES ON THE INDUSTRIAL REVOLUTION
(For teachers. All but one are paperbacks)

1. Ashton, T. S. The Industrial Revolution 1760-1830. New York: Oxford University, 1964. 119 pp. A paperback.
2. Heilbroner, Robert L. The Making of Economic Society. Englewood Cliffs, N.J.: Prentice-Hall, 1962. 242 pp. Stresses the economic aspects. Chap. 4.
3. Gustavson, Carl G. A Preface to History. New York: McGraw-Hill, 1955. 222 pp. Chap. 11 on "Inventors and Inventions." For methods of teaching.
4. Mantoux, Paul. The Industrial Revolution in the Eighteenth Century. New York: Harper, 1961. 528 pp. A classic in its field. A paperback.
5. Toynbee, Arnold. The Industrial Revolution. Boston: Beacon, 1962. 139 pp. Written in 1882 by the uncle of the famous historian.

OTHER VOLUMES
(For students who read at grades 7-10)

1. Neal, Harry E. From Spinning Wheel to Spacecraft: The Story of the Industrial Revolution. New York: Messner, 1964. 191 pp.
2. Spencer, Cornelia. More Hands for Man: A Brief History of the Industrial Revolution. New York: John Day, 1960. 192 pp.

Some Reasons for the Power
of England as a Nation

For well over 300 years, England was the most powerful nation in the world. "How could this happen?" you may ask. As you explore the answers to this important but baffling question and help students to analyze the reasons for England's power, these "leads" may prove helpful:

1. ITS GEOGRAPHICAL LOCATION. As an island, it was comparatively free from invasion. The English Channel served as a real line of defense. England did not have neighboring nations that continually threatened to invade. (See also Point 7 on its navy.)

2. ITS EARLY UNIFICATION. England became unified long before most nations of Europe. Perhaps 1066 is the earliest date you can pick for the beginning of the process; it is difficult to pick one date at which the unification ended. Because of its size and the fact that it was an island, England was relatively easy to unify. It is not divided by mountains, as many countries are (Greece and Italy, for example). Its compactness simplified the development of communications and transportation, both factors in fostering unity. Its single language also helped to unify England. Despite early language differences, a common language—English—developed fairly soon. Although variances based largely on class rather than on geographical lines persisted, one language helped to unify the country.

3. ITS COMPARATIVE RELIGIOUS HOMOGENEITY. After a long period of religious animosity and warfare, England became primarily a Protestant country, with the Church of England assuming religious and political leadership. In later years, England was not torn apart by religious differences.

4. ITS EARLY INDUSTRIAL REVOLUTION. It was in England that the Industrial Revolution took place. This factor cannot be emphasized too much. It is a key explanation of England's power for a long period. What caused the revolution there is difficult to say. Among the key factors were capital, raw materials, climate, and a spirit of inquiry resulting in inventions. (See also Point 6.)

5. ITS COLONIAL POSSESSIONS. Despite our aversions to colonialism today, it cannot be denied that England's colonies helped to make it a world power. The colonies supplied many of the raw materials for industrialization and, to some extent, provided markets for finished products.

6. ITS RESOURCES AT HOME. England had coal and iron in the early days, timber for its ships and navy, and people with inquiring minds, all of which aided in its early industrialization.

7. ITS NAVY AND SHIPS. Certainly without ships for defense and trade, England would not have accomplished what it did. These factors were essential to power.

8. THE EDUCATION OF AN ELITE. A society based upon an elite needed a special kind of education for its members. That kind of education developed in English "public schools" (private schools in our use of the term) and universities.

9. THE SENSE OF RESPONSIBILITY OF WEALTHY FAMILIES. A strong factor in England's power and prestige was the keen sense of social and political responsibility that developed in many wealthy families—a sense that has appeared in the United States only in relatively recent times.

10. EDUCATION FOR FOREIGN SERVICE. Realizing that many Englishmen would be engaged in the foreign service, educators early developed a special type of training for overseas work. This training, in turn, provided an outstanding diplomatic corps through the years.

11. ITS INQUIRING SPIRIT. A questioning approach to life has long characterized British society. The roots of this inquiring spirit are difficult to determine, but a search for them can be interesting and educative.

12. THE HIGH VALUE PLACED UPON SELF-DISCIPLINE AND WORK. The English have long emphasized self-discipline and work and have ranked these values high. This attitude may have resulted from the Puritan tradition, the climate, or a combination of these and other factors.

13. ITS LONG EXPERIENCE WITH DEMOCRACY. Although democracy did not extend to everyone and did not include social and economic democracy until recently, the English have felt involved with their government for a long time and have developed a high degree of political democracy.

14. ITS STRONG CIVIL SERVICE. Despite frequent changes in government, a strong civil service has brought continuity and a great deal of know-how to the English government.

15. ITS TRADITIONS AND AGE. A sense of tradition and age has given a feeling of security to most Englishmen. This security has been important, especially in times of crisis.

16. THE IMPORTANCE OF VOLUNTARY GROUPS. England has been strengthened in many respects by the role of individuals and groups working on a voluntary basis.

17. ITS EMPHASIS UPON SLOW AND PEACEFUL CHANGE. Drastic changes have occurred in England in recent times, but they have come slowly, without violence, and with a fairly strong degree of consensus among the people.

Revolutions

In any course in history, the idea of revolutions looms large. The first great political revolution took place in England in the 17th century. The late 18th century brought more revolutions, with the United States and France as focal points. But, in a very real sense, we are living in the most important period of revolutions in world history. The 20th century is a century of revolutions. Some of these have passed; we are in the midst of others; there are undoubtedly more to come.

Students, then, need to be confronted with this relatively recent and significant phenomenon of history. They need to study some of the important revolutions as analyzed and interpreted by various scholars of these movements. They need to learn more than the simple pattern teachers usually use—the underlying causes, the immediate causes, the major personalities and events, and the results. This approach oversimplifies revolution and leads students to misinterpretations.

In the introduction to his chapter on ''Revolution'' in A Preface to History, Professor Carl G. Gustavson of Ohio State University, writes a brief summary of revolutions as freshmen would write about them at the beginning of their work in history. According to him, they would say:

> A revolution is caused by the misery of the people. A strong and tyrannical government persists in its misrule until the people can endure it no longer. Then, moved by spontaneous zeal and righteous indignation, the multitudes rise. They assault the citadels of power and expel the ruling class in a bloody civil war. As a consequence of the revolution, liberty is restored to the people.

He points out that ''every sentence in the above paragraph proves to be a gross over-simplification.''

In order to present a more accurate picture, teachers can turn to several sources of information, among them:

1. Arendt, Hannah. On Revolution. New York: Viking, 1963. 343 pp.
2. Brinton, Crane. The Anatomy of Revolution. New York: Knopf, 1938 and 1952. Also available as a Vintage paperback. 300 pp.
3. Carr, E. H. Studies in Revolution. London: Macmillan, 1950. 226 pp.
4. Nomad, Max. Apostles of Revolution. New York: Collier, 1961. 414 pp.
5. Palmer, R. R. The Age of Democratic Revolution: A Political History of Europe and America, 1760-1800. Princeton, N.J.: Princeton University Press, 1959. 534 pp.

Crane Brinton's Anatomy of Revolution is probably the most helpful to the history teacher. In it, he mentions these uniformities in the causes and events of revolutions:

1. Societies that are on the <u>upgrade</u> economically but are struck by financial crisis.
2. Societies filled with bitter class struggles between classes that are fairly close rather than far apart. (Haiti is an exception to the rule that slaves and outcasts do not revolt.)
3. Societies in which the government machinery has not kept pace with changes, including industrialization.
4. Societies in which some of the ruling class and/or intellectuals are alienated and "desert" to the new movement.
5. Relatively new ideas are "let loose" and gain acceptance.
6. Some organization of the discontented occurs.
7. The power of the government to quell rebellion is markedly weak.
8. Only a minority, although a militant minority, really rebels.
9. The moderates usually come to power at first but are replaced by the extremists. The rebellion moves from right to left, assisted by an urge for strong centralized power that the moderates cannot provide. This movement is usually called "the crisis period."
10. The crisis cannot be sustained; the radicals are ousted, and the moderates regain power. Men's minds are more easily changed than their habits.
11. Changes take place but not radical ones. Government becomes more efficient, cultural achievements occur, the church's power loosens. The society is stronger at the end than at the beginning.

These are Brinton's conclusions; not everyone agrees with him. Students should examine these and other views critically.

In the study of any revolution (or of several revolutions as a unit), the following chart may prove helpful. Teachers should adapt it to their own purposes, however, for use with students of varying abilities.

	Revolution in	Revolution in	Revolution in
Economic conditions			
Areas of discontent			
Major ideas "let loose"			
Leaders			
Organization of the opposition to government			
Attempts to gain control of the government			
Takeover by extremists			
Takeover by moderates			
Fairly permanent results			

This chart can be used as an exhibit during a unit or series of lessons. It can be the basis of a chalkboard summary. Or students can prepare individual copies, allowing additional room for each item.

Nationalism

Nationalism is certainly one of the key concepts of any course in world history and, to a lesser extent, of any course in United States history. Barbara Ward, in her book Five Ideas That Change the World, speaks of nationalism as "the strongest, most pervasive force of our day."

At first, it seems fairly easy to teach about nationalism, but a longer and deeper look at this topic reveals that it is very complex. It cannot be taught in a few minutes. It requires analysis and reflection.

Here are six ideas you may want to consider as aims or goals in teaching about nationalism.

1. The importance of nations and nationalism in today's world.
2. The meaning of nationalism.
3. Conditions giving rise to nationalism.
4. How nationalism is fostered.
5. Values to be cherished in nationalism.
6. Difficulties growing out of intense nationalism.

Today's textbooks cover most of these topics adequately. This Background Paper is devoted primarily to areas that the textbooks have slighted.

Many teachers start a discussion of nationalism with a definition. Although that approach is probably the easiest, it may not be the most satisfactory. Too often students memorize definitions and ignore or slight their meanings. It seems much better to start with an analysis of what nationalism means to the pupils. A good introductory question is "You all say that you are American. What do you mean by that statement?" This may be followed by the question "What makes you American rather than . . . ?" A similar approach is "Suppose you woke up tomorrow morning and discovered that you were Japanese (or some other nationality). In what respects would you be different from what you are today as an American? How would you be Japanese?" From there, you can proceed to a discussion of nations and nationalism.

Early in any discussion of nationalism, you will want to bring out the factors that contribute to a feeling of nationalism or of being a nation. Here are a few generally accepted ingredients of nationalism.

1. A common enemy (usually a strong factor in the beginning).
2. A common language (although this is not always true).
3. A common religion (true in Israel and Pakistan to the largest degree, but not true of most nations).
4. Some common and usually contiguous territory. (Pakistan and the United States are exceptions to this idea of contiguous territory.)
5. A common history or "myths."
6. Some common goals.
7. A feeling of "belonging" together and of facing the future together.
8. Some common symbols (a flag, a national anthem, heroes, etc.).
9. Color or race.

10. Educational practices that foster nationalism.
11. Nationalistic propaganda used in mass communication.
12. Transportation that promotes national travel.

Students may develop these and other points, or you can give this outline to them for a check list, to analyze nationalism in any part of the world during any given period.

Discussions of nationalism in the past or at present should lead to thinking about the relationship of nationalism and internationalism today. Quotations like the following may prove useful to teachers at this point:

The whole intellectual life of mankind revolts against this intolerable, suffocating, murderous nuisance—the obsolescent national state. (H. G. Wells)

Love of country is eternal. It is on the same plane as love of family, love of one's native town or village, of all the fundamental realities that in our heart of hearts we hold nearest and dearest. But I am quite sure that there is nothing incompatible between patriotism and humanism—or if you like, between national and international loyalties. Love of a nation and love of the human race . . . can co-exist in the same conscience, as naturally as patriotism and love of family, or as patriotism and religious belief. (Leon Blum, For All Mankind)

There are many references available for teachers on nationalism. Here are a few you may want to use:

1. Binkley, Robert C. Realism and Nationalism 1852-1871. New York: Harper, 1935. 338 pp. Also available as a Harper Torchbook paperback.
2. Carr, Edward H. Nationalism and After. London: Macmillan, 1945. 74 pp.
3. Hayes, Carleton J. H. Essays on Nationalism. New York: Macmillan,1928. 279 pp.
4. Kohn, Hans. American Nationalism: An Interpretive Essay. New York: Macmillan, 1957. 272 pp. Also available as a Collier paperback.
5. Kohn, Hans. The Idea of Nationalism. New York: Macmillan, 1944. 735 pp. Also available as a Macmillan paperback.
6. Kohn, Hans. Nationalism. Princeton: Van Nostrand, 1955. 191 pp. An Anvil paperback.
7. Shafer, Boyd C. Nationalism: Interpreters and Interpretations. Washington: Service Center for Teachers of History, 1959. 12 pp. A summary of the thinking and books on this topic.
8. Shafer, Boyd C. Nationalism: Myth and Reality. New York: Harcourt, 1955. 319 pp.
9. Ward, Barbara. Five Ideas That Change the World. New York: Norton, 1959. 188 pp. Chapter on nationalism.

Napoleon

One or more exciting, informative lessons can emerge from the two quotations about Napoleon on the back of this page. Here are some ways in which you might use them.

1. Read short excerpts from the two quotations, without mentioning who the authors are. Immediately throw the class open for discussion of who was right in his evaluation of Napoleon. Get several comments quickly. Then begin to explore why the pupils think one or the other author was correct. As the period advances, you may want to have a student write the pros and the cons on the board, freeing you to lead the class discussion, which should be lively.

2. Duplicate the two quotations and give them to members of the class at least two days before you plan to discuss Napoleon. (You could include a brief reading list for bright students.) Ask the pupils to decide which of the two statements is more nearly correct, with reasons for their choice. In class, you may want to spend a few minutes on general reactions, then proceed to the board work.

3. Select a panel of students to discuss or evaluate the life of Napoleon. Have the chairman read these two quotes at the beginning; then have the panel members discuss their evaluation of the quotations for a few minutes. Finally, involve the entire class with their comments. The next day you may want to go on to material not included by the panel.

4. Ask a slow group to decide whether they would include Napoleon in a Hall of World Heroes. Eventually, you will need to discuss what is meant by "great" or "hero."

In using these quotations, you may want to identify the two authors if the class does not know them. Heine was the German poet—Wells, the English popular historian. Heine wrote his account near the time of Napoleon, whereas Wells wrote his in the 20th century from a different perspective.

Your discussions might include material on Napoleon's boyhood as one critical factor in his life. You also could compare Napoleon and Hitler—or some other dictator. There are numerous possibilities in this lesson.

"Hosannah, The Emperor!"

. . . The trembling trees bowed towards him as he advanced, the sunbeams quivered, frightened yet curious, through the green leaves, and in the blue heaven above there swam visibly a golden star . . . . He rode a white steed that stepped so proudly, so confidently, so nobly . . . . Carelessly and easily sat the Emperor, one hand holding the reins, the other good-naturedly patting the horse's neck. It was a glittering marble hand, a mighty hand, a hand that had bound fast the many-headed monster of anarchy and had let loose the war of nations—and it good-naturedly patted the horse's neck. His head reminded one of the marble busts of the Greeks and Romans; his features were as noble as those of the ancients, and on his face was written, "Thou shalt have no gods before me." A smile, which warmed and soothed every heart, flittered over his lips. Yet all knew that these lips had but to whistle and the entire priesthood was done for; they had but to whistle and the Holy Roman Empire tottered. And these lips smiled. And the eye smiled too, an eye, clear as heaven, that could see into the hearts of men, that pierced at a glance, all the things of this world . . . . . His brow was not so clear; the phantoms of future battles were nestling there. Now and then a quiver flitted over that brow. Those were the creative ideas, the great seven league boot ideas, with which the spirit of the Emperor strode invisibly over the world. (Heinrich Heine)

The figure he makes in history is one of almost incredible self-conceit, of vanity, greed, and cunning, of callous contempt and disregard of all who trusted him, and of grandiose aping of Caesar, Alexander, and Charlemagne which would be purely comic if it were not caked over with human blood . . . . It would be difficult to find a human being less likely to arouse affection. One reads in vain through the monstrous accumulation of Napoleonic literature for a single record of self-forgetfulness . . . . Out of his portraits he looks at us with a thin scorn upon his lips, the scorn of the criminal who believes that he can certainly cheat such fools as we are, and withal with a certain uneasiness in his eyes. That uneasiness haunts all his portraits. Are we really convinced that he is quite right? Are his laurels straight? He had a vast contempt for man in general and men in particular, a contempt that took him at last to St. Helena, that same contempt that fills our jails with forgers, poisoners, and the like victims of self-conceit . . . . He had never a gleam of religion or affection or the sense of duty. He was, as few men are or dare to be, a scoundrel, bright and complete. (H. G. Wells)

Which man was Napoleon? Which author was right? What is your evaluation of Napoleon. What evidence do you have to support your point of view?

Imperialism

| The population of England – approximately 40,000,000 | The population of the British Empire – nearly 400,000,000 | The population of The Netherlands – approximately 5,000,000 | The population of the Dutch Empire – nearly 35,000,000 |

There are many ways to launch a study of imperialism, with particular reference to the "new imperialism" of the late 19th century. One of the most effective methods is to bring into class a very large chart with the data shown in the bar graphs above, or to copy this material onto the chalkboard at the beginning of the class. You can draw similar, even more striking charts of the areas of "mother" countries and their colonial possessions. For example, the land still ruled by Portugal is 25 times the size of Portugal itself!

A teacher who is very sure of himself and saturated in the subject matter can wait until someone in the class comments on the displayed bar graphs, taking up the study of imperialism with that comment.

A teacher who is less sure of himself, the class, and the subject matter may prefer to structure the lesson a little, asking various students to interpret this data, taking one graph at a time—then drawing conclusions from the comparison of two of them.

Any teacher will want to have the class add other nations that might be pictured. These nations would include Belgium, France, Germany, Italy, Portugal, Russia, Spain, and the United States.

The key question in any discussion of this kind should be "How could such a small group of people obtain and hold these large areas and enormous populations?"

The study of imperialism in Africa might feature a large outline map of that continent with all areas left white except for Ethiopia and Liberia. Those could be colored bright blue or red to indicate that they were independent nations while the rest of the continent was under the rule of some European power. Show the various rulers of these colonial possessions in different colors on a second map; then ask the same basic question about how this happened.

From that point on, you will undoubtedly want to structure the lessons, taking up first the causes of imperialism, then the manner in which colonial possessions were obtained, the methods used to rule them, the advantages and disadvantages to the ruler and the ruled, and eventually the ways in which colonies obtained their independence. (In some cases, they are still under colonial rule.)

Some books and review books use a "balance" and lump the advantages and disadvantages to the ruler and the ruled together. In every illustration that this writer has seen, the two sides come out evenly. Perhaps it would be better to use this illustration once for those who ruled and again for those who were ruled over. If different dates were selected for the former and the latter, the changes over the years in supposed advantages and supposed disadvantages could be illustrated.

One question that textbooks and review books seldom handle is whether the so-called advantages of imperialism could have been obtained without actual political control.

When discussing the advantages of imperialism, you must be careful to show that the economic benefits to the ruling country were usually limited to certain segments of the population, though other groups may have profited indirectly. Actually, there is controversy over the economic benefits of imperialism. This is one of the points on which economists and historians do not agree.

Many students tend to sympathize with the colonial rulers. A good device is to role play imperialism, assigning the more vocal defenders of imperialism to the roles of colonial subjects so that they get another viewpoint on this highly charged and important topic.

In all discussions of imperialism, teachers need to remember that during this period the white Europeans (and to some extent Russians and Americans) felt distinctly superior as a group to the rest of the world—a feeling that is still held, consciously or unconsciously, by a large part of that population.

Teachers also need to remind students of the rise and fall of empires, noting that the period of imperialism coincided with low points in the power and prestige of areas such as India and China.

At the close of any small unit on imperialism, you may want to discuss whether new forms of imperialism exist today, taking the form of indirect economic imperialism, cultural imperialism, and even educational imperialism.

This is undoubtedly the most important topic to consider in world history for the years around 1900. It should be linked, however, with current developments in Asia, the Middle East, Africa, Latin America, and Oceania.

Causes and Costs of Wars

In every history course, you need to teach about several wars. Too often teachers limit discussions of wars to their long-range and immediate causes, their major events, and their results. Since many of these wars were fought a long time ago, students do not see much sense in studying them—except to pass a test.

Sometimes, teachers group several wars together to study as a unit on the causes and costs of wars. Such a unit may include material on ways to end hostilities and take in current efforts to end the arms race and achieve world disarmament.

This method is not always feasible. Another approach, then, is to use a general outline for the study of several wars, trying to find their similarities and dissimilarities. In this way, students have a chance to see individual wars in a broad context.

THE CAUSES OF WARS

A list of the causes of wars may be devised by students themselves, or it can be presented by the teacher and used as a basis of student reading and discussion. Here is the beginning of a list. You and your students may want to revise it and use it in the way suggested above.

Some causes of wars	Those that apply to the war we are studying

1. Economic causes

    a. Desire for raw materials.
    b. Desire for markets and investments.
    c. Need for outlet to the sea or to strengthen a frontier.
    d. Desire to protect economic holdings of an ally.
    e. Differences in economic systems.

2. Political causes

    a. National patriotism.
    b. Secret diplomacy.
    c. International political policies—the "need" to have a foreign war.
    d. Desire for new territory.
    e. Political independence.
    f. Alliances with other nations.

3. Psychological Causes

    a. Propaganda.
    b. Sympathy for the oppressed.
    c. Religious difficulties.
    d. Racial difficulties.
    e. Fear.
    f. Belief in the philosophy
       of force to settle disputes.
    g. Ideological disagreements.

In using this or similar lists, students will soon discover that many causes are difficult to pinpoint and some causes overlap.

THE COSTS OF WARS

A study of the causes of war is often enhanced by a study of the costs of wars. Students may, again, discover some of these costs themselves, or material may be supplied to them. Here are a few typical statements on the costs of wars.

In World War I, 40 million people were killed directly or indirectly. Other millions were maimed or wounded. What other "costs" were there?

World War II, which lasted 44 months, cost an estimated total of one trillion, 300 billion dollars. That is 29½ billion dollars a month, 985 million dollars a day, 41 million dollars an hour. Figures come from Walter Reuther's "A Proposal for a Total Peace Offensive."

    In World War II, 1 in every 22 Russians was killed.
                1 in every 25 Germans was killed.
                1 in every 45 Japanese was killed.
                1 in every 150 British was killed.
                1 in every 500 Americans was killed.

On April 17, 1953, Eisenhower pointed out that the cost of a single modern bomber would provide:

    The cost of one modern brick school in more than 30 cities.
    Two electric power plants, each serving a town of 60,000 people.
    Two fine, fully equipped hospitals.
    Fifty miles of concrete highway.
    Homes for 8000 persons.

Newsweek magazine reported some years ago (August 31, 1953) on the American war casualties from 1776 to 1953 as follows (reproduced by permission).

American War Casualties — 1776 to 1953

	Revolution	War of 1812	Mexican War	Civil War	Spanish-American War	First World War	Second World War	Korea
Dead	5,000	2,000	13,000	495,573	3,000	130,500	393,385	25,604
Wounded	unknown	unknown	unknown	unknown	unknown	234,300	670,846	103,492
Missing								8,529
Total	5,000 plus	2,000 plus	13,000 plus	495,573 plus	3,000 plus	364,800	1,064,231	137,625

Settlements at the Close of Wars

The problem of how to teach about the settlements or peace treaties at the conclusion of wars arises in every history course.

These lessons may be based entirely on memorization of the terms of the settlements and be practically worthless to students, except to pass examinations. Or the subject can raise basic and fundamental questions about the relationships between victors and vanquished.

In discussing peace settlements, you can use the chart below or some modification of it, showing that the same or similar problems arise at the conclusion of every war. You may want to use this chart for more than one war, reinforcing learning and reviewing the philo- sophical, political, social, economic, and psychological considerations at the close of several conflicts. It will be important to see whether students use the same logic in handling different settlements—and their reasons for any differences in reasoning.

Here is a bare outline, which you may want to use or adapt. (You may prefer to show three positions instead of two.)

Winner(s):

Loser(s):

	Plan A Moderate treatment of defeated group Leader(s) and/or group taking this position:	Plan B Harsh treatment of defeated group Leader(s) and/or group taking this position:
War guilt		
Territory		
Colonies		
Armed forces		
Reparations		
Political control of defeated group		
Treatment of head of government		

43

You may want to mimeograph a chart like this, providing larger spaces than are used on this Background Paper, so that pupils may fill in the columns and retain them in their notes.

An excellent way to introduce this topic is to pose a situation for your students to handle in which two friends have a fight. At the close of the fight, one is on the ground. Ask your students what the victor should do—and why. Answers will probably vary from letting the defeated person go without exacting any penalty to very harsh treatment. The transition to a discussion of the relationship of the victors and the vanquished after wars is then easy. What should the victor do? Should he be lenient or harsh? Here are three areas in which to explore specific answers to those general questions.

CIVIL WAR IN THE UNITED STATES.   You can use this chart in conjunction with the settlement in the United States after the ''War Between the States.'' First, discuss the terms of Lee's surrender to Grant; then go into the larger problem of what the North should do to the South. The two major proposals will, of course, be the moderate plan of Lincoln and the harsher plan of the radical reconstructionists (led by Charles Sumner and Thaddeus Stevens) leading up to the Congressional Plan of Reconstruction in 1867.

WORLD WAR I.   The chart can also be used to advantage in a discussion of the settlement growing out of World War I. The position of Georges Clemenceau would represent the ''harsh'' approach, that of Wilson the ''moderate'' approach. In this discussion, you may want to add a third column to represent Lloyd George's position. An excellent way to handle this settlement is to have three students role play the peace conference leaders presenting their plans. Have the class ask questions of these men and discuss what the final settlement should be. You can discuss the results of the harsh policy imposed on Germany and its allies in another lesson.

WORLD WAR II.   The victors after World War II were more united then they had been after World War I, and their peace settlement with Germany and Japan was more moderate than the one concluding the first World War. Your students should be aware of the other proposals after World War II, including Morgenthau's plan to dismantle German industry and convert Germany to an agricultural nation.

A Brief History of Russia

It is difficult, but not impossible, to select a few highly significant dates in Russian history to use with secondary school students. Below is such a list. If it does not suit your purposes exactly, modify it as you desire.

You might want to mimeograph this list for your students' use; or perhaps you prefer that they develop a similar list of key dates. In that case, this list could serve as background for your work with them in outlining Russia's important persons and events.

You may also want to encourage someone in your class to draw a large time-line, based on this or a similar outline. It could be hung in the classroom and used frequently during any study of Russia.

988	Introduction of Christianity by Vladimir.
1147	Founding of Moscow, eventually replacing Kiev in importance.
1223	Invasion of the Tartars, who ruled Russia for almost 250 years.
1462-1505	Ivan the Great. Formal end of Tartar rule, reduction of the power of the nobility, extension of serfdom, and attempts to curb Polish power.
1530-1584	Ivan IV (Ivan the Terrible). Further reduction of power of the nobles. Further extension of serfdom. New law code and church system. Expansion north, southwest, and east. Defeated in attempts to move west by combined forces of Sweden and Poland.
1640s	Russia reaches the Pacific.
1682-1725	Peter the Great. Influenced by the Industrial Revolution in England. Established the Academy of Science, built factories, gave women more power, encouraged merchant and artisan classes—as part of an attempt to westernize Russia. Emergence of Russia as a European power. Acquired ports on the Baltic and Caspian. Added the Ukraine. Defeated by the Swedes under Charles XII.
1762-1796	Catherine the Great. Partitioning of Poland (1772, 1793, 1795). Victorious over the Turks. Annexed the Crimea in 1783.
1812	Napoleon's unsuccessful invasion of Russia.
1815	The Congress of Vienna.
19th century	Development of revolutionary movements; conflicts between Slavophiles and Westerners. Period of great Russian writers.

1861	Emancipation of the serfs.
1854–1856	The Crimean War.
1865–1881	Conquest of Central Asia.
1904–1905	Russo–Japanese War.
1905	Revolution.
1906	Establishment of the duma.
1917	Eradication of Nicholas II, October Revolution, Kerensky.
1918	Treaty of Brest-Litovsk.
1921	New economic policy.
1924	Death of Lenin.
1928	Beginning of the five-year plans.
1933	Recognition of Russia by the United States.
1941	Invasion of Russia by Germany. About 20 million Russians died.
1945	End of World War II.
1953	Death of Stalin. Ruled from 1926 to 1953.
1964	Deposition of Khrushchev; elevation of Brezhnev and Kosygin.

There are many books that deal with the history of Russia and the U.S.S.R. Three quite different volumes follow:

1. Clarkson, Jesse D. A History of Russia. New York: Random House, 1962. 857 pp. A lengthy, authoritative, and highly readable account.
2. Kirchner, Walther. History of Russia. New York: Barnes, 1955. 329 pp. An outline book.
3. Pares, Bernard. Russia: Its Past and Present. New York: Mentor, 1953. 221 pp. An inexpensive paperback.

Some Contributions
of China and Japan to the World

CHINESE CONTRIBUTIONS

AGRICULTURE

Rotation of crops	Intensive farming	Green manure
Use of legumes	Soy bean and rape	Bamboo and mulberry trees
Cattle breeding	Tea, fruits, nuts	Irrigation

ARCHITECTURE

Garden plantings, memorial arches, walls, tombs.

ART

Paintings of flowers and animals, birds, trees (especially bamboo); vases; scrolls and different types of paper; calligraphy; use of silk, jade, ivory, bronze, lacquer, porcelain, glass, enamel.
Painters: Hu K'ai-Chih and Wu Tao Tzu
Calligraphers: Wang Hai-Chih, Su Shih, and Mi Fei

EDUCATION

Classical education and civil service
Mass education movement after World War I, work of James Yen

GOVERNMENT

Civil service system

LITERATURE

Libraries; dictionaries and encyclopedias
Chinese classics: Li, Ili, and Hsiao Ching
Historical studies, such as Shi Chi of SSu-Ma Chien
Some poetry, ballads
Literary figures: Ch'iu, Tse Chaan, Tzu Chih T'ung Chien, Ssu mei Juang

MEDICINE

Massage, pharmacopoeia

PHILOSOPHY

Confucius, Mencius, Lao Tzu, Wang Yang-ming, Chi Hai, and others

RECREATION

Jugglers, acrobats, marionettes, lanterns, professional storytellers, dolls, kites, maj jong and other card games, chess theater for popular works

SOCIAL INSTITUTIONS

Certain aspects of "extended families," such as care of the old

SCIENCE AND INVENTION

Painting, mariner's compass, textiles (especially silks)

TRANSPORTATION

Canals and various kinds of crafts

47

JAPANESE CONTRIBUTIONS

ART AND ARCHITECTURE

Prints
Lacquered articles
Carved wood and ivory
Screens: Sesshu, Eitoku, Sessher, Korin, and others
Porcelain or "china," especially of Imari and Satsuma
Fans
Painting stressing use of gold and secondary colors, nature, and animals
Tea ceremony
Temples and pagodas
Storage walls
Hekussi and 36 views of Mt. Fuji
Hiroshige landscapes

BIOLOGICAL PRODUCTS AND NATURE

Maple tress (varieties like Japanese maples)
Azaleas
Water lilies
Ginko trees
Flowering trees—cherries, known in United States as Japanese cherries
Japanese barberry. All American barberries destroyed; Japanese variety, not
    host to rust in wheat, substituted.
Various varieties of goldfish

COMMERCIAL PRODUCTS

Kimono
Fruits: tangerine ("Satsuma" variety named after Japane province)
        persimmons
Chinaware
Toys
Canned fish
Green tea
Dried ginger (also Formosa)
Camphor and camphor wood (in Formosa under Japanese)
Cameras and electronics products

MEDICINE

Dr. Hideyo Noguchi, yellow fever research
Beriberi and cancer research
Drugs, such as ephedrine

RECREATION, DRAMA, SPORTS

Jujutsu
"No" dance, rhythmic posturing to music
Tea ceremony
Plays: Chikamatsu Monzaemon, the greatest playwright

RELIGION

Zen Buddhists and other sects
Kagawa and other Christian reform leaders

Teaching about World Religions

No study of the people of other lands can be adequate without a thorough analysis of their values, goals, or ideals. The ideals, goals, and values of a given group of people are highly important, affecting their attitudes toward family life, economics, social systems, politics, and other areas. We can best discover these attitudes by studying the leading religions (including philosophies) of those people.

The study of religion may be more important in other civilizations or cultures than in our own. As Oliver Caldwell has pointed out:

> Religion in many societies is of a different degree of importance from what it is in the United States. It determines what a man eats, how he lives, where he lives, and a great many other things which must be understood if one is to cooperate effectively with that man. Some of our individual and collective American failures, especially in Eastern countries, may be traced to the ignorance of our representatives in matters pertaining to religion. This poses a direct challenge to our schools.

Some teachers are fearful about teaching anything concerned with religion because of the Supreme Court's rulings on prayer in the schools. However, no one has suggested that these can be interpreted to include teaching about religions. Teachers need only be careful not to use their classrooms as a place for the propagation of any religious faith. One cannot ignore the importance of religion in any course of history or in the study of another culture. How could you omit the religious aspects of the Renaissance or the Reformation in teaching about those periods? How could you disregard the philosophies of Hinduism, Confucianism, or Buddhism in learning about South or Southeast Asia?

In studying other people and their cultures, either past or present, there are several major concepts about religion to keep in mind. This list, an elaboration of material from the writer's Guide to Social Studies for Secondary Schools, contains some basic guidelines.

1. All people seek a system of values, consciously or unconsciously.
2. People everywhere and in all times have sought an explanation of their existence on this planet.
3. People everywhere and in all periods of history have tried to explain what happens when people die.
4. There are many philosophies of life or religions in the world.
5. Almost all religions have one great leader.
6. Ways of worship and religious symbols vary from religion to religion.
7. Religion is often a factor in politics—locally, nationally, globally.
8. A few basic values are upheld by all of the major religions.
9. Some religions have a missionary outlook.
10. Terrible conflicts and persecutions have taken place in the name of religion; some continue today.
11. Religious groups tend to divide into orthodox, conservative, and liberal factions.

12. Believing in an organized faith helps most people.
13. Interreligious cooperation is increasing today.
14. Although many people develop their own values outside of organized groups, they are affected by organized religion.
15. Understanding and respect for the values or religions of others need not destroy or deemphasize the basic tenets of one's own faith.

The central idea to keep in mind constantly in developing ideas about world religions is man's search, in all periods of history and in all places, for "the good life." "What did these people believe was 'the good life'?" can be posed frequently as a key question.

Here are a few suggestions for treating this important topic in various courses.

1. Arrange for speakers on various world religions, selecting authorities who can talk effectively with young people.
2. Show films or filmstrips on world religions. (See especially the colored filmstrips of Life magazine on this topic.)
3. Have able students give brief reports on the major ideas of the world religions being studied.
4. Mimeograph some of the beliefs of the faith under consideration. (This can be combined with point 3 above.)
5. Collect and show pictures of some of the followers of major world faiths.
6. Prepare a bar graph showing the number of adherents of the major world faiths.
7. Discuss ways in which communism is similar to a world religion.
8. Prepare brief biographies of the "founders" of various world religions.
9. Prepare a large map of the world, showing the location of followers of the major philosophies of life or world religions.
10. Prepare a chart of world religions similar to this one.

	Buddhism	Christianity	Confucianism	Hinduism	Judaism	Zoroastrianism
Leader or leaders						
Sacred book or books						
Places of worship						
Time of worship						
Special prohibitions						

Teachers will find valuable information in such sources as Robert O. Ballou's Bible of the World (Viking, 1958), or his paperback The Portable World Bible; Life magazine's World's Great Religions (Simon and Schuster, 1958); the Mentor Religious Classics series of paperbacks on the various leaders of world faiths; Huston Smith's The Religions of Man (Mentor paperback); a series of little volumes by the Peter Pauper Press on the "Sayings of . . ."; and a series of paperbacks on each of the world religions, published by the Washington Square Press. There are, of course, many other books on this important topic.

Buddhism

THE BUDDHIST WORLD TODAY. Buddhism is the philosophy of life or the religion of approximately 500 million persons in South and Southeast Asia and the Far East. Its followers are chiefly in Ceylon, Burma, Thailand, and other parts of Southeast Asia, India, Tibet, China, and Japan.

BUDDHISM'S HISTORIC ROOTS. Buddha, who lived in the 6th century B.C., wanted to purify Hinduism rather than to found a new faith. He rejected certain aspects of Hinduism, such as the caste system and the excessive and involved rituals of that way of life.

A great deal of legend has grown up around the founder of Buddhism, but it is assumed that he was born around 560 B.C. in northern India. His real name was Gautama Siddhatha (The Successful One). His father was a prince and his mother a beautiful princess. As a boy, he lived in luxury in the palace, eventually marrying and having one child. At the age of 29, he fled the palace and learned about the suffering in the world by contact with poor people and old people, and by the sight of dead people. He went into retirement for six or seven years and finally decided that seclusion was not the answer to the riddle of life any more than a life of luxury had been. After sitting under a bo tree for many days, he decided upon the middle path as the way of life—neither asceticism nor license, but moderation. From then on, he lived as a wanderer, traveling over large parts of India to talk with people and to share his views with them. He lived to be 80.

BUDDHIST BELIEFS. The central concept of Buddhism is the search for the inner self—the stress on self-salvation.

It sees three great sins:
1. Self-indulgence.
2. Ill-will.
3. Ignorance.

It has nine precepts for its followers. They are to be incapable of:
1. Deliberately depriving a living creature of life.
2. Taking what is not given—a theft.
3. Sexual impurity.
4. Deliberately telling lies.
5. Saving up treasure for indulgence in worldly pleasure.
6. Taking a wrong course through partiality.
7. Taking a wrong course through hate.
8. Taking a wrong course through stupidity.
9. Taking a wrong course through fear.

It has four noble truths:
1. All existence involves suffering; suffering is universal.
2. Suffering comes from excessive desires.
3. Suffering ceases if one suppresses or controls desire.
4. Control comes from the eight-fold path. (See next page.)

The eight-fold path leads to nirvana—peace of mind and soul.

1. Right views.
2. Right aspirations.
3. Right speech.
4. Right conduct.
5. Right effort.
6. Right livelihood.
7. Right mindfulness.
8. Right contemplation.

These constitute the "wheel of the law."

Buddhists, like Hindus, believe in karma—the future incarnation as one strives to attain nirvana.

BUDDHISM'S SYMBOLS. The Buddhist religion is rich in symbolism. Some examples follow:

1. Temples located in beautiful spots.
2. Statues of the Buddha, many of them large.
3. Family altars.
4. Shrines built by persons grateful for events in their lives.
5. Priests' yellow robes and shaven hair.
6. Ceremony for children at the age of four—donning beautiful clothes, replacing them with rags, having their heads shaved—reliving the life of Buddha.
7. Entry of young men into the monasteries at adolescence. The boys wear saffron robes and have their heads shaved. Then they go to school in the monastery. This period in monasteries accounts for the relatively high degree of literacy in some Buddhist countries, such as Ceylon. The monks obtain their food by going from door to door in the nearby community, with their wooden rice bowls, asking for rice.

THE DIVISIONS OF BUDDHISM. Like other faiths, Buddhism has its divisions. There are two branches.

1. Hinayana or The Little Vehicle. In Ceylon and South Asia. It stresses individual austerity and individual piety.

2. Mahayana or The Great Vehicle. In China, Japan, Korea, Tibet, and Mongolia. It stresses faith and good works. It has developed elaborate rituals, especially those concerned with the importance of saying prayers, and even accepts mechanical prayer wheels that automatically say prayers for worshippers.

THE SACRED WRITINGS OF BUDDHISM. The three baskets of wisdom or The Tripitaka are

1. Vinaya Pitaka. Discipline basket. Rules for members of orders.
2. Sutta Pitaka. Teaching basket. Words of Buddha.
3. Abhidhamma Pitaka. Metaphysical basket. Points of doctrine.

Buddhism, especially Zen Buddhism, has aroused considerable interest in the United States in recent years, particularly for its emphasis upon peace of mind and soul.

Confucianism

CONFUCIANISM TODAY. Confucianism is a way of life that has brought culture and civilization to hundreds of millions of Chinese for over 2500 years. It is basically a philosophy or way of life rather than a revealed religion. However, insofar as it includes reverence for ancestors and a place for sacrifice and augury, Confucianism is a religion, too. Its focus is on the here rather than on the hereafter, on the earth rather than on heaven. It centers on the life of man. According to Confucianists, the social order is sound if it is in harmony with the order of nature.

The government of mainland China today is communist. Nevertheless, Confucianism is still an important influence in that nation as it is in some other places in Asia.

CONFUCIUS' BACKGROUND. Confucius was born in the Shantung province in the 6th century before Christ. (This was also the century of Lao Tzu's birth.)

The period in which he lived was one of social anarchy. Old customs and traditions, which had been automatically accepted, were no longer providing acceptable answers. Reflective thinkers were challenging old views.

As a young man in a poor but aristocratic family, Confucius was absorbed in the history, poetry, and music of ancient China. He aspired to political life, but he spent several years as a teacher and as an editor, editing the classical writings of China. He wrote very little himself, considering his task that of "a transmitter."

CONFUCIUS' PHILOSOPHY. Confucius rejected the two extremes that had been proposed as answers to criticism of Chinese thinking. One was force; the other was love unbounded by social order. In his solution, Confucius placed the classics at the center of learning, but he subtly reedited, modified, and interpreted them. According to his views, tradition, once acceptable simply because it was tradition, would thereafter be acceptable with critical intelligence to serve it in choosing ends and means.

THE CULT OF CONFUCIANISM. Like most other founders of world religions, Confucius did not envisage a new philosophy, faith, or religion. But the school of thought that he represented became, in time, a cult or philosophy. He became a sage and ideal, and his views were a code of ethics for most Chinese. By 136 B.C., the Emperor Wu had made Confucianism the basic discipline for the training of government officials. In less than a hundred years, sacrifices were made to Confucius in urban schools. Later on, shrines were built honoring him.

THE CONFUCIAN DOCTRINE. Confucianism was concerned with three aspects of behavior:

1. Self: to be a gentleman, striving for the supreme good.
2. Family: to be an effective member of the family, working for its happiness and prosperity.
3. Humanity: to be an active participant in world society, dedicated to the realization of The Golden Rule—"Do not unto others what you do not like done with yourself."

THE GOALS OF THE CONFUCIAN TRADITION.   The five goals of the reconstructed Chinese tradition, according to Confucius, were

1. Jen. Human-heartedness, revealed in the respect one has for himself and others. The marks of jen are magnanimity, empathy, courtesy, and charity.

2. Chun-tzu. True manhood or the superior man or manhood-at-its-best. A far deeper meaning of the word "gentleman" than the one we use in the Western world today.

3. Li. The "rationalizing principle of social order," which supplies the total pattern of response for every life situation and enables one to lead the good life. The following teachings provide one with this virtue:
   a. Rectification of names. The need to keep a constant check on relationships between words, thought, and reality.
   b. Doctrine of the mean. The need to avoid extremes and to seek harmony and balance.
   c. Five key relationships. Through proper dealings with others, man discovers himself. These relations are between father and son; older brother and younger brother; husband and wife; elder friend and younger friend; ruler and subject.
   d. Family. The key to the good society lies in proper rearing.
   e. Respect for age.

4. Te. Power, generated through ideal examples, set especially by those at the top of the social order.

5. Wen. The art of peace, as opposed to the art of war. It is the cultured way of music, art, and poetry, which is essential for the moral education of the individual and which leads one nation to attain hegemony over others.

SOME SAYINGS ATTRIBUTED TO CONFUCIUS

Man is by nature good.

Within the four seas, all men are brothers.

The princely man thinks of virtue; the mean man of gain.

Yu, shall I tell you what true knowledge is? When you know, to know that you know, and when you do not know, to know that you do not know—that is true knowledge.

When you see a good man, think of emulating him; when you see a bad man, examine your heart.

Men who differ in principles cannot help each other in their plans.

He who requires much from himself and little from others will be secure from hatred.

We ought to have a wholesome respect for our juniors. Who knows but that by and by they may prove themselves equal to the man of today?

A man's character is formed by the odes, developed by the rites, and perfected by music.

Do not unto others what you do not like done unto yourself.

Virtue cannot live in solitude; neighbors are sure to grow up around it.

Hinduism

THE HINDU WORLD TODAY.   Hinduism is the broad philosophy or way of life of over 300 million Indians and about 15 million people in other parts of South Asia.

ITS HISTORIC ROOTS.   Hinduism's origins are unclear.   Probably the confluence of the conquering Aryans and the conquered Dravidians produced this system, which combines the intellectual and the abstract with demon worship.   Hinduism is steeped in antiquity.   Because of the lack of a formal creed, church organization, and formal priesthood, it has taken myriad forms.   Its flexibility has made it able to absorb many points of view, and no one person is considered the founder or the great leader of the faith.

ITS CHIEF BELIEFS.   Hinduism advocates belief in an absolute, all-embracing spirit—the Brahma—which is the only reality, the unconditioned, the original cause, and the ultimate goal of all living souls.   This is an abstract concept for most people, and so a whole galaxy of gods, with whom more people can identify this spirit, has evolved.   These gods represent the various aspects of God.

The three leading gods, who comprise the Triad, are Brahma—the creator, Siva—the destroyer, and Vishnu—the preserver.

Among the other highly honored gods are Rama, the hunter, and Krishna, the poet, musician, and lover.

There are also eight "world guardians" representing the regent of the East, the god of fire, the god of death, the god of the heavens, and others.

Many persons, particularly those who are not formally educated, believe in village and family gods, with whom they can closely identify.

There are temples but few set times of worship; people drop into the temple as they desire. Family altars to one or more of the chief gods, and possibly to more local gods, are common.

The various aspects of the virtuous life are clear in Hinduism, but each person is left free to develop his own theology, worshipping God in whatever way he chooses. However, an account is kept of each man's actions on the "wheel of life" as he works toward the goal of nirvana. Since reaching this goal may take endless years and many reincarnations, time is not an important factor in parts of the world where Hinduism flourishes.

HINDU SYMBOLISM.   In a sense, idol worship represents a degeneration of Hinduism, which came about because of the need for definite objects with which people could identify their religious beliefs and actions. But symbols are far more important than simply as objects of worship; they are a part of the Indian way of life. Indians think symbolically. Thus, a god may be pictured with two or more heads, four or more arms, or with large breasts, because those are the really important aspects of the particular gods.

THE ORIGINS OF CASTE. Over the centuries, the Hindus of India worked out a pattern of caste or a functional system of division of labor, just as the people in medieval Europe and ancient China did. This hierarchy included the following broad categories:

Brahmins—priests and teachers.
Kshattriyas—kings and warriors.
Vaisya—merchants and artisans.
Sudra—laborers and farmers.
Outcastes or untouchables—scavengers and sweepers.

Caste also developed from the conquerors' desire to prevent intermarriage with dark-skinned people of Southern India. Thus, the upper three castes were light-skinned. Through the dramatic intervention of Gandhi and a changed outlook on society, new India has down-graded and officially outlawed caste, although vestiges of it persist in many places.

SOCIAL THEORY. Among the important concepts with which each individual must deal throughout his life are the following. Again the individual determines how he will work out these precepts in his own life.

Varna—caste, kin, color.
Dharma—duty or function according to varna.
Karma—destiny, according to how one performs his dharma.
Samsara—the bondage of repeated births and deaths, moving from impurity and ignorance to illumination.
Nirvana—the undifferentiated whole, the union of Atman and Brahman, the release from rebirth.

DEBTS OR DUTIES. The five debts or duties for the expiation of sin in Hinduism are

1. Studying and teaching the Vedas (offering to Brahma, the creator).
2. Giving food and water (offering to the ancestors).
3. Pouring ghi oblations in the fire (offering to the gods).
4. Giving food to animals, to the sick, to the needy (offering to nature's elements).
5. Hospitality to guests and begging students (offering to humanity).

SACRED LITERATURE. Hinduism has a wealth of religious literature through which one can trace the development of this philosophy or religion. It includes the following:

Vedas	about 200–1000 B.C.	early nature worship
Brahmanas	about 1000–800 B.C.	priestly Hinduism
Upanishads	about 800–600 B.C.	philosophical Hinduism
Kataka	late centuries B.C. early centuries A.D.	pre-Buddhist tales and legends
Laws of Manu	late centuries B.C. early centuries A.D.	legalistic Hinduism
Puranas	early centuries A.D.	popular Hinduism legends
Ramayana	early centuries A.D.	popular Hinduism lengends
Manabharata	early centuries A.D.	popular Hinduism epic and devotional Hinduism

Islam

THE ISLAMIC OR MOSLEM WORLD TODAY.   Somewhere between 400 and 500 million people in the world today are Moslems or Muslims. The Moslem world extends from West and North Africa across the Middle East and as far east as China and Indonesia. The largest groups of Moslems are in Pakistan and India. Other large groups are found in Nigeria and other West African nations, in Morocco, Algeria, Tunisia, Libya, Egypt, the Sudan and East Africa, Arabia, Syria and Lebanon, Jordan, a few in Israel, Turkey, Iran and Iraq, the U.S.S.R., Afghanistan, China, and Indonesia.

The religion of those who are "at peace" with God and with man is called "Islam." Followers are known as "Moslems" or "Muslims," not "Mohammedans." They do not worship Mohammed but Allah, whose prophet Mohammed was.

MOHAMMED.   Mohammed, meaning "the greatly praised one," was born in Mecca in Arabia, on April 20, 571 A.D., at a time when that city was a trading center on the lucrative spice routes. There were many shrines in the city, including the Kasbah or Cube, for which his tribe was responsible. His father died before he was born, and his mother died when he was a young child, so he was raised by relatives. As a young man, he was a camel driver for a rich widow, whom he later married. Some of his wife's cousins were members of a group of Hanifs, penitents interested in the reformation of the tribal religions of the Arabs. Mohammed also came in contact with many Jews and Christians and was impressed with their beliefs, especially in a monotheistic God. He pondered these varied religious ideas and had numerous revelations in one of which he felt that God had selected him as a prophet. He had doubts about himself, but cast these doubts aside after a second revelation. He did not aspire to the formation of a new religion but gathered adherents among the Hanifs and other Arabs. Attacked by those who disagreed with him and warned of what would happen if he continued his preachings, he fled on July 16, 622 A.D., in what is celebrated as the Hegira. He became the local ruler in Medina as well as the prophet. He hoped to win even the Jews to his faith, and the early Moslems prayed facing Jerusalem rather than Mecca. The world religion that grew up around his life and beliefs is the newest of the major world faiths based on Judaism and Christianity and is probably the most simple and clear-cut of the major faiths in the world today.

ISLAMIC BELIEFS.   There are five pillars of Islam:

1. Shahada means witness—declares that there is no God but Allah and that Mohammed is his prophet.

2. Salat means prayer. Moslems must pray, facing Mecca, five times a day— at sunrise, noon, afternoon, sunset, nightfall.

3. Zakat means alms. Moslems must give to the poor during the last half of the month of Ramadan.

4. Siyam means fasting. Moslems fast from sunrise to sunset daily during the month of Ramadan.

5. Hadj. Moslems hope to make a pilgrimage to Mecca once in their lifetimes.

In addition to the pillars of Islam, Moslems believe in:

1. Moses and Jesus, as other prophets.
2. The Koran as the final revelation—the sacred scripture.
3. Angels.
4. The resurrection.
5. The day of judgment—heaven and hell.

ISLAMIC CUSTOMS.   Among the important religious customs that Moslems observe are these:

1. Worship in the mosque every Friday noon by men and boys.
2. Prohibition from idols, adultery, gambling, injury to others, eating pork, drinking alcoholic beverages (including wine).
3. Four legal wives permitted if they can be justly treated; divorce allowed but strictly regulated.

ISLAMIC SYMBOLS.   Moslems consider the following symbols particularly significant:

1. The Kasbah or Cube in Mecca.
2. The Koran, written in Arabic with 114 surahs or chapters, including 25 references to Jesus.
3. The mosques, with their minarets or towers from which the call to prayer is made five times a day.
4. Green as a special color of Moslems.
5. Mecca as the holy city to which pilgrimages are made and toward which worshippers face when praying.

DIVISION WITHIN ISLAM.   Islam is divided into two chief groups:

1. The Sunnis.   Followers of the Sunna, the traditions of the prophet as recorded in the Hadith, and belief in the succession of caliphs through election from the Koreish clan.

2. The Shiahs.   Followers of Ali, with hereditary spiritual leaders known as Immaams, decendants of Ali and Fatima. Largest center in Iran.

FAMOUS UNIVERSITIES OF ISLAM.   There are two of these: Al-Azhar in Cairo, Egypt (founded in 969 A.D.), and Aligarh near Agra in India (founded in 1875 A.D.).

FAMOUS MOSLEM RULERS.   Harun al-Rashid, Caliph from 786-802 in Baghdad. A contemporary of Charlemagne. Suleiman the Magnificent, Caliph and Sultan in Istanbul from 1520 to 1566. Contemporary of Queen Elizabeth.

THE APPEAL OF ISLAM TODAY.   Today Islam is once more a missionary religion seeking and gaining followers in many parts of Africa as well as in some other parts of the world, including the United States. Its appeal in Africa is in its simplicity, its lack of a history of race prejudice, and its acceptance of polygamy.

Judaism

JUDAISM TODAY. About 12 million people, of all races and colors, follow the precepts of Judaism, the religion of the Jews. Since the Diaspora, begun in 70 A.D., Jews have made their homes on all the continents except Antarctica. Today, large numbers of Jews live in the United States, the U.S.S.R., and, to a lesser extent, in Israel. Smaller numbers live in many other countries.

Their influence, however, is much more profound and extensive than their numbers indicate. With a strong emphasis upon education and learning, they have contributed far out of proportion to their numerical strength.

PEOPLE OF THE BOOK. The Jews have been called "the people of the Book." They regard the Book, the Old Testament, as revelation, gained not through their merit nor through man's insight, but revealed by God through his deeds. God revealed himself most clearly through "the chosen people" for the good of all men. Such an incomparable responsibility can at times include an incomparable suffering. To accept pain so that others may be spared is, then, the distinguishing characteristic of "the chosen people."

THE REVELATION OR DISCLOSURE

1. God is a single, omnipotent, omniscient, transcendent being—righteous and loving, holy and great. His name is unutterable.

2. Creation, or the universe, which is a reflection of its maker, is good. It is intelligible, though the meaning may not always be apparent. Existence in the universe is good—real, not illusory.

3. Man was created as lord of the universe. He was granted his freedom, the power of choice—the capacity to prove or disprove his worth within the realm of history.

4. History is a realm of useful and meaningful activity; it is not a realm of illusion. Further, it is bound by neither mechanical laws nor inexorable fate. God stretched his hand out to man in historical events rather than in natural phenomena, for holiness exists in history. Man, in turn, reaches out to God by living his law in daily life. Life on earth provides an opportunity and responsibility for every person (both as an individual and as a member of society) to bring God's will into being by the way he feels, thinks, and acts every moment—in the marketplace as well as in the temple.

5. The Ten Commandments are the ethical measuring rod for man's social action. They set minimum standards. Man gains full knowledge and understanding of God's law only through living the Ten Commandments.

6. Justice is the inalienable right of man, the child of God. This right is not limited to justice in the narrow sense; as the Psalms reiterate, it is loving and merciful justice.

7. <u>Suffering</u> is as much a mark of life on earth as is happiness or joy. However, to those who abide by the law of the Lord, suffering not only punishes but provides opportunity for learning — even for redemption.

8. <u>The way</u>. Judaism has no official creed; its stress is not on dogma but on ritual. Ritual, of course, can be as dry as dust. But it can also be a means of growing in awareness, a means of remembering God's sanctifying grace. God's grace, Jews believe, reaches into every nook and cranny of creation and into every infinitesimal and insignificant moment of time. Ritual, to them, is a means of vivifying life through sharing its every aspect with God.

JUDAISM'S DIVISIONS. Like the other major world faiths, Judaism is divided into branches. The three major groups are known as the Orthodox, the Conservative, and the Reformed. These three differ primarily in their observance of Jewish ceremonial customs.

AUTHORITY IN JUDAISM. No individual or group speaks for all Jews. There is no pope, bishop, or Sanhedrin. Rabbis resemble Protestant ministers. They do not act as intermediaries between individuals and God nor do they perform sacramental functions. They are "teachers," distinguished from laymen by their superior scholarship in Jewish law and lore. Orthodox rabbis interpret the rabbinic law, grant religious divorces, and decide on matters of ritual. Liberal rabbis are ordained to preach and teach. Authority rests in books. The Halacha or rabbinic law is found in the Torah, the Talmud, the Codes, and the divinely inspired Bible. Thousands of Jewish organizations exist, bound together frequently in federations of community councils.

SOME FAMOUS PASSAGES FROM THE OLD TESTAMENT

Hear, O Israel, the Lord Our God, the Lord is one.

Thou shalt love the Lord thy God with all thy heart, with all thy soul, and with all thy might. (Deuteronomy 6:5.)

Thou shalt love thy neighbor as thyself. (Leviticus 19:18.)

And they shall beat their swords into plowshares,
And their spears into pruning hooks;
Nation shall not lift up sword against nation,
Neither shall they learn war any more. (Isaiah 2:2-4.)

...whether a man accomplish great things or small, his reward is the same if only his heart be set upon heaven.

Have we not all one father?
Hath not one God created us?
Why do we deal treacherously every man against his brother,
Profaning the covenant of our fathers?

The Lord giveth and the Lord taketh away; blessed be the name of the Lord.

The stranger ... you shall love ... as yourself .... (Leviticus 19:34.)

The Golden Rule
in the World's Great Religions

In courses in world history, world geography, and world cultures, it is important to deal with the religions or philosophies of a given area in any period of history. A comparison of world faiths is often a valuable exercise, for students should become aware of the basic similarities and differences between religions.

One outstanding example of similarities is The Golden Rule, which is found in some form in all of the major faiths in the world today. Although stated in different words, the basic or underlying idea is the same in each principle.

The boxed material on this and the next page might well be mimeographed and distributed to students. Let the students read the passages to themselves; then ask if they have any comments or questions on this material. Wait for what seems a long time. If comments or questions are not forthcoming, make your question more pointed, asking "Why do you think these statements are similar?" or "What do you notice about these statements?" A lively discussion should take place. Some students will be surprised that the beliefs are so much alike.

THE   GOLDEN   RULE

Hurt not others with that which pains yourself. (Buddhism.)

All things whatsoever ye would that men should do to you, do ye even so to them, for this is the law and the prophets. (Christianity.)

Is there any one maxim which ought to be acted upon throughout one's whole life? Surely the maxim of loving-kindness is such. Do not unto others what you would not they should do unto you. (Confucianism.)

That is the sum of duty; do naught to others which if done to thee would cause thee pain. (Hinduism.)

No one of you is a believer until he loves for his brother what he loves for himself. (Islam.)

In happiness and suffering, in joy and grief, we should therefore refrain from inflicting upon others such injury as would appear undesirable to us if inflicted upon ourselves. (Jainism.)

What is hurtful to yourself, do not to your fellow men. That is the whole of the Torah and the remainder is but commentary. Go learn it. (Judaism.)

As thou deemest thyself, do deem others. Then shalt thou become a partner in heaven. (Sikhism.)

Regard your neighbor's gain as your own gain; and regard your neighbor's loss as your loss. (Taoism.)

There are various listings of these quotations in similar form. The above arrangement was taken from page 87 of the Kidger-Dunwiddie Problems Facing America and You (Boston: Ginn, 1956. 638 pp.) and is reprinted here with the permission of the copyright owners.

Major Concepts in Geography

What are the major concepts in geography that should be kept in mind when teaching that or related subjects? Professor Douglas Eyre, Chairman of the Department of Geography of the University of North Carolina, has provided one valuable list.

You may want to use his outline as a check list to see if you are stressing the major points from a geographer's point of view. You can add to or subtract from it for your particular class or classes.

Or you may prefer to work out subtopics for these major themes in terms of your own teaching.

Dr. Eyre's concepts or generalizations follow:

1. Geography is concerned with the arrangement (patterns) of people and their works on a physical base.

2. The geographical pattern involves both location and interaction (such as the movement of people, goods, ideas).

3. Geographic patterns change with time (like a chess game or a series of family photos).

4. Man is an active agent in reshaping the natural environment. Results are mixed—some negative, some positive.

5. The ways in which man reshapes the natural environment involve both the physical base and the culture (goals, needs, technology) present.

6. Extreme environments (tropics, polar lands, deserts, and mountain areas) tend to restrict the scope, and often the success, of human activity.

7. Coasts, rivers, plains are the main locations of human activity.

8. Men and their works are distributed unevenly. There are areas of dense, intermediate, and sparse population, and some population blanks.

9. A natural resource is not a natural resource until man has a use for it and a technology capable of handling it.

10. No country is self-sufficient in resources.

11. Great inequities occur in the degree of national self-sufficiency in raw materials and foodstuffs. "Have" and "have-not" nations result.

12. Differences in national economies are a basis for the exchange of goods.

13. Countries are human creations whose size and shape change through time. New countries are created; others are modified; some go out of existence.

14. Each country, or other spatial unit, is composed of distinctive parts or regions, each of which has a distinctive combination of physical and human patterns.

15. Regional patterns constantly change. Differences stimulate interaction (movement of people, goods, etc.) between them.

16. National boundaries are man-made; they often cut across physical and social lines and are often hard to maintain.

17. Each place (town, city) has distinctive functions. The bigger the place, the more complex the functions.

18. Towns and cities are arranged in distinctive patterns that reflect site, historical development, and functions.

19. Towns and cities have inseparable relations with their hinterlands (support areas). There is a relationship between city size and size and quality of the hinterland.

20. The city is the "nerve center" that attracts people, goods, and new growth.

21. The function of a city can change and effect growth rates and patterns.

22. Much industry tends to be market oriented, that is, locates near the market and attracts raw materials to it.

23. Transportation (kind, speed, cost) and power (kind, costs) are keys to industrial development.

24. Specific locations on a map are possible by use of the earth grid.

How would you revise this list? What additional concepts or generalizations would you add?

25.

26.

27.

28.

29.

30.

The Concept of Culture

A few years ago, Stuart Chase asked several hundred social scientists in the United States about new ideas in their fields. By an overwhelming vote, the concept of culture was mentioned as the most important idea to be developed in recent years.

The following notes on the concept of culture are taken from a document of the Foreign Service Institute of the Department of State, prepared by Edward A. Kennard.

1. The term "culture" is used by social scientists to refer to the totality of the behavior of any particular group of people, whether they be tribes, villages, or nation-states. It is equivalent to the ordinary meaning of "civilization" in its broadest sense, or what is meant by "a way of life."

2. Technically, culture is defined as the configuration of learned behavior and the results of behavior whose component elements are shared and transmitted by members of a particular society.

3. The great problem in international relations and in everyday dealing with foreign people is that most of us tend to identify our traditional ways of meeting problems, of organizing life, and of reacting to situations as human nature, whereas all those ways are learned. Other peoples have developed different solutions to the same universal problems and consequently have different human natures.

4. Every culture is ethnocentric. This term refers to the fact that each people tends to regard its own particular culture as either the best or the only proper solution and to think of all others as quaint, queer, or "cussed."

5. Culture is not only a way of life to which people emotionally adhere and conform, but it is also a set of solutions to the universal problems of life.

6. The various aspects of culture that can be analyzed and described—economic, technological, political, social, and psychological—are all delicately interlinked. There are not only overt behaviors, which can be observed directly, but also attitudes, feelings and other components that are often referred to as "sentiments." Sentiments of any culture also have structure and organization and can be determined by inferences from observed behavior.

7. Every culture embodies certain stated assumptions or hypotheses that vary tremendously in different societies. All Americans assume that every chain of action is directed toward a goal. To those who do not share this assumption, but rather see life as a series of activities that are satisfying in themselves, our behavior is meaningless and quixotic.

8. A culture is also a series of expectancies. Not only do we learn prescribed ways to behave toward others in terms of their sex, age, and status, but we also learn what we may expect from them in return.

9. Every culture embodies a social myth, which is a set of rationalizations and beliefs that give coherence and meaning to the activities of the society.

10. Cultures tend toward integration. Certain dominant ways of organizing activities or of phrasing issues characterize all the activities of the society and color the people's approach to economic, political, and social activities alike. As a corollary, changes that occur in one aspect of any culture either will produce concomitant changes in other aspects or will bring on serious social disorganization.

11. No culture is ever completely static. The rate of change may be so slow as to produce apparent stability, or relatively rapid, as in Western Europe and the United States during the last 150 years.

12. Every culture is selective. No great civilization, with all its diversity, embodies in its institutions all of the possible ways of defining situations and meeting problems. Consequently, as a person moves about the world, he will always be discovering new "normals" and new standards.

13. Most of the sentiment structure characteristic of any given culture never rises to the consciousness of individuals but is assumed as a universal. Usually, it cannot even be verbalized.

14. There is no psychological scale against which to evaluate the different cultures of the world. Each culture may be satisfactory to the members of the society that embodies the traditions. Consequently, problems must be seen from the point of view of the individual of the other nation, as well as in terms of American assumptions and American solutions. It may be that different courses of action from those we are accustomed to could be reconciled with the traditional ones.

The Earth as the Home of Man

At some time during junior or senior high school, students should study the earth as a whole. Usually this study serves as an introductory unit in a course in world geography, but it can also be used as a summary, bringing together all that the students have learned about countries and regions.

Since a unit on the earth may be your students' first glimpse of world geography, it should be an exciting experience—concentrating upon man, the earth, and the interrelationships of these two concepts. The focus should be on people—where they live and why, what they do and why. Probing these two questions makes geography functional in students' minds. These ideas make geography live, make students want to learn more about it.

While various types of maps should be used, it is not necessary to teach the names of the projections at this point. Confine definitions to such broad terms as "longitude" and "latitude." Point out the climatic zones if you like. But don't let an emphasis on technical terminology kill your students' interest in earth as the home of man. Use physical geography, but stress human geography.

Among the many ideas that you will certainly want to include are the following:

1. The high percentage of the earth that is water (about 75 per cent).

2. The distribution of the world's people, stressing three major spots: East Asia, Western Europe, and North America. You may also want to point out a few smaller areas with high concentrations of population, such as Taiwan, Java, Malaya, and Puerto Rico.

3. The different types of climate and weather in different parts of the world.

4. The variety of land forms in the world—mountains, deserts, plains, plateaus, etc.

5. How the factors above have influenced men throughout the centuries and how men have adapted their food, clothing, shelter, farming, transportation, and other aspects of life to these conditions.

6. How men have destroyed large parts of the world through lack of conservation.

7. How men have changed the land by reclaiming deserts, planting trees and crops, improving the soil, building canals, bridges, dams, tunnels, and by terracing and irrigating.

8. The earth as a rich storehouse of resources (bauxite—aluminum—coal, copper, gold, and silver, iron, petroleum—oil—natural gas, tin, uranium, and water) as well as agricultural products, such as barley, corn, cotton, potatoes, rice, and wheat.

9. The earth as a workshop where man has learned to produce a vast array of products and to live different kinds of lives according to the environment.

10. The earth as man's playground.

11. The importance of water (or the lack of it) in men's lives, stressing the role of a few important rivers.

12. How men are currently exploring the secrets of inner space and the oceans.

13. How men are exploring outer space—the earth and the universe.

14. Conservation as a universal obligation.

15. Philosophically, the idea that "the same sky covers all of us, the same sun and stars revolve about us and light us all in turn." (Comenius.)

16. Globes and maps as symbols that help us talk about and study the earth.

Any study of the earth as the home of man should include examples of each of these factors as preparation for study in depth of selected countries as well as for a general understanding of basic concepts. To give one example: the Netherlands, having little in the way of resources, turned to shipping, dairying, and manufacturing as leading industries. It is a sandy country; its houses have utilized this basic resource—being predominately brick. The sandy soil has enabled the Dutch to grow vegetables, fruit trees, flowers, and to graze cattle. This part of the world turned early to the use of the wind for power. And to enlarge their territory, the Dutch became adept at salvaging the earth from the sea. You will find other illustrations to show the interrelation of man and the earth in that country.

To motivate interest in this unit, you could talk to your students about inspecting a new house from basement to attic and relate this structure to a study of the earth. Or you could plunge into the question of where most of the earth's people live today and why. Most students will find this approach more exciting than the conventional one that starts with the universe, goes on to examine our galaxy and solar system, and finally pinpoints the earth as a single small planet.

In developing an overall unit on earth as the home of man, you will want to use even more pictures than you use in other units. These may be films, filmstrips, slides, or pictures. Students can help you build a good collection and mount them on cardboard for preservation.

You will also want as many world maps as possible. You can buy some of these; you and your students can make others. Some can be cut out of magazines and newspapers and used in an opaque projector.

There is no shortage of materials on this topic. Encyclopedias are full of interesting maps, charts, and pictures as well as textual material. Good geographies will help. Also, many high-quality supplementary or trade books are available.

Above all, bear in mind that you are teaching about people and the earth, not just about the earth alone.

Studying Various Countries

Many high schools include a study of individual countries in their social studies curriculum. Because these studies should encourage depth rather than superficial coverage, the number of countries to be examined should be drastically limited. The following criteria may help you decide upon the 12 to 15 nations you want to consider in any year:

1. World powers.
2. Countries of the future, such as China, India, Canada, Brazil, Nigeria.
3. Neighboring nations.
4. Nations representing the world's major cultures.
5. Countries from which ancestors of the class came.
6. Countries against which there is the most prejudice.
7. Countries representing different world religions.
8. Countries representing different types of economy and government.
9. One or more "new nations."
10. Countries representing the cultural heritage of the United States.
11. Countries that you can teach with relative objectivity.
12. Countries on which there are adequate materials.

Having decided upon the countries you plan to study, you must further consider which characteristics to stress for each. This chart plots one approach to the detailed study of any nation.

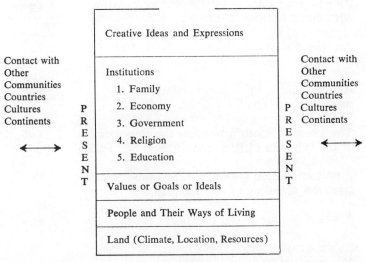

In most cases, it is wise first to consider the modern country in all these ramifications, then turn back to its history to show how that country developed. You are more likely to arouse the pupils' interest in this way than by using the past as an introduction.

However, everyone will be bored if you follow the same pattern for each country. Without distorting the picture of any country, you might vary the approach like this.

Country	Dominant Theme and Second or Third Themes	All Other Themes
England	Reasons for its long rule of the world; the history of its democracy.	Yes
Germany	A nation that developed late, and the results of that fact.	Yes
Sweden	Its middle-road economy and government.	Yes
Italy	The rise and fall of a nation; its many contributions to the world.	Yes
U.S.S.R.	Its geography, with special emphasis upon size; its communist economy and government, and their effects on the world.	Yes
Egypt	Its geography; the battle between land or sand and water throughout the ages.	Yes
Iran	Its long history and current problems.	Yes
Israel	Pioneering in a new nation; Judaism.	Yes
India	Its variety of geographical forms and varied peoples; how to achieve unity.	Yes
Thailand	Its long history as an independent nation; its cultural life; Buddhism.	Yes
Indonesia	Its geography as an island nation; relations with other nations of the world.	Yes
Japan	An island nation turns to the West and industrializes; the old and the new.	Yes
China	Its size and long history; position in the world today—and tomorrow.	Yes
Brazil	The giant of South America; the importance of the triangle of Rio, Santos, and São Paulo.	Yes
Mexico	A nation well on its way toward modernization; the blending of old and new.	Yes
Canada	A world leader in the making?	Yes
Nigeria	Its geography and tribal groups; problems of a new nation.	Yes

What changes would you make in the above list of nations and in the themes for each?

The Rivers of Europe

Rivers are extremely important in the study of any region. Through the ages, they have provided man with (1) highways for raw materials, finished products and people; (2) boundaries and lines of defense, especially in the past; (3) places to have pleasure, fun; and (4) sources of water power and electricity.

One way to begin a study of the rivers of Europe is to refer to leaves. "Have you ever examined a leaf? What did you notice about it?" you might ask. Most people notice the veins. When some student mentions this feature, ask, "In what way are the rivers of Europe like the veins of a leaf?" Let the students locate the main rivers on a map of Europe. You can either stop and discuss each river as it is found, or you and the students can list all the major rivers on the Continent and discuss them individually later.

The location of key cities (Rotterdam, Hamburg, Bremen, etc.) in relation to major rivers is another significant aspect to discuss.

Don't overlook the development of canals to link sources of supply to major rivers and to link small rivers to larger ones. This could be a separate topic in itself. Canals have been built primarily as links with the Rhine and the Seine. Although canals are still very important, pipelines are beginning to replace them as means of transporting raw materials.

The following data may be helpful in studying the rivers of Europe.

THE LONGEST RIVERS IN EUROPE

Volga	2287 miles
Danube	1835
Don	1220
Vistula	860
Rhine	822
Elbe	722
Loire	632
Tagus	626
Ebro	575
Oder	565
Rhone	503
Seine	481
Po	404

Length is not necessarily the most significant factor about a river. More important ordinarily are the river's location in relation to sources of raw materials, its harbors, and its depth.

THREE OF THE MOST IMPORTANT RIVERS OF WESTERN EUROPE

1. THE RHINE. This river starts in Switzerland and passes through a large and important section of Central Europe. Men straightened and deepened it, making a "new Rhine" in the 19th century. Only fifth in length, the Rhine is Europe's busiest river. Some of the largest cities of Europe are on its sides. Castles line its banks. It flows through the busiest industrial section of Germany. In fact, that section developed in part because of the Rhine. Major cities on the Rhine or its tributary, the Main, are Cologne and Frankfurt.

    Several nations are interested in the Rhine: Germany; France, as an outlet for products of the Northeast; the Netherlands; Switzerland.

    Its most important tributaries are the Moselle and the Main.

    Free navigation on the Rhine was introduced at the time of the French Revolution, but this has had to be reasserted many times.

2. THE DANUBE. In one form or another, a twig or leaf from the Black Forest ends up 1800 miles away in the Black sea. Its journey is made on the Danube—Europe's second largest river and Western Europe's longest.

    The Danube crosses eight countries: Germany, Austria, Czechoslovakia, Hungary, Yugoslavia, Rumania, Bulgaria, and Russia.

    Long an important river, it has sometimes been called "the Highway of Races." The Danube formed a boundary line and a defense line for the Roman Empire. The Huns, the Slavs, the Magyars, and others have used it.

    Although famed as "The Blue Danube," it is brown.

    Coal, iron, oil, fertilizers, food products, textiles are transported on it.

3. THE SEINE. This is one of the smallest and shortest rivers of Europe but one of the most important. Rising in Burgundy in eastern France, the Seine is the most navigable river of France.

    Paris is built on its banks, as are Rouen and Fontainebleau. Deep dredging of the Seine for 50 miles makes Rouen a seaport city.

    The Marne, Oise, Aube, and Yonne are all tributaries of the Seine.

    Canals have been built to improve its value as a water highway.

Scandinavia

Although we are greatly concerned in social studies with teaching about the areas of the world that were slighted for so long (Africa, the Middle East, Asia), we should not bypass those that have always provided students with valuable study. Scandinavia is such a region. It has contributed richly to world culture. Many of its sons have emigrated to the United States. Possibly most important, the countries of Scandinavia have developed a way of life—sometimes known as "the middle way" between communism and free enterprise—that is worthy of deep consideration. Their experiments with government planning in a liberal, semi-socialistic framework have made the entire world watch them. Your students can learn a great deal by studying Scandinavia, either as a unit by itself or in conjunction with other units in world geography and modern problems courses.

"Scandinavia" is a term used loosely to group certain countries. Basically, it takes in Denmark, Norway, and Sweden. Often Finland is added. Sometimes Iceland, Greenland, and the Faeroe Islands are included.

COMMON TRAITS. Despite differences between them there is a great deal of homogeneity in these countries. Some of the things they have in common are

1. Climate. Because of their location, most of these nations have long, harsh winters and short, pleasant summers. Denmark, of course, is farther south than Finland, Norway, and Sweden, and is, therefore, warmer.

2. Constitutional monarchies and democracies. All these nations are democracies. Denmark, Norway, and Sweden have kings with little power but much prestige.

3. High degree of literacy. Illiteracy is almost unknown. Even the nomadic Lapps are literate. In the past, the Folk High Schools have been prominent in adult education. They still exist but are less dominant than in the 19th century. Sweden's recent school reform program is outstanding. Paying fees to high school students is a revolutionary part of that program.

4. Social legislation. All these nations have extensive social programs, including old-age pensions, unemployment insurance, workingmen's compensation, and similar measures. They are all socialist democracies or welfare states.

5. Religious background. Lutheranism is the major denomination and the state church.

6. Importance of cooperatives. Producer and consumer cooperatives are very important in Scandinavia and are utilized to a greater degree than in most nations.

7. Economic cooperation. The Scandinavian nations work together economically through the Nordic Council, a loose confederation of five countries. They jointly own and run the Scandinavian Airlines System.

8. Similarity of languages.   Danish, Norwegian, and Swedish are very similar, and people can understand each other in these three tongues. Finnish is quite different, being similar to the Magyar of Hungary.

9. No gross inequalities in wealth.   Because of their social outlook and economic setup, there are few rich and fewer poor in these nations.

DIFFERENCES.   Despite their similarities, each nation in Scandinavia is unique. Here are a few examples of their characteristics.

1. Finland.   A country of woods and lakes. Seventy per cent of the nation in forests, hence lumbering and related industries predominate. Much of the paper used in the United States comes from Finland. Tree farming a science. Finland has excelled in modern architecture. It has to walk a tightrope continuously in its relations with the U.S.S.R. Reparations to the U.S.S.R. included 17,680 square miles and $300 million in goods.

2. Norway.   A mountainous country that is only 3 per cent arable. People work and live on fjords or, in the summers, in the mountains. Because of the scarcity of arable land, many Norwegians have emigrated, with large numbers going to the United States. Tremendous supply of electricity from its waterfalls. Some electricity exported.

3. Denmark.   A flat land, consisting of many islands and the peninsula jutting out from the northern part of Europe. Once a great wheat-growing nation, it converted its economy in the 19th century to hogs and dairy products, with a high degree of specialization. Three-quarters of its land arable.

4. Sweden.   A farming and manufacturing nation. Greatest reserves of high-grade iron ore in Europe. Considerable water power. Raises grain, potatoes, sugar beets. Traditionally non-aligned, as it was in World Wars I and II. Some friction with Denmark and Norway on this score.

Scandinavia has produced many outstanding leaders.

Denmark. Grundtvig, Kristen-Kold, Dalgas, Hans Christian Andersen, Bohr, Finsen, Oerstad, Kierkegaard, Thorvaldsen.
Norway. Amundsen, Bjornson, Grieg, Hamsun, Ibsen, Munch, Nansen, Undset, T. Lie, and Vigeland.
Sweden. Branting, Johannson, Lagerlöf, Laval, Milles, Myrdal, Nobel, Söderblom, Strindberg, Wallander, Hammarskjöld.
Finland. Aalto, Cajander, Runeberg, Saarinen, Sibelius, Stanvall, Topelius, and Wrede.

In studying Scandinavia, especially in a world geography class, it might be profitable for the entire class to study the area as a whole, then to divide into committees to study Denmark, Finland, Norway, and Sweden individually.

Germany

The way you teach about Germany depends upon your specific aims in the course, your interest and background, and your pupils' needs and enthusiasms.

However, there are certain key ideas that teachers need to keep in mind in any study of Germany. These include the following:

1. ITS LOCATION IN CENTRAL EUROPE. The location of Germany in Central Europe has given it the feeling of being hemmed in by strong powers, hence the need for "lebensraum" or space. This location, together with other factors, has meant a series of struggles with other countries.

2. ITS LATE UNIFICATION. Germany was one of the last nations of Europe to become unified. This placed it in a poor position in the power struggle. It felt it had to make its way against nations like England and France, which already held positions of leadership and power.

3. ITS GOOD RESOURCES. Much of the power of Germany grows out of the valuable coal and iron deposits in the Ruhr valley. Together these made possible the steel industry upon which Germany's industrialization is based. There are also good farming and timber areas, especially in the South.

4. ITS TRANSPORTATION SYSTEM. The Germans are blessed with several rivers, of which the Rhine is the most important. It is the main water highway of the nation and placed in a strategic position, flowing through the Ruhr region. Cologne developed on it. Frankfurt was built on one of its major tributaries—the Main.

    Other rivers include the Weser and the Elbe, which flow from south to north; the Main, which flows from east to west; the Moselle and the Danube, which flow from west to east.

    Germany's excellent railroad system also enhanced its economy.

5. ITS EDUCATIONAL SYSTEM. German education developed the thoroughness that was necessary for survival in Central Europe. Training was especially strong in scientific subjects—chemistry and physics—an aid to economic development. Germany has long had a high literacy rate.

6. INTEREST IN THE ARTS. Germany should not be considered merely in geographic or economic terms. It also has a high degree of culture, with outstanding contributions in music, literature, art, and allied fields.

What other key ideas do you think should be stressed in any study of Germany?

7.
8.
9.

A BRIEF BIBLIOGRAPHY ON GERMANY

New books about Germany are being published constantly for adult readers. Some high school and junior high school pupils can utilize these volumes. The materials listed below are shorter, much easier references for junior high school readers:

PAMPHLETS AND ALLIED MATERIALS

1. Conly, Robert L. "Modern Miracle—Made in Germany." National Geographic, June 1959. Pp.735 - 791. Black and white and colored illustrations.
2. Deutsch, Harold C. Our Changing German Problems. Chicago: Science Research Associates through Laidlaw, 1956. 64 pp.
3. Epstein, Klaus. Germany after Adenauer. New York: Foreign Policy Association, 1964. 64 pp. A Headline book.
4. Kohn, Hans. West Germany: New Era for German People. New York: Foreign Policy Association, 1958. 62 pp. A Headline book.
5. Office of the Armed Forces Information and Education, Department of Defense. A Pocket Guide to Germany. Washington: Government Printing Office, 1956. 104 pp. Prepared primarily for servicemen in Germany.
6. "West Germany as a World Power." Current History, January 1960. A special issue devoted to West Germany.

BOOKS FOR YOUNG READERS

1. Holbrook, Sabra. Capital without a Country. New York: Coward-McCann, 1961. 121 pp.
2. Larson, Egou. Young Traveler in Germany. New York: Dutton, 1955. 228 pp. Grades 6-9.
3. Lobsenz, Norman. The First Book of West Germany. New York: Watts, 1959. 66 pp. Grades 5-8.
4. Savage, Katharine. People and Power: The Story of Three Nations. New York: Walck, 1959. 250 pp. Grades 6-9. One country is Germany.
5. Savage, Katharine. The Story of the Second World War. New York: Walck, 1958. 271 pp. Grades 6-9.
6. Seger, Gerhart. Germany. Grand Rapids, Mich.: Fideler, 1956. 160 pp. Profusely illustrated with black and white pictures. Grades 5-8.
7. Shirer, William L. The Rise and Fall of Adolph Hitler. New York: Random House, 1961. 185 pp. A Landmark book. Grades 6-9.
8. Tor, Regina. Getting to Know Germany. New York: Coward-McCann, 1954. 64 pp. Grades 4-7. For slow readers in junior high school.
9. Wohlrabe, Raymond, and W. Krusch. The Land and People of Germany. Philadelphia: Lippincott, 1957. 128 pp. Grades 6-9. In the Portraits of Nations series.

FREE MATERIALS

Some free material is available from the German Information Center (410 Park Avenue, New York 22, N.Y.). Some materials (films, filmstrips, and art exhibits) may be borrowed from the Carl Schurz Memorial Foundation (420 Chestnut Street, Philadelphia 6, Pa.).

Italy

Italy's history is long and its accomplishments are illustrious. How can one study Italy for only a few days and get much understanding of it? One answer is to concentrate on a few aspects of that nation, using as much visual and auditory material as possible, so that pupils are touched at feeling, as well as fact, levels. Four aims you may want to develop follow. You can add others if time permits.

1. ITS GEOGRAPHY.   Certainly every study of Italy should emphasize geography. A thorough study of its geography leads into almost all phases of the story of Italy yesterday and today.

    Location.   A peninsula in the southeastern part of Europe. Nearness to Greece. Effect later on its closeness to North Africa. Partial separation from the rest of Europe geographically—and the effects of that separation.

    Bodies of water.   Almost surrounded by water: Adriatic sea, Ionian sea, Tyrrhenian sea, Ligurian sea, and the Mediterranean. Importance in the development of Venice, Genoa, and Pisa near northern European markets and at heads of Adriatic and Ligurian seas. The location of Italian cities on major bodies of water, including the two major rivers—the Po and the Tiber.

    Climate.   Warm, sunny climate, due to the protection of the Alps from northern winds; the seas' influence on weather.

    Soil.   The difference between the soil of the northern areas, the Lombardy and Emilia plains, and the South.

    Terrain.   The fact that Italy was divided geographically by mountains, especially the Apennines, accounts in part for its belated unification.

2. ITS CITIES.   A study of Italy might well be based on its cities and their hinterland areas. In fact, the cities are an important part of any study of Italy. Among the major cities: Assisi, Florence, Genoa, Milan, Naples, Rome, Palermo, Venice. Study each in some detail.

3. ITS LONG HISTORY.   Probably a time-line, with illustrations prepared by pupils, is the best way to show the long history of Italy. Key periods should be marked off to represent the early period of settlements, the Etruscan period, the Roman period, the period of city-states, the period of foreign rule, the period of Italian unification, the period from World War I through World War II, and present-day Italy.

4. CONTRIBUTIONS OF ITALIANS TO WORLD CULTURE. Italy's contributions to world culture are as great as those of any European nation. Approached biographically, a survey of Italy's culture might include these outstanding Italians: da Vinci, Michelangelo, Giotto, Raphael, Vivaldi, Corelli, Monteverdi, Verdi, Rossini, Dante, St. Francis and the various Popes, Galileo, Columbus, Marconi, Volta, Fermi, and Montessori.

A BRIEF BIBLIOGRAPHY ON ITALY

Senior high school students should be able, in many instances, to read the books written on Italy for adults. Some pupils in junior high schools may also be able to use them. The references below are largely for junior high school readers. Some books, written for elementary school pupils, are included for slow readers in junior high schools.

BOOKS

1. Craz, Al. Getting to Know Italy. New York: Coward-McCann, 1961. 64 pp. Grades 4-7.
2. Epstein, Sam and Beryl. First Book of Italy. New York: Watts, 1958. 68 pp. Grades 4-7.
3. "Italy." A special issue of Holiday magazine for April 1960. Reading material for adults; pictures for anyone.
4. Keating, Kate and Bern. A Young American Looks at Italy. New York: Putnam, 1963. 126 pp.
5. Kish, George. Italy. Garden City, N.Y.: Doubleday, 1956. 62 pp. Grades 7-10. With many colored illustrations. There is also a school edition prepared by Rand McNally.
6. Kish, George. Italy. Grand Rapids, Mich.: Fideler, 1957. 160 pp. Grades 5-8. Many large black and white photographs.
7. Kubly, Herbert. Italy. New York: Time, Inc., 1961. 160 pp. Magnificent illustrations. In the Life World Library series. Reading material for adults.
8. Toor, Frances. Made in Italy. New York: Knopf, 1957. 209 pp., Grades 7-10. On the fine arts in Italy.
9. Winwar, Francis. Land of the Italian People. Philadelphia: Lippincott, 1961. 130 pp. Grades 7-10. In the Portraits of Nations series.

FILMS

"Italy-Peninsula of Contrasts." Encyclopedia Britannica Films. 1961. 17 minutes. Sound, color. For sale or rental.
"Italy: The Post-War Renaissance (Our World of the Sixties)." 1961. United World Films. 17 minutes. Sound, color. For sale.

FILMSTRIPS

"Life in Italy." 1960. Pictorial events. 45 frames. Color.
"Italy." Eye Gate House. Color.

The Balkans

The area of Europe called the Balkans is probably the least-known part of Europe to Americans. Nevertheless, you will undoubtedly need to teach about it in world history, in world geography, and in conjunction with current events. Here are some background ideas and data on the Balkans.

1. COUNTRIES IN THE BALKANS: Albania, Bulgaria, Greece, Yugoslavia, Turkey. Sometimes Hungary is included.

2. IMPORTANCE OF THE BALKANS. Meeting place today of communism and Western democracy. United States' interest because of our allies—Greece and Turkey.
   Historically: melting pot of peoples as a result of migrations; battleground of of empires of East and West; tinderbox or powder keg of Europe in recent times (small nations supplied the kegs; great powers, the powder).

3. GEOGRAPHICAL LOCATION AND IMPORTANCE. A peninsula jutting out of the southeastern part of Europe in the shape of a triangle. An area of mountains and river valleys. "Balkans" means mountains in Turkish. The mountains divided the peoples of the area for centuries. Dominated geographically by the Danube River and its tributaries. A land bridge from Europe to the Middle East and Asia—and vice versa.

4. THE PEOPLE OF THE BALKANS are largely Slavs: Serbs, Croats, Bulgarians, Macedonians, Ruthenians, Slovenes. The Rumanians, Hungarians, and Greeks have some Slavic background but do not speak Slavic languages. There are also Turks, Albanians (a separate group), Germans, Jews, and gypsies.

5. RESOURCES OF THE AREA. This is not a wealthy area compared to many parts of the world.
   Bulgaria: largely agricultural.
   Albania: primitive farming and herds.
   Greece: tobacco, raisins, olive oil.
   Hungary: grain (especially wheat), bauxite, textiles, machinery.
   Rumania: lumber, grain, oil, shipping.
   Turkey: tobacco, cotton, wheat, chromium.
   Yugoslavia: lumber, lead, chromium.

6. A THUMBNAIL SKETCH OF THE HISTORY OF THE BALKANS. This region has a long and very complicated history. Centuries of migrations, during the time of Greece's supremacy. From the third century on—the Slavs—followed by Macedonian leadership; Roman domination; Byzantium control of most of the area; Turkish control for five centuries; Austria's push southeast; Russia's push southwest (stopped by England in the Crimean War); formation of the Balkan League; World Wars I and II.

79

A BRIEF BIBLIOGRAPHY OF THE BALKANS

Good readers in junior high schools and many students in senior high schools may use books written for adults. Most of the references given here are for grades 6–10, as it is assumed that most studies of the Balkans will be in world geography courses.

GENERAL
1. Chubb, Thomas C. Slavic Peoples. Cleveland: World, 1962. 128 pp. Grades 7-10.
2. Joy, C. R. Young People of the Eastern Mediterranean. New York: Duell, 1959. Grades 7-10.
3. Kostich, Dragos D. The Land and People of the Balkans: Albania, Bulgaria, Rumania, Yugoslavia. Philadelphia: Lippincott, 1962. 160 pp. Grades 6-9.
4. "Hungary, Romania, Bulgaria." New York: American Geographical Society, 1960. 6 pp. An issue of Focus.
5. Scholastic Publications. The Soviet Satellites of Eastern Europe. New York: Scholastic Book Services, 1963. 160 pp. Intended as a text. A paperback.
6. Wolff, R. L. The Balkans in Our Time. Cambridge, Mass.: Harvard University Press, 1956. 618 pp. For advanced students in secondary schools.

GREECE
Some material is available free from the Greek Embassy Information Service (2211 Massachusetts Avenue, N.W., Washington 8, D.C.).
1. "Greece." New York: American Geographical Society, 1958. 6 pp. An issue of Focus.
2. Gianakoulis, Theodore. The Land and People of Greece. Philadelphia: Lippincott, 1952. 117 pp. Grades 6-9.
3. Gidal, Sonia and Tim. My Village in Greece. New York: Pantheon, 1960. 76 pp. Grades 5-8. For slow readers. Gives some interesting information on village life.
4. Pocket Guide to Greece. Washington: Government Printing Office, 1960. 95 pp. Written originally for the armed forces.
5. Tor, Regina. Getting to Know Greece. New York: Coward-McCann, 1959. 64 pp. Grades 5-7. For slow readers.
6. Visual Geography Series. Greece in Pictures. New York: Sterling, 1962. 64 pp. About half of the material is pictorial—black and white.

HUNGARY
Pounds, Norman J. G. Hungary, Bulgaria, and Rumania. Garden City, N.Y.: Doubleday, 1961. 64 pp. Pictures in color. Around the World series.

TURKEY
1. Brock, Ray. Ghost on Horseback: The Incredible Ataturk. Boston: Little, 1954. 408 pp. Grades 9-12.
2. Davis, Fanny. Getting to Know Turkey. New York: Coward-McCann, 1957. 64 pp. Grades 5-8.
3. Melamid, Alexander. Turkey. Garden City, N.Y.: Doubleday, 1957. 56 pp. Includes many colored pictures.
4. Pocket Guide to Turkey. Washington: Government Printing Office, 1960. 96 pp.
5. Spencer, William. The Land and People of Turkey. Philadelphia: Lippincott, 1958. 128 pp. Grades 6-9.

YUGOSLAVIA
1. Armstrong, Hamilton Fish. Tito and Goliath. New York: Macmillan, 1951. 300 pp.
2. Gidal, Sonia and Tim. My Village in Yugoslavia. New York: Pantheon, 1957. 74 pp. Grades 4-7.
3. Halpern, Barbara and Joel. Yugoslavia. Garden City, New York: Doubleday, 1956. 64 pp. Many pictures in color.

The U. S. S. R.

SOME   STEREOTYPES   TO   SHATTER

A great many stereotypes about the U.S.S.R. have developed in the minds of Americans. Your students are likely to believe some of these generalizations, with varying degrees of conviction. As a social studies teacher, devoted to the discovery and propagation of the truth, you will want to try to correct misimpressions. The best way to do so is to help students find out what the facts are. In some instances, you will have to tell them the facts, but, wherever possible, they should discover them for themselves. Here are a few of the stereotypes about Russia that are common; you will undoubtedly discover others as you teach about the country.

1. ALL RUSSIANS ARE COMMUNISTS.   Three to five per cent of the population, or around ten million Russians, are members of the Communist party. A large majority of the populace support the communist regime, despite their criticisms of some aspects of it.

2. ALL WEALTH IN THE U.S.S.R. IS EVENLY DIVIDED.   This idea has arisen from the theory that communism "divides the wealth." Actually, there is an increasing amount of private enterprise, such as incentive wages in factories, and there are wide ranges in salaries.

3. ALL RUSSIANS ARE ALIKE IN APPEARANCE AND BACKGROUND.   There is probably as much variation in types of people in Russia as exists in any country of the world. They range from Europeans to Mongolians. The backgrounds of Russians vary tremendously, too, from the people in remote villages to the people of large metropolitan cities.

4. THERE IS NO RELIGIOUS LIFE IN THE U.S.S.R.   The Communist party has combated the idea of religion with varying degrees of intensity at different periods. Many churches are still open, and some groups, such as the Baptists, are actually growing in numbers.

5. THE RUSSIAN SYSTEM OF EDUCATION SURPASSES OURS. This stereotype began about the time of Sputnik, as an attempt to explain the strides of the Russians in space science and to discredit American education. There are many fine aspects to Russian education, but it is a type of education developed for their society and their aims—not ours.

6. COMMUNISM APPEALS ONLY TO THE POOR AND IGNORANT.   Although communism has had a great appeal to the poor of the world and to those who want rapid change, its appeal is wide. Many highly educated people in different parts of the world have espoused communism because of its philosophy in its most idealistic form.

SOME POINTS TO STRESS IN STUDYING THE U.S.S.R.

The U.S.S.R. is a vast country with a long and complicated history. It merits considerable time in any social studies curriculum. If your time for such a study is limited, you will have to decide upon major points to stress in the course of study. Here are a few significant topics.

1. The enormous size of the U.S.S.R. Three times the size of the United States and three-fourths the size of the African continent.

2. The wide variations in topography, from the frozen northern areas to the tropical southern ones.

3. The wide variety of people in the U.S.S.R. and the problems arising from this variety. Includes the Russians, the Ukrainians, the Uzbeks, the Tartars, and others. Differences in languages, in culture.

4. The effect of its vast plains in "inviting" invasions.

5. The lack of warm-water ports and the search for them over the centuries.

6. The fear of "containment." This is best illustrated by a world map with a polar projection showing the various alliances of the Western world surrounding the U.S.S.R.

7. The authoritarian pattern of organization of its institutions over the centuries, including the governments and the church.

8. The excesses of the church, resulting in attacks upon it. Alliance of the church and the Czarist regimes and the lack of social consciousness of the church in Russia.

9. The conflicts between westernization and Pan-Slavism. The big question throughout history: "Is Russia Eastern or Western?"

10. Its expansion over the centuries, including that in recent times.

11. Its contributions to world culture, especially in music, art, architecture, literature, and the ballet.

12. Its tremendous resources and vast industrialization.

13. Its firm belief in state planning.

14. Its overriding belief or feeling that it is "behind" and must "catch up."

15. The importance of its education, both formal and informal.

16. Its appeal to the economically underdeveloped areas of the world as they see how fast the U.S.S.R. has developed. Its ability now to export economic know-how.

Source Materials
for Studying the U.S.S.R.

There is a wealth of materials today on the U.S.S.R., ranging from translated Russian materials to books, pamphlets, and articles written by Americans who know the U.S.S.R. well.

You can cull much good material from magazines and newspapers but take heed as to its authenticity. Materials representing a variety of points of view should be saved and used by pupils as well as teachers.

Some of the most current materials are listed below. The author has paid special attention here to pamphlets written for secondary school students and to paperback books, although the entries in this reading list include other items.

PAMPHLETS FOR SECONDARY SCHOOL STUDENTS
(Most of these items cost less than $1)

1. Editors of Scholastic Book Services. The Soviet Union. New York: Scholastic, 1962. 160 pp.
2. Griffith, William E. World Communism Divided. New York: Foreign Policy Association, 1964. 48 pp. A Headline book.
3. Isenberg, Irwin. The Soviet Satellites. New York: Scholastic, 1963. 160 pp. In the same series as No. 1 above.
4. Judy, Richard. Communist Agriculture: Crisis and Change. New York: Foreign Policy Association, 1963. 62 pp. A Headline book.
5. Lengyel, Emil. The Soviet Union: The Land and Its People. New York: Oxford, 1956. 92 pp.
6. McNeal, Robert H. The Russian Revolution. New York: Holt, 1960. 62 pp. In their Source Problems in World Civilization series.
7. Midesell, R., and D. Wells. The Soviet Economic Offensive. Toronto, Canada: Canadian Institute, 1959. 17 pp.
8. Petrovich, Michael B. The Soviet Union. Boston: Ginn, 1964. 122 pp. A very comprehensive, well-balanced account, well written and well illustrated.
9. Platig, E. Raymond. The United States and the Soviet Challenge. River Forest, Ill.: Laidlaw, 1960. 64 pp.
10. Raymond, Ellsworth. Soviet Economic Progress. New York: Holt, 1960. 56 pp. in their Source Problems in World Civilization series.
11. Red China and the U.S.S.R. Washington: Government Printing Office, 1963. 35 pp.
12. Salvadori, Massimo. The Rise of Modern Communism. New York: Holt, 1963. 220 pp.
13. Schwartz, Harry. The Soviet Union: Communist Economic Power. Chicago: Scott, 1963. 72 pp.
14. "The Soviet Union. 1964." Current History. Special issue for November 1964. 63 pp. Usually such an issue each year.
15. The Soviet Union and Eastern Europe. New York: Foreign Policy Association, 1960. 18 pp.
16. Whitney, Thomas P. Has Russia Changed? New York: Foreign Policy Association, 1960. 96 pp.

SELECTED BOOKS FOR SECONDARY SCHOOL STUDENTS
(Largely for junior high readers or slower readers in the high schools)

1. Gunther, John. Meet Soviet Russia: Land, People, Sights. New York: Harper, 1962. 182 pp. From Inside Russia Today. Also a paperback.
2. Gunther, John. Meet Soviet Russia: Leaders, Politics, Problems. New York: Harper, 1962. 180 pp. From Inside Russia Today. Also a paperback.
3. Hoff, Rhoda. Russia: Adventures in Eyewitness History. New York: Walck, 1964. 207 pp.
4. Nazaroff, Alexander. The Land of the Russian People. Philadelphia: Lippincott, 1960. 128 pp.
5. Salisbury, Harrison E. The Key to Moscow. Philadelphia: Lippincott, 1963. 128 pp.
6. Thayer, Charles W., and the editors of Life. Life World Library: Russia. New York: Time, 1960. 152 pp. Magnificent color photographs as well as textual material.

SELECTED PAPERBACKS
(For teachers and good readers in secondary schools)

1. Cantril, Hadley. Soviet Leaders and Mastery Over Man. New Brunswick, N.J.: Rutgers University Press, 1960. 173 pp. A brilliant analysis, by a psychologist, of the ideology and the manner in which it is implemented.
2. Gorer, Geoffrey, and John Rickman. The People of Great Russia: A Psychological Study. New York: Norton, 1962. 236 pp.
3. Kennan, George F. Russia and the West under Lenin and Stalin. Boston: Little, 1961. 409 pp. A Mentor paperback, too.
4. Kechan, Lionel. The Making of Modern Russia. Baltimore: Penguin, 1963. 335 pp.
5. Lawrence, John. A History of Russia. New York: Mentor, 1962. 320 pp.
6. Levine, Irving R. Main Street U.S.S.R. New York: Mentor, 1962. 190 pp. On many phases of life but emphasizes the people.
7. Mager, N. H., and Jacques Katel, eds. Conquest Without War. New York: Pocket Books, 1961. 550 pp. On Khrushchev.
8. Mandel, William. Russia Re-Examined: The Land, the People and How They Live. New York: Hill and Wang, 1964. 244 pp.
9. Mehnert, Klaus. Soviet Man and His World. New York: Praeger, 1962. 310 pp. Impressions of the people and their attitudes towards family life, collectivization, religion, and other fields of human endeavor.
10. Miller, Wright W. Russians as People. New York: Dutton, 1961. 205 pp. A most interesting comparison of Americans and Russians as people.
11. Pares, Bernard. Russia: History, People, Politics. New York: Mentor, 1958. 200 pp. A favorite of many people for many years.
12. Rostow, W. W. The Dynamics of Soviet Society. New York: Mentor, 1958. 264 pp.

OTHER MATERIALS

1. George Kirk's Economic Atlas of the Soviet Union (Ann Arbor, Mich.: University of Michigan Press, 1960. 96 pp.) is expensive but an excellent volume for a school library.
2. A map of the geography of the U.S.S.R. in color is sold by World Affairs Materials, Brooklyn College, Brooklyn 10, N.Y.
3. Warren B. Walsh has three volumes in Readings in Russian History (Syracuse, N.Y.: Syracuse University Press, 1963. 867 pp.) for those who want to delve deeply.

The European Community

The development of the Common Market and the European Community are events of tremendous importance in today's world. Social studies teachers must include them in studying Europe, current events, the foreign policy of the United States, the U.S.S.R, and other topics.

Average and below-average students need to be aware of the European community. You can show this best by comparing it with the states of the United States, showing what happens when there are tariffs and when there are not tariffs. Gifted students should certainly study the European Community in detail.

Some big ideas to stress include the European Community's effect on living standards in Europe, on world trade, on the United States, the U.S.S.R., and Great Britain.

BASIC BACKGROUND. The "Inner Six" of the Common Market are France, Belgium, Luxembourg, the Netherlands, West Germany, and Italy. The "Outer Seven" include Norway, Sweden, Denmark, the United Kingdom, Portugal, Austria, and Switzerland—associated in the European Free Trade Association (EFTA). Some of the overseas possessions and former possessions of the members of the Common Market are related in a special capacity.

The three main parts of the European Community (see chart on reverse side) are

1. The European Coal and Steel Community (ECSC).
    Started in 1952. Aim—to pool resources of coal, iron ore, scrap, and steel.
2. The Common Market (officially the European Economic Community—EEC).
    Started in 1958. Aim—to reduce tariff barriers over a 12-year period and to eliminate them eventually.
3. The European Atomic Energy Community.
    Started in 1958. Aim—to develop nuclear energy in the member states for peaceful purposes.

IMPORTANT STATISTICS ON THE EUROPEAN COMMUNITY. The materials below, taken from official publications of the EEC, should serve as provocative data for students. You could write these statistics on the chalkboard or give mimeographed copies to each pupil.

Topic	Community	UK	USA	USSR
Area in thousands of square miles	449	94	3,600	8,600
Population in the mid-60s in millions	179	53.7	189	225
Active working population in millions	74	23	72	99
Gross National Product at market prices in 1963	248.8	84.2	585.4	No data
Steel production in millions of metric tons	73.2	22.9	101.2	80.2
Imports in millions of dollars	24,653	13,496	17,014	No data
Exports in millions of dollars	21,618	11,854	22,922	No data

THE INSTITUTIONS
OF THE EUROPEAN COMMUNITY

ECSC
EUROPEAN COAL AND STEEL COMMUNITY

COMMON MARKET
EUROPEAN ECONOMIC COMMUNITY

EURATOM
EUROPEAN ATOMIC ENERGY COMMUNITY

THE EXECUTIVES

Consultative Committee

HIGH AUTHORITY

European Investment Bank

Monetary Committee

European Social Fund

Overseas Development Fund

COMMISSION

Economic and Social Committee

COMMISSION

Supply Agency

Scientific and Technical Committee

Joint Nuclear Research Center

COUNCILS' OF MINISTERS

DEMOCRATIC CONTROL

EUROPEAN PARLIAMENT

JUDICIAL CONTROL

COURT OF JUSTICE

EUROPEAN COAL AND STEEL COMMUNITY

EUROPEAN ECONOMIC COMMUNITY

EUROPEAN ATOMIC ENERGY COMMUNITY

Source Materials
on the European Community

Events are transpiring so rapidly in the European Community that you will need to keep a good file of current newspaper and magazine articles to keep abreast of them. The following sources provide free materials:

1. The Atlantic Council of the United States, 1616 H Street, N.W., Washington 6, D.C.
2. E.E.C. Information Service, 808 Farragut Building, Washington 6, D.C.
3. European Free Trade Association, 711 Fourteenth Street, N.W., Washington 5, D.C.

The information bureaus of the governments of Europe involved in the European Community also supply data.

The most inclusive listing of materials is collected in a special issue of Intercom magazine (345 East 46th Street, New York 17) for February–March 1962. ($1.) This list includes many sources to which one can write, as well as titles of books and pamphlets.

Sidney N. Barnett outlines teaching about the European Community in an article on "One More Unit of Social Studies Work: The European Community," in The Social Studies (November 1964, pp. 221-228). The article includes a full listing of books and other materials, as well as an outline and explanation of a unit of work for senior high school.

BOOKS

1. Albrecht-Carrie, Rene. One Europe: The Historical Background of European Unity. New York: Doubleday, 1965. 345 pp.
2. Barach, Arnold B. The New Europe and Its Economic Future. New York: Macmillan, 1964. 148 pp. For the Twentieth Century Fund.
3. Benoit, Emile. Europe—At Sixes and Sevens. New York: Columbia University Press, 1961. 275 pp.
4. Birrenbach, Kurt. The Future of the Atlantic Community: Toward European American Partnership. New York: Praeger, 1963. 94 pp. Also available in a paperback edition.
5. Brinton, Crane. The Temper of Western Europe. Cambridge, Mass.: Harvard University Press, 1962. 118 pp.
6. Frank, Isaiah. The European Common Market. New York: Praeger, 1961. 324 pp.
7. Henderson, W. O. The Genesis of the Common Market. Chicago: Quadrangle, 1962. 201 pp. From the 18th century on.
8. Humphrey, Dan D. The United States and the Common Market. New York: Praeger, 1962. 176 pp. Emphasizing United States trade with Europe.
9. Kitzinger, U. W. The Challenge of the Common Market. New York: Praeger, 1963. 250 pp. A revised edition.
10. Lichtheim, George. The New Europe: Today and Tomorrow. New York: Praeger, 1963. 232 pp.

11. The New Europe: Implications for the United States. Entire issue of The Annals of the American Academy of Political and Social Science for July 1963.

12. Polach, Jaroslav G. Euratom: Its Background, Issues and Economic Implications. Dobbs Ferry, N.Y.: Oceana, 1964. 232 pp.

13. Shanks, Michael, and John Lambert. The Common Market Today—and Tomorrow. New York: Praeger, 1962. 254 pp. Also in a paperback.

PAMPHLETS

1. Calderwood, James D. Western Europe and the Common Market. Chicago: Scott, 1963. 72 pp. Junior and senior high school readers.

2. Clayton, William L. U.S. Trade and the Common Market. New York: Foreign Policy Association, 1962. 62 pp. 75¢. A Headline book.

3. Coppock, Joseph D. The European Economic Community and United States Trade Policy. Washington: Government Printing Office, 1962. 12 pp. 10¢.

4. Deutsch, Harold C. The New Europe and the Common Market and the United States. River Forest, Ill.: Laidlaw, 1964. 67 pp. A booklet intended as a text in senior high schools. Revised edition of an earlier booklet. Emphasizes United States relations.

5. "The European Common Market." Current History magazine for November 1963. Usually one issue per year on this topic.

6. "European Economic Community." New York: American Geographical Society, 1962. 6 pp. 25¢. A special issue of Focus.

7. Heilbroner, Robert L. Forging a United Europe—The Story of the European Community. New York: Public Affairs Committee, 1961. 32 pp. 25¢.

8. MacDonald, H.I. The European Economic Community: Background and Bibliography. Toronto, Canada: Canadian Institute, 1962. 16 pp. 20¢.

9. MacDonald, H.I. A Guide to European Economic Community. Toronto, Canada: Canadian Institute, 1962. 20 pp. 20¢.

10. A Remodelled Economic Organization: A Report by the Group of Four. New York: Committee for Economic Cooperation and Development, 1960. 78 pp. 50¢.

11. Stewart, Maxwell S. The European Common Market and the United States. New York: Public Affairs Committee, 1962. 20 pp. 25¢.

KIT

The International Communications Foundation, 870 Monterey Pass Road, Monterey Park, California, sells kits of materials on the Common Market. There are two kits, priced at $100 and at $50, including filmstrips, colored maps, narrative recordings, and teachers' study guides. Previews may be arranged for a few days.

FILM AND FILMSTRIP

1. A filmstrip is sold by the New York Times Office of Education Activities (229 West 53rd Street, New York) on "Europe's Common Market and U.S. Trade." 51 frames. Black and white.

2. A film on "Europe Without Frontiers" is available on free loan from Association Films, 347 Madison Avenue, New York 17. 22 minutes. Color

3. The International Cooperation Administration has a free film on "Europe Looks Ahead." Write to that organization, Washington 25, D.C. The emphasis, however, is on the Marshall Plan.

Studying Africa

SOME STEREOTYPES TO SHATTER

Here are some of the stereotypes about Africa that your students may believe. If they are to obtain an accurate, realistic picture of that continent, you will have to replace generalizations with facts.

The Stereotype

1. Africa is a country.

2. Africa is mostly jungles and deserts.

3. Africa is filled with wild animals.

4. All African countries are rich in minerals.

5. Africa is hot and humid.

6. Africans are naked, drum-beating savages.
7. Africans are African "natives" with a few Europeans.
8. Africans live in small tribes.

9. Africans live in villages.

10. Africa had no great civilizations.
11. Africa has no industrialization.
12. Africa is filled with race problems.

The Facts

1. Africa is a continent, with 50 countries and territories.
2. The Sahara is about one-fourth of Africa, and the Kalahari is relatively small. The extent of jungles has been grossly exaggerated. Most of Africa is not desert and jungle.
3. There are many wild animals in Africa but not in all parts, especially not in the western regions. They are fast disappearing.
4. All African countries are not rich in minerals. Some of its nations do have wonderful mineral resources.
5. The coastal plains are hot and humid, but most of Africa is plateau country and is not hot and humid.
6. This is the worst stereotype of Africans, and you should try to erase it.
7. There are large numbers of Indians and Pakistani in East and South Africa and Lebanese and Syrians in West Africa.
8. Some do, but some tribes are very large: the Fulani of Nigeria, the Ibo, and the Yoruba.
9. Many do, but in parts of East Africa they live on small plots of land; many Africans live in cities, too.
10. Africa had the civilizations of the Ghana, Songhai, and Mali empires.
11. There are some very large industries, such as the copper and gold industries.
12. Actually, race is a major issue in only a few sections—Kenya, South Africa, and Rhodesia.

SOME   POINTS   TO   STRESS

From the following list, you should be able to select a few points to stress in any study of Africa. Each point, of course, should be elaborated. Here are some significant points to consider.

1. Africa is an increasingly important part of the world today.

2. Africa is a continent of great diversity.

3. Africa has many natural and mineral resources.

4. There is a great variety of people in the African continent, and there are many differences between the Africans themselves.

5. The variety of languages makes communication difficult. People often use European languages, such as English and French, for communication among different groups. Hausa and Swahili are two local languages used in more than one area of Africa.

6. The ways of living differ radically in Africa.

7. There are many value systems and religions in Africa, including Moslem and Christian.

8. The extended family and the tribe have been central in the lives of Africans in the past but are decreasingly important today.

9. African value systems are being eroded.

10. Racial conflicts exist in some parts of Africa and are acute in such areas as Kenya, Rhodesia, and the Republic of South Africa.

11. Africa is developing rapidly economically, with the building of dams and factories.

12. The standards of living are very low in most parts of the continent, with a per capita income of less than $100 a year for most people.

13. There are many patterns of government, but most of the new countries are democratic, even though one-party democracies are developing.

14. Africa has a long and interesting history, including the famous empires of Ghana, Mali, and Songhai.

15. The African people, like people everywhere, enjoy and create many kinds of beauty.

16. Our contacts with the African continent and its people will increase markedly in the years ahead.

Nigeria

Social studies students need to study some countries of the world in depth in order to come close to understanding them. In the continent of Africa, or Africa south of the Sahara, Nigeria is perhaps the best nation to select for intensive study because

1. It has the largest population in Africa, about 40 million persons.
2. It has a wide variety of people, from villagers to city dwellers, from Christians to Moslems, and from very small tribal groups to tribes numbering five to six million.
3. It has a broad-based economy, with considerable agriculture, some mining, and an increasing amount of manufacturing.
4. It has a relatively stable government and many educated leaders.
5. It represents the majority of African nations that have no special race problem.
6. It is a country with a promising future.

SIZE AND LOCATION. Nigeria is like a keystone wedged into the western side of Africa just north of the equator, bordered by Dahomey, Niger, Chad, the Cameroun Republic, and the Gulf of Guinea. It is 650 miles from the coast to the northern border and 700 miles east to west at the broadest point. It is about the size of Texas and Arizona combined, three times the size of Norway, four times the size of the United Kingdom, ten times the size of Portugal, and thirty-five times the size of Belgium.

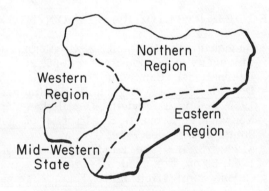

REGIONS AND GEOGRAPHY. Nigeria is divided into three relatively distinct regions by the Niger river in the West and the Benue river in the East, which combine to form the Niger river in the southern part of the country. To these three regions, a fourth political unit—the Midwest State—has been added since independence. Geographically, there are four strips or bands of land starting in the south: the mangrove swamps and delta; the forest belt or region; the grasslands, savannah, and plains; and, in the far north, the desert and thorn forest. The southern part of Nigeria is a coastal plain and is hot and humid much of the year. The northern region is subtropical—hot and dry. The rainy season, from April to November, is characterized by southwestern monsoon winds.

PEOPLE.   Contrary to popular belief, some of the tribes in Africa are extremely large. This is especially true in Nigeria. The Hausas, in the North, number about 6 million; the Ibos, in the East, about 5½ million; the Yorubas, in the West, about 5 million; the Fulanis, in the North, 3¾ million; the Kanuris 1½ million; and the Ibibios a million.

AGRICULTURE AND INDUSTRY.   Nigeria is predominately an agricultural country, with about 80 per cent of its people cultivating farms and forests. For years to come, Nigeria must depend primarily on those farms and forests. Among the products grown are cacao, cotton, groundnuts or peanuts, yams, cassava, beans and rice, and rubber. Farm holdings are often only one to two acres. The discovery of petroleum and natural gas has enhanced Nigeria's wealth. A little coal is mined. Some tin ore exists, and some iron has been found recently. New factories are being built rapidly for industry such as cotton-ginning, piece-cotton manufacture, palm oil extraction, plywood and veneer production, fruit juice and soft drink bottling. A six-year plan of development (1962 to 1968) has high targets for electricity, trade and industry, transport and communications, education, health, and other aspects of the nation.

GOVERNMENT.   Because of the strong attachment to the various regions, Nigeria developed a system of regional government inside a federal framework. In each region, there is a governor, a premier, and a bicameral legislature: a House of Assembly and a House of Chiefs. At the federal level, there is a governor-general and a prime minister, a House of Representatives and a Senate elected by universal adult suffrage. Up to the present time, a combination of the Northern and Eastern Region parties has controlled the central government.

CITIES.   There are more large cities in Nigeria than in most countries of Africa. The largest center is Ibadan, with over 800,000 inhabitants. Next comes Lagos, the capital, with over 500,000. The third largest city is Kano, a trading center in the North, with a population of 150,000.

HISTORY.   Students should learn something of the high development of culture in early Nigeria, centered in Ife and Benin with their advanced work in bronze. They should learn about the slave trade in this part of the world. The period of British control began with the colony of Lagos in 1861 and gradually included other parts of present-day Nigeria. Finally, Nigeria won independence on October 1, 1960. This is a skeleton outline of a long, and often illustrious, history.

A SELECTED BIBLIOGRAPHY ON NIGERIA

1. Buchanan, K. M., and J. C. Pugh. Land and People of Nigeria. London: University of London Press, 1955. 252 pp. For adults.
2. International Bank for Reconstruction and Development. The Economic Development of Nigeria. Baltimore: Johns Hopkins University Press, 1955. 686 pp. For adults. Detailed.
3. Kenworthy, Leonard S. Profile of Nigeria. New York: Doubleday, 1960. 96 pp. For grades 7-10.
4. Niven, C. R. The Land and People of West Africa. New York: Macmillan, 1959. 84 pp. For grades 8-10.
5. Olden, Sam. Getting to Know Nigeria. New York: Coward-McCann, 1959. 60 pp. Grades 8-10.

Studying Kenya

If you want to learn about the world, Kenya is a good country to study. In a way, it is the world in miniature. It has representatives of the three major races of mankind—the Mongoloids, the Caucasoids, and the Negroids—or the Asians, Europeans, and Africans. It has most of the major religions. It has a variety of land forms, from deserts to mountains. It has almost every stage of industrial development from nomadic tribes to modern factories. It has most of the problems of the world—including poverty, prejudice, lack of education, capital, and water.

Here are some of the salient facts about Kenya. Others may be obtained from the references on the back of this page.

1. GEOGRAPHY. Three-fifths of Kenya (the northern part) is desert and bush country. In that area live nomadic tribes, such as the Somalis and the Masai. The southern strip of Kenya contains most of its 6½ million people. It is mostly highland or plateau country, except for a narrow coastal plain along the Indian ocean. Lake Victoria, the world's second largest, inland, fresh-water lake, is in the southwest. Mt. Kilimanjaro is just across the border of Kenya in Tanganyika.

2. PEOPLE. Approximately 6,200,000 of the people of Kenya are Africans. The Asians number 170,000. They came to Kenya from India and Pakistan to build the railroad from Mombasa on the coast to Lake Victoria and thence into Uganda. There are only about 60,000 Europeans, but, until recently, they earned about two-thirds of the cash income of the country. The relations between these three groups is one of Kenya's chief problems. In fact, the rise of Mau-Mau a few years ago stemmed primarily from the Africans' inability to advance in the face of white control. After independence, some whites left the country, fearing what might happen to them under an African government. The place of the Indians and Pakistani in the "New Kenya" is still open to question. In the past, they have been primarily the small shopkeepers.

3. EARNING A LIVING. Kenya has been, and probably will remain, primarily an agricultural country because it has almost no minerals, except a little soda ash. It has little water and must get its water power from Uganda and Tanganyika. Therefore, it is essential to improve the state of agriculture and to develop secondary industries based upon agriculture, such as meat canning.

4. EDUCATION. At the time of independence, Kenya had 620,000 children in grades 1 to 4; 100,000 in grades 5 to 8; and only 5500 in grades 9 to 12. The bottleneck in education is the lack of teachers and of secondary school pupils. Most teachers are only eighth grade graduates. A branch of the University of East Africa (with sections in Kenya, Tanganyika, and Uganda) is located in Nairobi.

5. MODERN HISTORY OF KENYA. The history of Kenya in modern times began around 1900 when England built a railroad from Mombasa to Lake Victoria. England wanted to offset the growing influence of Germany in East Africa (especially in Tanganyika), protect the headwaters of the Nile river, cut down on the slave traffic carried on in caravans from Uganda, and obtain the valuable ivory from East Africa. Settlers were encouraged to go to Kenya and settle along the railroad. Soldiers from England, in World War I and again in World War II, found the highlands of Kenya a beautiful and promising area, and many of them returned there to live. In 1963, Kenya won its independence; in 1964, it proclaimed itself a republic but remained a member of the Commonwealth.

6. KENYA AND EAST AFRICA. Kenya works with Uganda and Tanganyika (now called Tanzania) in the East African Common Services, the extension of a union started by the British. There was hope for a while that these three areas (or four, if one includes the former Zanzibar) would unite in a federation, but that step has not come about yet.

A brief study of Kenya might be carried on in several ways. One method is to start with the building of the railroad and to see what happened as a result of this major event and the arrival of the whites and the Asians. Another way is to follow the chart in Leonard Kenworthy's Guide to Social Studies Teaching (Wadsworth). Start with the land, then take up the people, their values, their institutions, their creative ideas and expressions, and their contacts with other lands and peoples. Conclude with the story of their history. A third way is to divide the class into Africans, Asians, and Europeans for role playing the data students discover about these three groups. Of course, the majority of the class should be assigned to the role of Africans.

A BRIEF BIBLIOGRAPHY ON KENYA

1. Barker-Benfield, M. A. The Land and Peoples of East Africa. New York: Macmillan, 1960. 104 pp. Chapters 11 and 12 on Kenya. Grades 6 and up.
2. Carter, Gwendolen. Independence for Africa. New York: Praeger, 1960. 172 pp. Chapters 1 and 2 on Kenya. Available as a paperback.
3. Delf, George. Jomo Kenyatta. New York: Doubleday, 1961. 214 pp. A very favorable account of this highly controversial figure.
4. Gunther, John. Inside Africa. New York: Harper, 1955. 952 pp. Chapters 18-21 on Kenya.
5. Ingalls, Leonard. Getting to Know Kenya. New York: Coward-McCann, 1963. 64 pp.
6. Kenworthy, Leonard S. Profile of Kenya. New York: Doubleday, 1962. 96 pp. Grades 6-9. Many black and white photographs included.
7. Melady, Thomas P. Profile of African Leaders. New York: Macmillan, 1961. 186 pp. Pages 46-59 on Tom Mboya.
8. Savage, Katherine. The Story of Africa South of the Sahara. New York: Walck, 1961. 184 pp. Grades 6-9. Chapter 12 on Kenya.
9. Wood, Susan. Kenya: The Tensions of Progress. New York: Oxford, 1960. 108 pp. Grades 9-12.

Studying South America

You will probably find in studying South America that pupils have gained a good many mis-conceptions about that part of the world from movies, television, previous school work, and other sources. Among the misconceptions you may find are the following:

1. ALL SOUTH AMERICANS SPEAK SPANISH. Actually, most Brazilians speak Portuguese. Many other persons speak a variety of Indian dialects. Still others speak European and Asian languages.

2. SOUTH AMERICANS HAVE EITHER EUROPEAN OR INDIAN BACKGROUNDS. This assumption overlooks the large numbers of persons of African and Asian origin.

3. SOUTH AMERICA'S CULTURE IS EXCLUSIVELY SPANISH. Actually, it is a combination of Indian, Portuguese, Spanish, and other cultures. Some-times one dominates; often two or more combine influences.

4. SOUTH AMERICANS ARE ALL ARDENT CATHOLICS. In reality, only a small proportion are ardent Catholics, although most South Americans are communicants of the Catholic faith.

5. SOUTH AMERICANS OF VARIOUS COUNTRIES KNOW EACH OTHER WELL. The chances are that South Americans still know more Europeans or North Americans than people from other countries of South America, although there is more travel and exchange among South American nations now than formerly.

6. SOUTH AMERICANS LIVE LARGELY IN VILLAGES. A high proportion of South Americans today live in cities, many of them very large cities, such as Bogotá, Buenos Aires, Caracas, Lima, Montevideo, Rio de Janeiro, Santiago, and São Paulo.

7. MOST SOUTH AMERICANS ARE ENGAGED IN PRODUCING OR MINING OIL, TIN, COFFEE, AND OTHER PRODUCTS FOR EXPORT. These are all important products of South America, but only a small percentage of the people work with these products.

8. MOST OF BRAZIL IS A VAST JUNGLE. Parts of that huge country are jungle, but much of it is grassland or scrub country.

9. THE AMAZON RIVER IS A WONDERFUL HIGHWAY FOR TRADE. Un-fortunately, the Amazon does not run through the parts of Brazil that produce farm products or minerals, and it is not a vast highway of trade.

10. SOUTH AMERICAN UPRISINGS ARE ALL COMMUNIST-INSPIRED. Some revolts are led by Communists or Communist sympathizers. More often, persons who are interested in removing the obstacles of poverty, unjust land tenure laws, and other evils, and who are not Communists, have led the revolts.

11. SOUTH AMERICAN GOVERNMENTS ARE ALL DICTATORSHIPS. Some are, but their number has decreased in recent years.

No one can frame a list of aims or ideas for you to stress in studying South America without knowing your class—its interest and its needs. But the following major ideas might help you outline your study plan.

1. The importance of geographic factors.

2. The relation between geography and transportation.

3. The tremendous variety of people in South America.

4. The importance of the extended-family system and the inroads into its strength brought about by changes in South America.

5. Some of the social values stressed by many South Americans.

6. The crippling effect of one-product economies in most South American countries.

7. The many ways of earning a living in South America.

8. The disastrous effects of the land-ownership system and the concentration of wealth and power in the hands of a few people. In recent years, this power concentration has been attacked in parts of South America.

9. The effects of poverty on education, politics, and other phases of life.

10. The condition of education, with special attention on the lack of secondary schools.

11. The importance of the church as a political factor as well as a religious institution.

12. The rapid and almost phenomenal growth of cities in South America.

13. The changing patterns of parties and governments, with a trend toward more democratic governments.

14. The history of South America, including its long and often fascinating history under Indian control.

15. Relations with North America over the centuries.

16. The important role of the Organization of American States (formerly the Pan American Union).

17. The importance of the Alliance for Progress and its work.

18. The varied forms of creative expression, fun, and beauty in this part of the world.

The material on these two pages has been excerpted from Leonard Kenworthy's Studying South America in Elementary and Secondary Schools, rev. ed. (New York: Teachers College Press, 1965).

Brazil

Every student in our schools should study about Brazil. It is extremely important today and may well become one of the major powers of the world in the years ahead.

There are several reasons for its importance. Among them are (1) its size and population— fifth in area and eighth in population in the world; (2) its leading position in South or Latin America; (3) its strong political and economic ties with the United States; (4) its outstanding record in race relations; (5) its remarkable progress as a "developing" country; (6) its contributions in architecture, music, medicine, and aviation in the past and today; and (7) its potentialities for the future.

For these reasons, you should devote two or three weeks to Brazil, longer if possible, even if you must omit other countries entirely. It is certainly better to study a few well-selected nations in depth than to treat many superficially.

Too many teachers begin the study of a country with the question "Why are we interested in . . . ?" At that point, the pupils don't know enough about the country to be interested in it at all. Ideally, they could answer that question at the _end_ of a study unit.

Wiser teachers start by assigning reading that supplements the text and arouses interest in the new topic. They include guide questions to focus attention on key concepts. (This is a good time to review the students' note-taking skills. Suggest using a separate card or notebook page to deal with each question.)

Toward the end of the unit, there should also be individual reading on topics of special interest. Reports need not be oral.

These points should be stressed in any study of Brazil.

1. ITS SIZE.   Compare Brazil with the rest of South America, with the United States, and with Europe. See how many European countries can be "dropped" inside Brazil. Make a map showing this.

2. ITS REGIONS.   Various authors divide Brazil into different regions. Charles Wagley divides it as follows: (1) the Amazon lowlands, (2) the arid northeastern sertao or backlands, (3) the northeastern coast, (4) the eastern highlands, (5) the Far West, and (6) the South. Each of these regions has had its period of prominence:

Northeast	Sugar cane and cattle	16th and 17th centuries
Eastern highlands	Gold	18th century
Southwest	Coffee and cattle	19th century
Amazon lowlands	Rubber	Late 19th and early 20th centuries
Rio - São Paulo	Industry	Mid-20th century

   Pupils need to study how the one-product economy of Brazil has been a drawback in its development.

97

3. ITS PEOPLE. Brazil is a "melting pot" of peoples and one of the world's most successful laboratories in human relations. Its population includes Indians (American), Africans (originally brought as slaves to work on the sugar cane plantations), Europeans, Asians (especially Japanese in recent years), and persons of mixed background. While there is prejudice, it stems from socio-economic rather than racial considerations.

4. ITS RESOURCES. Brazil is potentially a rich country. It has about one-fourth of the world's iron deposits, large and unexplored deposits of bauxite (for aluminum), possibly the largest amount of manganese in the world, precious stones, phosphates, thorium (next to uranium in importance for atomic energy), and other minerals. There is good farming land to be developed. Some experts estimate that Brazil could have 500 to 900 million persons if its territory werd developed. One major drawback is a shortage of coal and oil. However, there is some coal and hope of discovering oil deposits. A second handicap is the lack of adequate transportation facilities. (See point 6.)

5. ITS CITIES. Most Brazilians still live on the land or in small towns, but the drift to the cities is marked. São Paulo has around 4 million people and is the ninth largest city in the world; Rio has around 3½ million and is the fourteenth largest city in the world. Individual pupils might make a study of these two cities plus Santos, Salvador, Recife, Natal, Fortaleza, Belém, Manaus, Porto Alegre, and Brasília, the new capital.

6. ITS TRANSPORTATION. The Amazon (unlike the Mississippi and the Rhine) is located in the wrong place to be used as a giant waterway. The mountains have made highways difficult to construct and railroads almost impossible. Highways are now being built at great expense. Airplanes are more widely used than in most countries of the world.

7. ITS CLIMATE. You may find that students think of Brazil as being totally hot and humid. Although this is true of parts of that nation, the elevation of the country makes much of it more mild than most people imagine.

8. ITS EDUCATIONAL SYSTEM. Two points need emphasis: (1) the widespread illiteracy—about 50 per cent, and (2) the recent attempts to improve free education for more people.

9. ITS CONTRIBUTIONS. Resource materials spell out Brazil's contributions to the world, including the music of Carlos Gomez and Villa Lobos, the paintings of Portinari, the yellow fever work of Oswaldo Cruz, and the achievements of other eminent Brazilians.

10. ITS PROBLEMS. A thorough study of Brazil should include a look at its many problems as it faces the future: the class system, lack of education, transportation difficulties, inflation, and difficulties in opening the western regions. These would provide a good discussion at the conclusion of the unit.

You will undoubtedly want to develop other concepts. These are a start.

Source Materials on Brazil

Teachers should have a file of clippings about Brazil from newspapers and back copies of current events magazines.

They should also have general books on Latin or South America and encyclopedias available for pupils, especially for research topics.

A picture collection would be extremely useful.

A few items are available free from the Brazilian Government Trade Bureau, 551 Fifth Avenue, New York 17.

SPECIAL MATERIAL FOR TEACHERS

"Brazil." World Book Encyclopedia. 1960. 12 pp. 25¢.
"Study Kit on Brazil." Pan American Union. 25¢. Pamphlets on Brazil, coffee, and the Amazon.

BOOKS ABOUT BRAZIL
(For teachers and good high school readers)

1. Alexander, Robert J. Prophets of the Revolution. New York: Macmillan, 1962. 322 pp. (See pages 219-245 on Vargas, "Father of the Poor.")
2. de Azevedo, Thales. Social Change in Brazil. Gainesville, Fla.: University of Florida Press, 1963. 83 pp.
3. de Jesus, Maria. Child of the Dark: The Diary of Carolina Maria de Jesus: My Life in the Slums of São Paulo. New York: Dutton, 1962. 190 pp. A grim account of living in the slums. Not for most students.
4. Freyre, Gilberto. The Mansions and the Shanties. New York: Knopf, 1963. 431 pp. By Brazil's leading sociologist.
5. Freyre, Gilberto. The Masters and the Slaves. A Study in the Development of Brazilian Civilization. New York: Putnam, 1956. 537 pp. Brazil's Negroes and their life on Brazilian plantations. A classic.
6. Freyre, Gilberto. New World in the Tropics. New York: Knopf, 1959. 285 pp.
7. Gold, Ellen B. Portrait of a Great Country. New York: Viking, 1960. 172 pp.
8. Horowitz, Irving L. Revolution in Brazil: Politics and Society in a Developing Nation. New York: Dutton, 1964. 430 pp.
9. Schurz, William L. Brazil: The Infinite Country. New York: Dutton, 1961. 346 pp.
10. Wagley, Charles. An Introduction to Brazil. New York: Columbia University Press, 1963. 322 pp. An excellent introduction to this nation.

PAMPHLETS AND ARTICLES ON BRAZIL

1. The Amazon. Washington: Pan American Union, 1959. 20 pp. 10¢.
2. "Brazil." New York: American Geographical Society. November 1964 issue of Focus. 6 pp. 25¢.
3. Brazil. Washington: Pan American Union. 1959. 46 pp. 15¢.

4. Brazil: Which Way Half a Continent?   Foreign Policy Association, 1962. 12 pp. 20¢. Fact Sheet No. 3.
5. Cunha, Luiz de Almeida.   Art in Latin America Today: Brazil. Washington: Pan American Union, 1960. 60 pp. 75¢.
6. de Sa, Hermane Tavares. "Brasilia: Metropolis Made to Order." National Geographic, May 1960. Pp. 704-724. Colored illustrations.
7. Economic Developments in Brazil.   Washington: Government Printing Office, 1961. 8 pp. 15¢.
8. Education in Brazil.   UNESCO, 1958. 22 pp. 20¢. Through UNESCO Publications.
9. Faust, Augustus F.   Brazil: Education in an Expanding Economy. Washington: Government Printing Office, 1959. 142 pp. 50¢.
10. Introduction to Brazil.   Washington: Pan American Union, 1962. 2 pp. Single copy free. Others 2¢ each.
11. Mutual Security in Action: Brazil.   Washington: Government Printing Office, 1960. 16 pp. 10¢.
12. "Spectacular Rio de Janeiro."   National Geographic, March 1955.
13. U.S. Department of Commerce.   Economic Developments in Brazil. Washington: Government Printing Office, 1960. 8 pp. 15¢.
14. White, Peter T. "Brazil, Oba!" National Geographic, September 1962. Pp. 299-353. Colored illustrations.

OTHER BOOKS ABOUT BRAZIL
(For junior high and elementary school pupils)

1. Brown, Rose.   The Land and People of Brazil. Philadelphia: Lippincott, 1960. 128 pp. Grades 6-9.
2. Caldwell, John C.   Let's Visit Brazil. New York: John Day, 1961. 64 pp. Grades 5-8.
3. Kenworthy, Leonard S.   Brazil. New York: Holiday, 1954. 24 pp. Includes colored illustrations. Grades 5-8.
4. MacDonald, N. P.   The Land and People of Brazil. New York: Macmillan, 1959. 96 pp.
5. May, Stella B.   Brazil. Grand Rapids, Mich: Fideler, 1963. 127 pp. Especially good for black and white photographs. Grades 5-8.
6. Sheppard, Sally.   The First Book of Brazil. New York: Watts, 1962. 64 pp. Grades 5-8.
7. Wagley, Charles.   Brazil.   Chicago: Nystrom, 1964. 64 pp. Includes several colored photographs. Grades 5-8. A teacher's guide accompanies this booklet.
8. Wagley, Charles.   Brazil: Crisis and Change. New York: Foreign Policy Association, 1964. 62 pp. Grades 9-12.
9. Webb, Kempton E.   Brazil. Boston: Ginn, 1964. 120 pp. Grades 9-12. Suitable as a text for good readers in junior high school or senior high school readers.
10. Hall, Frederick.   Land of Coffee. Chicago: Encyclopedia Britannica, 1964. 36 pp. Grades 3-5. Colored illustrations.
11. Cavanna, Betty.   Paulo of Brazil. New York: Watts, 1962. 63 pp. Grades 3-5.
12. Maguere, Francis, and Dominique Darbois.   Parana: Boy of the Amazon. Chicago: Follett, 1959. 47 pp. An Indian boy and his life.

Mexico

Mexico is a "must" in any social studies program in the United States. It should be studied several times with different emphases. For example, a child might learn about selected Mexican families in the primary grades, selected Mexican villages and cities in the middle grades, and Mexico as a country in the upper elementary or junior high school years. Other aspects should be explored in courses in world geography, world history, and United States history.

A unit on Mexico can begin in many ways: with a film or filmstrip; with an exhibit of pictures; with the song "South of the Border—Down Mexico Way"; with a pooling of current knowledge about it; or with a look at its geography, thinking about how to develop a country with its particular location, climate, and resources. Mexico is one of the few countries in which the history can be used to motivate interest in the present, so you may decide to introduce Mexico historically.

The central emphasis in any study of Mexico will vary from class to class. It might be on the blending of past and present (old and new) there, or on the tremendous changes and progress.

Here are a few points to remember as you develop your study plan for Mexico.

1. ITS IMPORTANCE. (a) One of our neighboring nations; (b) a country with which we have had conflict in the past; (c) the eleventh most populous nation of the world and the most populous of the Spanish-oriented countries of Latin America; (d) a place from which many of our imports come and to which some of our exports go; (e) a colorful country with a remarkable past and an emphasis on the arts; (f) a leader in Latin America; and (g) the scene of incredible changes in recent years.

2. ITS GEOGRAPHY. Largely mountainous, its mountains forming a V, with the Central Plateau, inhabited by about two-thirds of the people of Mexico in the center. Three types of climate: the hot coastal plain, the temperate plateaus and valleys, and the cold area above sea level.

3. ITS REGIONS. The metropolis (Mexico City), the core (the hinterland of Mexico City), the West, the North, and the South.

4. ITS PEOPLE. About 35 million in 1964. Out of every 100 persons approximately 30 are pure Indian, 55 mestizo, and 15 pure white. Over 2.75 per cent increase in population—among the highest in the world. Little immigration over the centuries.

5. ITS WAYS OF LIFE. Spanish and Indian ways in the past. Divisions between rich and poor. Importance of family life, the church, festivals, art, and music. A culture of poverty, past and present. Increasing urbanization today. One-third of populace urban; Mexico City the fifth largest city of the world. Urban and rural cultures today. Other cities. Languages.

101

6. ITS ECONOMY. Boom in recent years, with agriculture and industry both improving, but half of the populace still in agriculture. Special boom in cotton and coffee. Endowed with rich mineral resources (although mining not increasing as rapidly as other sectors of the economy): gold and silver, iron and steel, oil and gas. Considerable government ownership (petroleum, natural gas, railroads, and electric power) and domination. Tremendous development in land reclamation and irrigation, with the Falcon Dam as the the most important factor.

7. ITS GOVERNMENT. A federal republic, with 29 states, 2 territories, and the Federal District (Mexico City). A strong President, a Senate and Chamber of Deputies, with a judiciary branch. Almost a single-party democracy, with the Institutional Revolutionary party in control for years. No merit system in the civil service. Strength of organized labor. Government ownership and domination of some industries.

8. ITS EDUCATION. More funds spent on education than on national defense. Great progress in recent years, yet 35 to 45 per cent illiteracy still. Most educational growth has been in the cities; rural schools seldom go beyond third grade. National Autonomous University and National Polytechnic Institute (Mexico City) at top of educational apex. Mexico has been a world leader in adult-education movements.

9. ITS CHURCHES. Ninety-seven per cent of the population Roman Catholic. Many of them nominal adherents, yet no country in the world has had a more bitter struggle between church and state. State now uppermost. Better relations between these two institutions now than in the past.

10. ITS HISTORY. Remarkable prehistory civilizations of the Mayans, Toltecs, Aztecs. History often divided into four periods: (a) precolonial or pre-conquest, (b) colonial from 1519 on, (c) nationhood from 1821 on, and (d) revolutionary from 1910 on. Juarez and the revolution.

11. ITS RELATIONS WITH THE UNITED STATES. Often turbulent. Lost over one-half of its territory to United States from 1846 to 1852. Vera Cruz incident in 1914. Pershing expedition in 1917. Problem of Mexican-Americans in southwestern United States. Problem of "wet-back" immigration. Friendlier relations in recent years. Cooperation on Falcon Dam and other projects.

12. ITS CONTRIBUTIONS TO THE WORLD. Its early history of Indian civilizations. Its music—Carlos Chavez and Miguel Bernal Jiménez. Its artists—expecially mural painters—Rivera, Orozco, Siqueiros, Tamayo. Its adult education and "cultural missions." Its modern architecture, such as the University of Mexico and the Hydraulic Resources Ministry Building. What others?

Source Materials on Mexico

Some up-to-date materials may be purchased inexpensively from the Pan American Union. Write to them for a list. (Pan American Union, Washington 25, D.C.).

BOOKS ON MEXICO
(For teachers and good readers in high schools)

1. Adams, Richard N., and others. Social Change in Latin America Today. New York: Knopf, 1960. 352 pp. Also a Vintage paperback. Chapter 6 on "Mexico Since Cardenas."
2. Aid in Action—Mexico. Washington: Government Printing Office, 1962. 13 pp. 10¢.
3. Cline, Howard F. Mexico Revolution to Evolution. New York: Oxford University Press, 1963. 374 pp. A comprehensive and recent account.
4. Cline, Howard F. The United States and Mexico. Cambridge, Mass.: Harvard University Press, 1953. 452 pp.
5. Crawford, W. Rex. A Century of Latin American Thought. Cambridge, Mass.: Harvard University Press, 1961. 322 pp. Chapter 9 on "The Mexican Revolution."
6. Education in Mexico. Washington: Government Printing Office, 1956. 135 pp. 55¢.
7. James, Preston. Introduction to Latin America: The Geographic Background of Economic and Political Problems. New York: Odyssey, 1964. 362 pp. Chapter 3 on Mexico.
8. Kneller, George F. The Education of the Mexican Nation. New York: Columbia University Press, 1951. 258 pp.
9. Lewis, Oscar. The Children of Sanchez: Autobiography of a Mexican Family. New York: Random House, 1961. 499 pp. The life of a family in a slum tenement in Mexico City, portraying the culture of poverty.
10. Lewis, Oscar. Five Families. New York: Basic Books, 1959. 351 pp. Also a paperback—Science Editions, 1962. The lives of four families in Mexico City and one migrant family.
11. Lewis, Oscar. Pedro Martinez: A Mexican Peasant and His Family. New York: Random House, 1964. 507 pp. Life of rural Indians.
12. Mayer-Serra, Otto. The Present State of Music in Mexico. Washington: Government Printing Office, 1960. 47 pp. 50¢. English and Spanish on opposite pages.
13. "Mexico." A special supplement to Harper's magazine for February 1964. On various phases of contemporary culture.
14. Redfield, Robert. The Little Community and Peasant Society and Culture. Chicago: University of Chicago Press, 1962. 265 pp.
15. Toor, Frances. A Treasury of Mexican Folkway. New York: Crown, 1947. 566 pp. A remarkable collection, profusely illustrated.
16. Von Hagen, Victor W. The Aztec Man and Tribe. New York: Mentor, 1957. 224 pp. A paperback.
17. Von Hagen, Victor W. World of the Maya. New York: Mentor, 1962. 224 pp. A paperback.

BOOKS ON MEXICO
(For younger and/or slower readers)

The Pan American Union (Washington 25, D.C.) has three especially valuable booklets: The Aztecs, (10¢); The Mayas, (10¢); and Mexico, (15¢). Suitable for use by junior high pupils.

1. Bleeker, Sonia. The Aztec Indians of Mexico. New York: Morrow, 1963. 156 pp. Grades 6-9.
2. Epstein, Sam and Beryl. The First Book of Mexico. New York: Watts, 1955. 63 pp. Grades 4-6.
3. Larralde, Elsa. The Land and People of Mexico. Philadelphia: Lippincott, 1950. 128 pp. A well-balanced account.
4. Long, E. John. Mexico. Garden City, N.Y.: Doubleday, 1955. 62 pp. Includes many colored illustrations.
5. McDowell, Bart. "Mexico in Motion." National Geographic. October 1961. Pp. 490-539. Includes many colored illustrations.
6. "Mexico." American Geographical Society, 1959. 6 pp. 25¢. An issue of Focus magazine.
7. Mexico. Life magazine. 1963. 160 pp. 92 photographs, 33 of them in full color. Textual material fairly difficult, but the pictures can be used by almost anyone.
8. Ross, Patricia F. Made in Mexico: The Story of a Country's Arts and Crafts. New York: Knopf. 1958. 329 pp. Grades 6-9.
9. Von Hagen, Victor W. The Sun Kingdom of the Aztecs. Cleveland: World, 1958. 127 pp.

OTHER MATERIALS

The International Communications Foundation (870 Monterey Pass Road, Monterey Park, California) has a special kit of audio-visual materials on Mexico. It includes several color filmstrips with sound, six long-playing records, 40 artifacts, among them costumes, stringed puppets, rural kitchen utensils, and musical instruments. Write to the foundation for costs and details.

Records of Mexican music can be purchased from several sources.

Studying Asia

In any study of Asia, you will have to decide which aspects of this enormous continent to stress. Your decision will depend largely upon the subject you are teaching, your aims, and the abilities and backgrounds of your students. Here are some major points that you may want to consider in planning your treatment of Asia.

1. THE DIVERSITY OF ASIA. This large part of the world is characterized by tremendous diversity. Therefore, you may want to divide it into South Asia, Southeast Asia, and East Asia for teaching. There are many land forms, many types of governments, several major religions, widely varied stages of industrialization, and several cultures and subcultures. This diversity should be emphasized constantly.

2. ITS SIZE. Fifty-two out of every 100 people in the world live in Asia. It includes five of the seven most populous nations: China, India, Japan, Indonesia, and Pakistan—in that order. One other (the U.S.S.R.) is partially in Asia.

3. THE INFLUENCE OF GEOGRAPHY UPON HISTORY. Any study of Asia should include a study of geography that goes beyond locations to relationships—effects on history and contemporary affairs. The following are only examples of the geographical aspects of Asia you might explore. The major rivers and river-valley cultures: the Yellow and Yangtze in China; the Mekong in Southeast Asia; the Ganges and Brahmaputra in India; and the Indus in Pakistan. The mountains—especially the Himalayas—and the effect of the mountainous terrain (plus water supplies) on Japan. The earthquakes, typhoons, and tidal waves, and their effects. Japan as an island and its need for outreaching—economically and psychologically. The desert areas.

4. THE RESOURCES OF ASIA. The need for food is a tremendous problem today, especially in China and India. How does China's need for food affect its relations with Southeast Asia? You will need to stress the effect of resources on industrialization, on world trade, and on colonialism (the past and present desire of nations for the oil, rubber, bauxite, etc., of Southeast Asia). What effect does Japan's wood supply have on its culture and economy (such as ship-building, in which it leads the world today)?

5. PEOPLE AND THE POPULATION PROBLEM. Perhaps Asia's number one problem today is population. Almost everything hinges on what is done about this. In China and India, this problem is acute. Japan has attempted to solve it by legalizing abortions and fostering birth control.

6. VILLAGE LIFE AND INCREASING URBANIZATION. There are about half a million villages in India, a million in China. Life still is centered in villages, yet there is growing urbanization as shown by the size of Tokyo, Calcutta, and other cities. What are the effects of the movement to the cities?

7. THE IMPORTANCE OF FAMILY LIFE. Family life is far more important than in the United States and the Western world. Explain the importance of the "extended family." Include the changes in families, especially in China under communist rule.

8. STRATIFICATION OF SOCIETY. Each society has had its own form of stratification. The caste system began in India as an economic measure. Attacks upon it today are far-reaching. Stratification in China in the past established scholars at the top, but this has changed in recent times.

9. VALUE SYSTEMS. No one can understand Asia, even in an elementary way, without considering the value systems, religions, philosophies, ways of life of Buddhism, Confucianism, Hinduism, Shintoism, and communism. (See separate Background Papers on these world faiths.)

10. LINGUISTIC SIMILARITIES AND DIFFERENCES. Discuss the written language as a cohesive force in Chinese history. Language divisions in India have been a divisive force, with political overtones. Southeast Asia is broken into many language areas.

11. STANDARD OF LIVING. Closely linked to the importance of food, population, and resources is the problem of a very low standard of living in most of Asia (e.g., about $50 per capita per year in India). Japan is an exception to this rule. How can a nation raise the standard of living with a rapidly growing population? Consider the problems, such as health and education, that grow out of a low standard of living.

12. THE IMPACT OF THE WEST. This can be traced back to the early explorers from Europe and their reasons for going to Asia. Asia was divided into areas of influence by the Dutch, French, English, etc. How did the United States react to colonization? What is the effect today of increasing westernization, with Japan the prime example?

13. THE REVOLTS IN ASIA AND THE APPEAL OF COMMUNISM. Consider the revolt in Japan, Sun Yat Sen and revolts in China after the Boxer Rebellion, India's revolt and movement for independence, and others. What are the appeals of communism today? Emphasize the rapid changes in Russia and the ability of Asian countries to "identify" with those changes.

14. CONTRIBUTIONS TO WORLD CULTURE. See Background Paper No. 24, Contributions of China and Japan to World Culture.

15. ASIA AND CURRENT WORLD PROBLEMS. Many of the world's current problems relate to Asia. Some of these are foreign aid, Japan's place in the world, recognition of China by the United States, China's entry into the United Nations, wars in Southeast Asia, and difficulties over Malaysia.

16. HISTORY, GOVERNMENT, AND LEADERS. For suggestions on teaching the history of Asia, see Hyman Kublin's chapter in Social Studies and the Social Sciences (New York: Harcourt, 1962. 303 pp.).

China

Have you ever tried the word-association approach to a country? It might be an interesting method to use at the beginning of a unit on China. This approach not only arouses the students' interest in a country but provides a way to find out the stereotypes they believe about it. If you use the word-association game again at the end of your unit, you can measure changes in the students' knowledge and attitudes.

Start by putting on the board the name of a person or object familiar to everyone. Ask the class to name quickly some characteristics of that object. Write these words on the chalkboard under or around the name. (This prerun will show the students how word association is carried on.) Then, write the word "China" on the chalkboard and let them mention whatever comes to mind. After you have eight or nine items, stop and discuss whether or not those terms belong on the chalkboard and whether they should be modified or amended.

In many cases, the first items students mention are "Communists . . . big country . . . yellow peril . . poverty . . Taiwan . . Mao Tse-tung." With phrases like these on the chalkboard, stop to look at the total picture you have painted of China. Discuss with the pupils where they got their impressions and whether each of the characteristics is valid. When this is done, you are ready to move on to other associated words and phrases. Perhaps you should talk about the ideas yourself, pointing out how they are correct, incorrect, or distorted. Then you can assign reading material, either based on one or two of the board items or on topics that lead into a structured study of China.

What chief points do you want your students to gain from their study of China? Here are a few items to include or to use as a start of your own list. Perhaps you should read the chapter by Hyman Kublin on "Teaching about Asia" in The Social Studies and the Social Sciences as background for teaching about China. Most of the main points he makes in that chapter are included in the list below:

1. ITS IMPORTANCE IN TODAY'S WORLD AND IN THE PAST. Seven hundred million persons, or nearly one-fourth of the world's population; second largest area of the world; 4000 years of history; contributions to the world (see Background Paper No. 24); increasing role in world affairs and some problems in this connection.

2. ITS LAND AND RESOURCES. Extent of land and problems of transportation, communication, and government. Variety of climatic regions and effect on agriculture. Importance of its major rivers—Yellow, Yangtze, West. Importance of its mountains. The differences between North and South China. Deposits of coal, tin, tungsten, antimony. The richness of Manchuria in minerals. Agricultural program: wheat, millet, soy beans, corn, tea, rice, and cotton.

3. ITS PEOPLE AND POPULATION PROBLEMS. Over 700 million persons, plus 10 million in Taiwan and 12 million "overseas" Chinese. The great variety of Chinese. Language differences between Mandarin and Cantonese, but unifying effect of language for centuries. Fourteen million additional people a year to feed. Birth control campaign for a short time under present regime.

4. THE FAMILY. Importance of family life in China for centuries and the disruption of the family in People's Republic of China. Reasons for the desire to disrupt the family as a social unit; what was done. Social pyramid of China in the past.

5. FOOD AND PEOPLE. Life over the centuries on a submarginal basis. Problems today of feeding 700 million persons. Interest of China in Southeast Asia partly on basis of food from the "rice bowl." Attempts to accelerate industry and results on food supply. Development of communes and scientific farming. Contributions of China to scientific farming in the past.

6. ITS HISTORY. Early settlements by 2000 B.C. in Yellow river valley. Various dynasties since that time with stress on recent ones, especially Manchu dynasty for 250 years until 1911. The revolution of 1911 and Sun Yat-sen. China under the Japanese. The fight between Chiang Kai-shek forces and Communists. Reasons for the rise of communism and its eventual victory.

7. ITS EMPHASIS UPON THE PHILOSOPHY OF CONFUCIUS. Basis of Confucian philosophy. How it was perpetuated. Influence of Confucian scholars upon the government and the examination system for officials. Rise of Buddhism. Other philosophies in China. Communism as a "religion" today.

8. ITS VILLAGES AND CITIES. China long an agricultural country. Even with movement to the cities, 85 per cent of the people still in villages. Communes today and how they are changing Chinese life. Cities in the past and present—Canton, Peking, Nanking, Shanghai, and others. Hope of present government to achieve balance—50 per cent urban, 50 per cent rural—in future and reasons for that goal.

9. CONTRIBUTIONS OF CHINA TO THE WORLD. See Background Paper No. 24.

10. THE CURRENT REVOLUTION IN CHINA UNDER THE PEOPLE'S REPUBLIC. Reasons for the rise and appeal of communism. First state of recovery after the war. First five-year plan and the great leap forward. Efforts to industrialize, change family structure, provide more education and youth activities, reorganize governmental structure (with importance of the Communist party).

11. RELATIONS WITH THE WORLD. China's relations change with U.S.S.R. and the United States. China and the United Nations. China and Southeast Asia. China and other parts of the world.

Source Materials on China

BIBLIOGRAPHIES ON CHINA

1. "The China Problem." New York: Foreign Policy Association, 1965. A special issue of <u>Intercom</u> magazine.
2. Cole, Allan B. <u>Forty Years of Chinese Communism: Selected Readings with Commentary</u>. Washington: Service Center, 1962. 43 pp.
3. Hucker, Charles O. <u>Chinese History: A Bibliographic Review</u>. Washington: Service Center, 1958. 42 pp.

PAPERBACKS ON CHINA
(For teachers and some high school students)

1. Barnett, A. Doak. <u>Communist China in Perspective</u>. New York: Praeger, 1962. 88 pp. Three lectures on the Chinese revolution, its history, and problems of the future.
2. Boyd, R. G. <u>Communist China's Foreign Policy</u>. New York: Praeger, 1962. 147 pp.
3. Buss, Claude A. <u>The People's Republic of China</u>. Princeton, N.J.: Van Nostrand, 1962. 188 pp. Contemporary China through documents.
4. Chai, Ch'u and Winberg. <u>The Changing Society of China</u>. New York: Mentor, 1962. 253 pp. From the remote past to the present.
5. Chandra-Sekhar, Sripati. <u>Red China: An Asian View</u>. New York: Praeger, 1961. 230 pp. A topical analysis of contemporary China by a leading social scientist of India.
6. Clubb, O. Edmund. <u>Twentieth Century China</u>. New York: Columbia University Press, 1964. 470 pp. By the last United States consul in Peiping.
7. Feuerwerker, Albert. <u>Modern China</u>. Englewood Cliffs, N.J.: Prentice-Hall, 1964. 186 pp. Twelve themes in present-day China analyzed by experts.
8. Fairbank, John K. <u>The United States and China</u>. New York: Viking, 1958. 369 pp. One of the few books dealing with United States-Chinese relationships.
9. Hsieh, Alice L. <u>Communist China's Strategy in the Nuclear Era</u>. Englewood Cliffs, N.J.: Prentice-Hall, 1962. 204 pp. By an official of the Rand Corporation who formerly worked in the State Department.
10. Latourette, Kenneth S. <u>China</u>. Englewood Cliffs, N.J.: Prentice-Hall, 1964. 152 pp. In The Modern Nations in Historical Perspective series. By a leading writer on China for many years.
11. Li, Choh-ming, ed. <u>Industrial Development in Communist China</u>. New York: Praeger, 1964. 205 pp. By twelve economists.
12. Rowe, David N. <u>Modern China: A Brief History</u>. Princeton, N.J.: Van Nostrand, 1959. 191 pp. Largely documents, with some commentary.

BOOKS AND PAMPHLETS
(Primarily for students)

1. Armstrong, John P. <u>Chinese Dilemma</u>. Chicago: Laidlaw, 1959. 67 pp. Focuses on United States foreign policy in relation to China.

2. Barnett, A. Doak.   Communist China—Continuing Revolution. New York: Foreign Policy Association, 1962. 64 pp. A Headline book.

3. Bell, Oliver. The Two Chinas. New York: Scholastic, 1962. Written as a general text for grades 9-12.

4. Bisch, Jorgen. "This Is the China I Saw." National Geographic. November 1964. Pp. 591-639. Illustrated with many colored photographs.

5. Buck, Pearl. The Man Who Changed China: The Story of Sun Yat-sen. New York: Random House, 1953. 185 pp.

6. Chang, Perry P. China: Development by Force. Chicago: Scott, 1964. 80 pp. An economic approach. Grades 8-10.

7. "China in the World Today." Current History. Special issue of September 1964. Usually such an issue each year.

8. Creel, H. G. Chinese Thoughts from Confucius to Mao Tse-tung. New York: Mentor, 1960. 240 pp.

9. Durdin, Peggy. Mao's China. New York: Foreign Policy Association, 1959. 62 pp.

10. Fessler, Loren, and the editors of Life. China. New York: Time, 1963. 176 pp. Magnificent photos, partly in color, as well as a good text.

11. Joy, Charles R. Getting to Know the Two Chinas. New York: Coward-McCann, 1960. 64 pp. Grades 5-8. For slower readers in secondary schools.

12. Kenworthy, Leonard S. Twelve Citizens of the World. New York: Doubleday, 1953. 286 pp. Chapter 10 on Sun Yat-sen.

13. Kinmond, William. The First Book of Communist China. New York: Watts, 1962. 85 pp. Grades 5-8. For slow readers in secondary schools.

14. Payne, Robert. Mao Tse-tung: Portrait of a Revolutionary. New York: Abelard, 1962. 311 pp.

15. Red China and the U.S.S.R. Washington: Government Printing Office, 1963. 35 pp.

16. Seegers, Elizabeth. Pageant of Chinese History. New York: McKay, 1962. A revised edition of an old-time favorite.

17. Seligman, E., and R. L. Walker. Should the U.S. Change Its China Policy? New York: Foreign Policy Association, 1958. 78 pp. A Headline book.

18. Spencer, Cornelia. The Land of the Chinese People. Philadelphia: Lippincott, 1960. 128 pp.

19. Spencer, Cornelia. Made in China: The Story of China's Expression. New York: Knopf, 1952. 258 pp. The story of arts and crafts in Chinese history.

20. Steiner, H. Arthur. Communist China in the World Community. New York: Carnegie Endowment, 1961. 64 pp.

21. Swisher, Earl. China. Boston: Ginn, 1964. 122 pp. One of their Studies in Depth series. Especially good for grades 9-12.

22. Who Are They? Part 2: Mao Tse-tung and Chou En-lai. Washington: Government Printing Office, 1957. 6 pp.

23. Yutang, Lin. The Chinese Way of Life. Cleveland: World, 1959. 127 pp. A student edition of a popular adult book.

OTHER MATERIALS

A Guide to Films, Filmstrips, Maps and Globes, Records on Asia. New York: Asia Society, 1964. 87 pp. A carefully selected list, with brief annotations.

World Crops

In courses in world geography, the major crops of a particular area are significant. Students will not be familiar with many of them, such as sisal, pyrethrum (used in insecticides), and rice. In fact, many students are not at all familiar with farms and farming. As you discuss agriculture in the United States and around the world, you will need to help pupils consider the many factors involved in deciding what should be grown on specific pieces of land.

One excellent approach to this topic is to "give" each student a piece of land. Don't tell them anything about their land at first. Let them ask questions about it—where it is, how large it is, what kind of soil it contains, etc. As they ask questions about the land, you can begin a list of factors determining how to use land anywhere in the world. Your list might eventually look like this:

1. Location and terrain.

2. Climate and weather (including the length of the growing season).

3. Size of the farm or plot of ground.

4. The soil.

5. Tools (including their cost and suitability for this piece of land).

6. Capital available.

7. Knowledge about farming methods.

8. Markets.

9. Transportation.

10. Ownership of the land.

11. Government regulations and control (depending upon the country).

12. Prices for the product.

13. Number of workers in the family and other laborers.

14. Interest of the farmer in certain crops.

15.

16.

What shall I (we)
grow on this plot of ground?

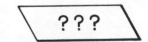

111

A teaching device like this chart can be given to students to use in a variety of ways. But they will learn much more if they develop the chart.

They can use it over and over for different kinds of land in different parts of the world. In this way, they are likely to "internalize" its contents and retain their knowledge.

When the class has developed a chart similar to the one on the previous page, you may want to have a student prepare a very large edition of it, suitable for mounting somewhere in the room. It can be used from time to time by the entire class, and individual students are likely to look at it occasionally when their minds wander from their lesson (as minds inevitably do).

A variation of this approach is to give students a list of different types of land and ask them to decide what crops they would grow on each piece if the land were theirs. The specific plots of ground can be selected according to the topic on which you are working. For example, if you are studying the geography of the United States, you can pick a small, hilly piece of land near a large city. Assume that it contains only fairly good soil and ask pupils what they would grow. Or select a sandy piece of land in a relatively hot part of the country and try to figure out what you could grow on it—whether the crop should be peanuts or vegetables.

Similar examples can be developed, of course, for any part of the world.

In order to further impress these factors on some students, you may want them to collect pictures of various kinds of farm land and crops and mount them for use in class, discussing why the particular crops are probably grown on the land pictured.

Or you may want to have your students develop a set of charts of different kinds of land and crops, using the drawings in other classes.

United States History:
Concepts and Propositions

What are the big ideas to keep in mind when teaching United States history? Are there a few ideas that should be stressed in such courses? In answer to these questions, Oscar O. Winther, Professor of History at Indiana University and managing editor of the <u>Journal of American History</u>, has suggested the following concepts or propositions:

1. Democracy is deeply rooted in American soil.
2. American institutions were transplanted from the European or Western world.
3. The practice of the separation of church and state is inherently American.
4. The new world environment produced what Crèvecoeur called "This new man, an American."
5. Mixture of peoples began during the colonial period.
6. European influences (transit of civilization) concentrated in colonial urban centers (see Carl Bridenbaugh's <u>Cities in the Wilderness)</u>.
7. The colonies were a haven for many seeking the right to practice religious freedom.
8. The frontier contributed toward the production of individualism, democracy, independence, and nationalism.
9. The principle of checks and balances emerged out of our colonial experience.
10. Our Bill of Rights is derived from British political philosophy (Locke and others).
11. Geography guided or influenced the direction and flow of much of American settlement.
12. British power triumphed over the French in 1763 and, as a result, Anglo-Saxon institutions became dominant north of the Rio Grande.
13. There were clashing vested interests represented at the Constitutional Convention, for example: debtor versus creditor; large versus small states; states' rights versus popular sovereignty.
14. The slavery problem, of course, has its roots in earliest colonial America.
15. The American party system also has colonial roots.
16. The tariff concept emerged with the birth of our nation.
17. Sectional conflict is inherent in American life.
18. Industrialism was accompanied by political power.
19. The Industrial Revolution began the gradual transformation of America from a rural, agricultural society to an urban one.
20. Large-scale industrialism contributed to the emergence of imperialism.
21. Industrialism brought about giant labor unions.
22. America is an idealistic nation and sought in World War I "to make the world safe for democracy," and, in World War II, to bring about "freedom from want and fear," as well as other freedoms.
23. Personal leadership and the role of the average citizen in American political and social life has always been pronounced.
24. Americans believe in public school education.
25. The United States is an affluent nation, but it harbors much poverty.
26. The urge to crusade, to bring about reform, is strong in American life.
27. Minority elements have always been a part of American culture, and, by and large, have had a rough time.

28. America's active role in world affairs grew out of bitter isolationist experiences after World War I.
29. The United States is learning the hard way that with leadership goes responsibility.

How would you modify this list?

Additional Concepts and Propositions

    30.

    31.

    32.

    33.

    34.

    35.

United States History:
Interpretations

Teachers of United States history should be conversant with the various interpretations of our national development. Inasmuch as the interpretations of men, events, and movements change from time to time, teachers need to subscribe to professional journals and to read new books on our history.

Most students will not be interested in or capable of handling the heavier works on the interpretations of history, but they should be aware that all historians do not agree in their estimate of men, events, and movements. More able students can read some of the inter- pretive materials.

There are many books that might be cited as background volumes for teachers. Three seem especially suitable.

1. Higham, John, ed. The Reconstruction of American History. New York: Harper, 1962. 244 pp. Sections written by different authors on "The Con- struction of American History," "The Puritan Strain," "The Revolutionary Era," "The Changing West," "The Age of the Common Man," "Disunion and Reunion," "The Working Class," "The Realm of Wealth," "The Progressive Tradition," and "The Quest for National Character." A paperback.

2. Kraus, Michael. The Writing of American History. Norman, Okla.: University of Oklahoma Press, 1953. 387 pp.

3. Wish, Harvey. The American Historian. New York: Oxford University Press, 1960. 366 pp. The subtitle is "A Social-Intellectual History of the Writing of the American Past." Chapters on most of the better-known historians— Bancroft, Parkman, McMaster, Turner, Beard, Parrington, Nevins, and others.

The Service Center for Teachers of History (400 A Street, S.E., Washington 3, D.C.) continues to issue a series of brief booklets on history. Many of these are on United States history. Each of them reviews the literature of a period or region and gives various interpretations of that part of history. A full list of titles may be obtained by writing to the Service Center. Here are a few typical titles in the series:

1. Berwick, Keith B. The Federal Age, 1789–1929: America in the Process of Becoming.
2. Billington, Ray A. The American Frontier.
3. Bridges, Leonard Hal. Civil War and Reconstruction.
4. Carter, Harvey L. The Far West in American History.
5. DeConde, Alexander. New Interpretations in American Foreign Policy.
6. Friedel, Frank. The New Deal in Historical Perspective.
7. Morgan, Edmund S. The American Revolution: A Review of Changing Inter- pretations.
8. Mowry, George E. The Progressive Movement, 1900–1920: Recent Ideas and New Literature.

9. Sellers, Charles G., Jr. Jacksonian Democracy.
10. Singletary, Otis A. The South in American History.
11. Wright, Louis B. New Interpretations of American Colonial History.

In the introductory chapter of The Reconstruction of American History, Higham refers to five noticeable trends in the writing of American history in recent years. He characterizes these as follows:

1. No great leaders. No one person now dominates the writing of American history as Turner and Beard did in their times.

2. Attraction of intellectual history. There is much more attention paid today to the history of ideas than in previous periods. Higham credits Vernon L. Parrington as the man who initiated this movement and mentions Curti, Gabriel, and Commager as experts in this relatively new field.

3. Decline of the economic interpretation. There is less emphasis today upon the economic interpretation of American history than in the period of Beard. This is especially true of such periods as the Revolution and the Civil War.

4. Beyond "scientific" history. The idea of rigid objectivity has become some-what outmoded, with the recognition that all historians "interpret."

5. The ambiguity of the American experience. Writers today are laying more stress on the homogeneity of our society and less emphasis upon the conflict between the few and the many than early writers did. Modern historians are trying to steer a middle course between consensus and conflict.

Another relatively new interpretation, not listed in the five points above, is the exploration of the influence of urban centers on our national life. According to some historians, this began even in the early colonial period. For more data on this interpretation, see Background Paper No. 70, The Importance of Cities in Early America.

United States History:
Important Decisions

Even though our history is not long when compared to that of other parts of the world, there is far too much of it to be adequately studied in a single year, at either the junior or senior high school level. Consequently, teachers need to select certain aspects of our history to emphasize. These aspects may be movements; they may be important turning points.

In considering which parts of our history to emphasize, you may find an article by Richard B. Morris helpful. The article, entitled "The Presidency: 10 Fateful Decisions," appeared in the New York Times magazine section on December 4, 1960.

Here are the ten decisions Morris selected, in abbreviated form.

1. Washington's decision to put down the Whiskey Rebellion.
2. Jefferson's decision to purchase the Louisiana Territory.
3. Monroe's decision to issue a warning (known as the Monroe Doctrine) to Europe.
4. Jackson's decision to assert federal supremacy over the states in the tariff issue growing out of South Carolina's nullification acts.
5. Lincoln's decision to save the union.
6. Theodore Roosevelt's decision to "take" the Panama area in order to build a canal.
7. Wilson's decision to support the League of Nations plan without accepting modifications suggested by the Senate.
8. Franklin Roosevelt's decision to help Britain in 1940.
9. Truman's decision to drop atomic bombs on Japanese cities at the end of World War II.
10. Truman's decision to support the Republic of Korea in 1950.

You may also want to read Oscar Handlin's volume on Chance or Destiny: Turning Points in American History. (Boston: Little, 1954. 220 pp.). Handlin colorfully analyzes eight historical turning points:

1. The battle of Yorktown.
2. The Louisiana Purchase.
3. The explosion on the Princeton and its effect on the Texas question.
4. July 4, 1863, at Gettysburg.
5. Seward's purchase of Alaska.
6. Theodore Roosevelt's cable to Dewey in 1898 leading to the entry into Manila Bay.
7. The sinking of the Lusitania.
8. The attack on Pearl Harbor.

There are several ways to use these and similar lists. At the end of the year, you may ask your students to select a few of the most important decisions they have studied. You may mimeograph one or both of these lists and use them for review, asking pupils why the events were important. You may want to go even farther, and organize your entire course around 25 to 35 great decisions. In studying these decisions, students will have to gather data on background, on the events themselves, on alternative proposals, and on the results. If this approach is well handled, your students will learn far more than just the events immediately surrounding each decision.

Here is the start of a list of 35 great decisions. You and your students may want to complete the list. For teaching purposes, the author has organized the topics in the form of questions, as follows:

1. Is there another water route to Asia?
2. Who shall control North America?
3. How should the colonies be governed?
4. Colonies—or a separate nation?
5. How can we defeat the British?
6. Is a loose confederation a practical government for us?
7. How shall we organize the old Southwest and the old Northwest?
8. Shall we be friends with England or France?
9. How can we extend our democracy?
10. Shall we fight Mexico?
11.
12.
13.
14.
15.
16.
17.
18.
19.
20.
21.
22.
23.
24.
25.
26.
27.
28.
29.
30.
31.
32.
33.
34.
35.

SOCIAL STUDIES BACKGROUND PAPER
NO. 60
FILE: U.S. HISTORY

The American Revolution:
Various Interpretations

If you haven't delved into it too deeply, the American Revolution may seem to be a part of our history that is easy to teach. Actually, it is a period about which there is still much controversy; therefore, you should know the various emphases placed on its causes and weave them into your teaching, without trying to make your students American Revolution experts.

Two highly readable, brief, up-to-date summaries of the varied interpretations of this period are available: (1) Edmund S. Morgan's The American Revolution: A Review of Changing Interpretations (1958, 20 pp., published originally by the American Historical Association; sold now by Macmillan); and (2) Wesley Frank Craven's chapter on "The Revolutionary Era" in John Higham's The Reconstruction of American History (Harper, 1962, 244 pp. A Paperback).

Both authors stress the importance of George Bancroft's 19th century account of this period. Although oversimplified and erroneous in some respects, it draws upon original sources and is written in a moving style. Briefly, Bancroft saw the Revolution as the result of a series of oppressive measures against a free people—a theory still popular in patriotic circles and one with some evidence to support it.

George Louis Beer and Charles M. Andrews were among the revisionist historians who placed the American Revolution in a broader frame of reference—that of British colonial policy. Both writers were much more critical of the American colonists and much more supportive of the British than Bancroft.

Charles A. Beard proposed an economic interpretation of the events of those years, summarized all too briefly in the statement "economic nationalism . . . led toward political nationalism." To him, the Revolution was a victory for the agrarians—the Constitution was a counter-revolution protecting the property interests of its signers and their cohorts. Despite attacks on Beard's theory, his work added a new dimension to the writings about the period.

About the same time, Carl Becker stressed the two issues of home rule and who should rule at home, and Philip Davidson emphasized the role of propaganda in his Propaganda and the American Revolution. Arthur M. Schlesinger showed, through incident after incident, how the colonial merchants shifted until they were finally arrayed with the aristocrats against the lower classes that came into prominence in the Revolution.

More recent revisionists have swung part of the way back to the Bancroft interpretation emphasizing a consensus among the colonists as they moved toward a fuller concept of democracy. Among these writers are Edmund S. Morgan in The Birth of the Republic, Louis Hartz in The Liberal Tradition in America, and J. Franklin Jameson in The American Revolution Considered As A Social Movement.

Can anyone say there is agreement among historians on this period?

119

BIBLIOGRAPHY ON THE CAUSES OF THE AMERICAN REVOLUTION

These books refer to materials on the causes of the American Revolution rather than on the revolution itself. A few of the references are to short accounts in general histories, which, it is assumed, are readily available. The other titles refer to more specialized accounts on this topic.

1. Andrews, Charles M. The Colonial Background of the American Revolution: Four Essays in American Colonial History. New Haven: Yale University Press, 1931. 220 pp. See also his The Colonial Period of American History. New Haven: Yale University Press, 1934-1938. Four volumes.
2. Bancroft, George. A History of the United States from Discovery of the American Continent. 10 volumes.
3. Beard, Charles A. An Economic Interpretation of the Constitution. New York: Macmillan, 1936. 330 pp.
4. Becker, Carl L. The Declaration of Independence: A Study in the History of Political Ideas. New York: Vintage, 1959. 286 pp. A paperback.
5. Chitwood, Oliver P., Rembert W. Patrick, and Frank L. Owsley. The American People: A History. Princeton, N.J.: Van Nostrand, 1962 edition. Vol. 1.
6. Davidson, Philip. Propaganda and the American Revolution. Chapel Hill, N.C.: University of North Carolina Press, 1941. 460 pp.
7. Friedel, Frank. The Golden Age of American History. New York: Braziller, 1959. 536 pp.
8. Gipson, Lawrence H. The Coming of the Revolution: 1763-1775. New York: Harper, 1964. 287 pp. A volume in the New American Nation series.
9. Handlin, Oscar. The Americans: A New History of the People of the United States. Boston: Little, 1963. 434 pp.
10. Jameson, J. Franklin. The American Revolution Considered as a Social Movement. Boston: Beacon, 1963. 105 pp. A paperback.
11. Lacy, Dan. The Meaning of the American Revolution. New York: New American Library, 1964. 308 pp.
12. Miller, William. A New History of the United States. New York: Dell, 1962. 466 pp. A paperback.
13. Morgan, Edmund S. The Birth of the Republic: 1763-1789. Chicago: University of Chicago Press, 1956. 177 pp. Also available from the same publisher as a paperback. A volume in the University of Chicago History of Civilization series.
14. Morison, Samuel Eliot, and Henry Steele Commager. The Growth of the American Republic. Vol. I. New York: Oxford University Press, 1962. 830 pp.
15. Nevins, Allan, and Henry Steele Commager. The Pocket History of the United States. New York: 1960. 593 pp. Pocket Books. A paperback in several editions.
16. Rossiter, Clinton. Seedtime of the Republic: The Origin of the American Tradition of Political Liberty. New York: Harcourt, 1953. 558 pp.
17. Schlesinger, Arthur M. The Colonial Merchants and the American Revolution: 1763-1776. New York: Ungar, 1957. 647 pp.

Leaders of the Revolutionary Period

Sometimes, when studying the Revolutionary period in United States history, a bright student asks why there were so many outstanding men in that era. If no one does, ask the question yourself, for there were men who emerged then who would stand out in any place and in any period. Among them were John Adams, Samuel Adams, Benjamin Franklin, Alexander Hamilton, Patrick Henry, Thomas Jefferson, John Marshall, George Mason, Tom Paine, Benjamin Rush, George Washington, James Wilson, and a good many others.

No one can answer this provocative question definitely, but it is an interesting problem to explore. It may well plunge you into the larger question of whether the men produce the times or the times the men.

Henry Steele Commager has wrestled with this question in a chapter on "Leadership in Eighteenth-Century America and Today" in Excellence and Leadership in a Democracy, edited by Stephen R. Graubard and Gerald Holton (Columbia University Press, 1962. 222 pp.).

Here are the five points by which Commager explains the outstanding leadership of the Revolutionary period.

1. "Such talent as there was, then, had no effective outlet except in public channels." Few people, according to Commager, became artists. The church was not as important in the colonies as it was in Europe and not as important as it had been in earlier America. Big business had not yet developed. Government was, therefore, the major arena for talented minds in that day.

2. "It is more to the point that they were all part of what we may call the American Enlightenment . . . " Commager points out that the men of that period had similar philosophies of life. There was a philosophical ferment in the colonies at that time. Despite differences of opinion, Hamilton and Jefferson and John Adams and Jefferson shared many common views.

3. A feeling of responsibility to posterity is another factor that explains these men's preeminence, according to Commager. He quotes Benjamin Rush's remarks about being "animated constantly by a belief that I was acting for the benefit of the whole world, and of future ages . . . " These leaders were inner-directed individuals, altruists, idealists.

4. Commager says that a fourth factor was the formal and informal education of the leading citizens. They were educated in history and philosophy, which led directly to an interest in colonial politics.

5. Similar to the fourth point is their knowledge of history and their outlook toward it. The founding fathers constantly referred to history in the Federalist Papers. They addressed themselves to great public questions, to broad general issues, and to profound moral problems, rather than to details.

A sixth point that might well be added is the burst of energy and the feeling of responsibility that often attends the gaining of independence. It is similar to the human change of growing up and assuming the responsibility of a family. While this phenomenon does not always occur in a nation's history, it is common enough to warrant examination as a cause for outstanding leadership. (India and Israel, examples of today's newly independent countries, have produced great leaders.)

So far as this writer can discover, no analysis of this question appears in a book suitable for the majority of students. Teachers will find some interesting material in the booklet by Stanley Elkins and Eric McKitrick on The Founding Fathers: Young Men of the Revolution (Washington: Service Center for Teachers of History. 1962. 28 pp.).

Numerous biographies of men of that period have been written for pupils. There are also several books of collective biography, including accounts of the leaders of the early republic. The following are excellent.

1. DaCruz, Daniel, Jr. Men Who Made America: The Founders of a Nation. New York: Crowell, 1962. 143 pp. Intended for pupils using English as a second language.

2. Foley, Rae. Famous Makers of America. New York: Dodd, 1963. 154 pp. Grades 6-9.

3. Padover, Saul K. The Genius of America: Men Whose Ideas Shaped Our Civilization. New York: McGraw-Hill, 1960. 369 pp. Grades 10-12.

A valuable exercise for teachers would be the preparation of a one-page bibliography of biographies of leaders of our new nation. After pupils have used the list a year or two, it could be revised.

Benjamin Franklin

Benjamin Franklin was certainly one of the great Americans of all times. In the early period of our country's history, he ranks with Roger Williams, William Penn, George Washington, Thomas Jefferson, and Alexander Hamilton.

Probably he was the most versatile of them all. He was a writer, publisher, propagandist, negotiator, humorist, philosopher, patriot, inventor, and scientist.

His sense of humor, satirical wit, ability to make and hold friends, adaptability, and flexibility were but a few of the characteristics that help to explain his greatness. He was able to absorb much from others and then to popularize it. He picked up many of his ideas while he was in England and France and adapted them to the American colonies.

As an inventor, he developed bifocal glasses, the Franklin stove, lightning rods, and the harmonica (which he really improved rather than invented).

As a politician, Franklin was a member of the English troops that fought in the French and Indian War in the Ohio valley, the originator of the Albany Plan of Union in 1754, president of the Pennsylvania General Assembly, a member of the Second Continental Congress and the Constitutional Convention, American representative in England and in France for nearly 30 years—including the years in which the treaty of peace after the Revolutionary War was negotiated.

He was a "modern" educator, starting the academy that later became the University of Pennsylvania. His "Junto" developed into the American Philosophical Society. He started the police and fire departments and street lighting in Philadelphia—ideas picked up in Boston and London.

Franklin's work as postmaster for the colonies built up communication and helped to tie the colonies together. He traveled extensively in this capacity and knew all parts of the colonies.

His Poor Richard's Almanac was one of the few pieces of writing read by a large percentage of the colonists. One writer has said that it was "a vital factor in uniting the colonies."

Perhaps Franklin ought to be portrayed to pupils as "the First American"—a man who helped to develop a unique American way of life. As Burlingame says, "He awakened Americans to their own intelligence." Van Doren points out that "he seems to have been more than a single man – a harmonious human multitude."

Franklin's life spanned all but 16 years of the 18th century. He was born in 1706 in Boston, but spent most of his life in Philadelphia. He died in 1790.

MATERIALS ON FRANKLIN
(For teachers and high school students)

1. Burlingame, Roger. Benjamin Franklin: The First Mr. American. New York: Signet, 1955. 127 pp. 25¢. A paperback.
2. Franklin, Benjamin. The Benjamin Franklin Sampler. New York: Premium. 35¢ A paperback. Excerpts from his writings.
3. Parrington, Vernon L. Main Currents in American Thought. New York: Harcourt, 1939. Pp. 164-178. This excellent book is also available in three volumes as a paperback.
4. Van Doren, Carl. Benjamin Franklin. New York: Viking, 1938. 845 pp. Considered the best of the full biographies of Franklin.

MATERIALS ON FRANKLIN
(For elementary and junior high school pupils)

1. Aulaire, Ingri and Edgar d'. Benjamin Franklin. Garden City: Doubleday, 1950. 47 pp. A picture book biography. Grades 2-5.
2. Cousins, Margaret. Ben Franklin of Old Philadelphia. New York: Random House, 1952. 184 pp. A Landmark book. Grades 6-9.
3. Crane, Verner W. Benjamin Franklin and a Rising People. Boston: Little, 1954. 219 pp.
4. Daugherty, James. Poor Richard. New York: Viking, 1941. 158 pp. With drawings. An interesting and extremely well-written text. Grades 7-10.
5. Eaton, Jeannette. That Lively Man, Ben Franklin. New York: Morrow, 1948. 253 pp. Emphasizes the grievances of American colonists. Grades 5-8.
6. Eberle, Irmengaarde. Benjamin Franklin: Man of Science. New York: Watts, 1961. 145 pp. Grades 5-8.
7. Epstein, Samuel, and Beryl Williams. Real Book About Benjamin Franklin. New York: Garden City, 1952. 192 pp. Grades 4-7.
8. Friedman, Estelle. Benjamin Franklin. New York: Putnam, 1961. 45 pp. Grades 2-4.
9. Grover, Eulalie O. Benjamin Franklin: The Story of Poor Richard. New York: Dodd, 1953. 267 pp. Grades 8-11.
10. Judson, Clara I. Benjamin Franklin. Chicago: Follett, 1957. 204 pp. Grades 6-9. Concentrates on his political activities.
11. Lawson, Robert. Ben and Me: A New and Astonishing Life of Benjamin Franklin As Written by His Good Mouse Amos. Boston: Little, 1951. 113 pp. Primary grades.
12. McKown, Robin. Benjamin Franklin. New York: Putnam, 1963. 192 pp. Grades 6-9.
13. Meadowcroft, Enid L. The Story of Benjamin Franklin. New York: Grosset, 1952. Grades 5-7. 182 pp. A Signature book.
14. Stevenson, Augusta. Ben Franklin: Boy Printer. Indianapolis: Bobbs-Merrill, 1962. 200 pp. Grades 4-6.
15. Tottle, John. Benjamin Franklin: First Great American. Boston: Houghton, 1959. 192 pp. Grades 4-6.
16. Weir, Ruth C. Benjamin Franklin: Printer and Patriot. Nashville: Abingdon, 1956. 128 pp. Grades 4-6.

The United States as a New Nation

Many students and a few teachers find the period of the formation of the United States dull, uninteresting, and without focus.

If you think of the United States as a new nation and compare it with the new nations formed after World War II, the period may take on significance. The analogy can be used if your students are aware of the basic differences between the two historical periods involved.

Students might enjoy a search for the weaknesses and strengths of their tiny nation in 1789, keeping separate notes on each. Perhaps the following will be helpful to teachers in using this approach.

SOME WEAKNESSES OR PROBLEMS

1. A tiny nation. Less than four million persons in 1789.
2. Surrounded by unfriendly or less than friendly nations—England, France, and Spain, including the West Indies.
3. Failure of the first government under the Articles of Confederation.
4. Difficulties in winning ratification of the new Constitution. Rhode Island delayed ratification for months. Ratification won in New York state by only three votes.
5. One area—Vermont—remained "independent" from 1777 until 1791.
6. The United States was faced very early with a "cold war" between France and England, in which she decided to remain neutral or independent.
7. Poor transportation facilities. Mostly waterways. More communication with Europe than among the colonies. A few stagecoaches on post roads, but journeys were rough, expensive, and sometimes dangerous.
8. Poor communications. A postal system, developed by Benjamin Franklin, but little else.
9. No universal language. English was a common language, but it was not spoken by everyone. Dutch and Swedish spoken, considerable French in certain areas, and much German. German was even considered as a national language.
10. Some of the minority, who opposed the war and independence, left the country. Others of the minority remained. Loss of some outstanding people.
11. Disagreement on the form the new government should take and the power it should have.
12. Much regional or state feeling. Strong loyalty to the colony rather than to the new central government. A long fight between Virginia and Massachusetts for domination in the new central government.
13. The Whiskey Rebellion, somewhat analogous to the Cocoa Rebellion in Ghana at the time of independence after World War II. The role of the federal government was challenged. Alexander Hamilton led a force of 15,000 men (a large number in those days) to quell the rebellion.
14. An Alien and Sedition Law, somewhat similar to the Deportation Acts of Ghana after independence.

SOME STRENGTHS AND UNIFYING FACTORS

In spite of the weaknesses, there were enough unifying factors and strengths to make it possible for this tiny nation to survive—and grow. Among them were these.

1. The geographic isolation of the nation from Europe.
2. The comparative homogeneity of the people. In 1790, 49 per cent were English and 63.6 per cent came from Great Britain. The largest minority were the Germans, and even they had ties with the British.
3. Homogeneity in religion. Despite the differences in beliefs, worship, and church organization, most Americans in that period were Christians and Protestants. Catholics were a minority in Maryland, and there were only a few Jews in the country.
4. A common language. English was the common language of most people, despite the fact that many spoke other languages. Language was not the great problem that it is in some of the new nations today.
5. A high percentage of literacy. Figures are impossible to find, but some authorities feel that the United States had the largest percentage of literacy in the world in that day. This factor was an enormous help in building an educated electorate.
6. Excellent land and good harbors.
7. Many common values: hard work, especially a Puritan heritage; emphasis upon individualism, competition, despite much cooperation; little class consciousness compared with Europe; adaptability and ingenuity; high value placed upon education.
8. A frontier to serve as a "safety valve." (Some authorities doubt that this was a great factor, pointing to the need for money and equipment to strike out anew.)
9. Experience in self-government, especially in some of the colonies.
10. Outstanding leadership. Few nations have had as many able leaders in proportion to their population as the United States had in its early years. General Washington, who was an able administrator, is a significant example.
11. The ability to compromise, highlighted in the great compromises in writing the Constitution and in adding the Bill of Rights.
12. A fairly adequate land system. The large estates of the Tories and others were broken up after the Revolution. Primogeniture laws abolished early. Widespread ownership of land by the people.
13. Some post offices and post roads. Developed by Benjamin Franklin in an earlier period.
14. The necessity and desire to succeed. The "release of new energy" that sometimes comes with independence of persons or nations.

You may want to add other items to these two lists.

The next period in United States history could be studied by examining ways in which unity and strength were fostered. The basic question "How did we develop national unity and national strength?" can be the focus of many lessons, directly or indirectly. Or it can be used to summarize the next period. Some attention should, of course, be given to the forces that still divided the nation.

Democracy in the United States

Although the concept of democracy is learned best in action, the idea also needs to be raised to the level of pupils' consciousness by discussions. Here are a few points to consider in discussing democracy.

1. Democracy is more than a form of government. It is a way of life, permeating every aspect of human endeavor. Democratic government rests upon democracy in other areas of life.

2. Democracy is based on belief in the unique worth of <u>all</u> individuals. All people are important. In the words of Harold Laswell, democracy is a "commonwealth of mutual respect." Its aim is to help all people to grow and develop to their fullest possible extent.

3. Democracy attempts to find a balance between security and freedom, between freedom and responsibility.

4. Democracy assumes that the judgment of many people is better on most issues than the judgment of one person or group.

5. Democracy depends, to a large extent, upon an educated electorate.

6. Democracy vests its supreme power in the people. In some respects, they share directly—in others, indirectly—in the choices to be made by their elected representatives.

7. Democracy is based upon the rule of the majority, with protection of the minorities. In popular language, it is based upon "counting heads" rather than "cracking heads."

8. Democracy demands means that are consistent with ends; means are at least as important as ends.

9. Democracy achieves changes by peaceful, reasonable, and lawful means—by persuasion rather than by force.

10. Democracy, at its best, encourages both cooperation and competition.

11. Democracy demands some planning in the public interest.

12. Democracy guarantees all people various freedoms—of religion, of press, of assembly, and of speech.

13. Democracy demands a live interest in public affairs by everyone; each person has responsibilities as well as rights.

14. Democracy entails interest in closing the gap between the ideal and the real. There is always "unfinished business" to be carried on.

METHODS OF ILLUSTRATING THE GROWTH OF DEMOCRACY

It is not easy to teach the idea of the growth of democracy. It is an idea, a concept, a way of life with many facets.

In developing the idea of democracy and its growth, you will want to use graphic illustrations. Here are a few examples from which you can select the most appropriate. You and your pupils may want to figure out others.

1. A HIGHWAY. Democracy was only a path at first. Who was on the path in Greece, in Rome, in other places? Later it became a narrow road, widening to include more people. Not always a straight road ahead, democracy wound back sometimes. Weeds and even trees grew on it. When was it widened? Who else was allowed to travel on it? Who were its social engineers? Who is still excluded? What improvements need to be made on the road?

2. A TREE. Where was the seed of democracy discovered? By whom? Where was it planted? Under what conditions does it thrive? What are its roots? Does it have one tap root, like some trees, or several roots, like other trees? What winds have blown against it? What storms have whirled around it? Are there any new "seedlings" today? Where? Who is sheltered by the tree?

3. A HOUSE. Democracy was only a crude, small house at first. Who built it? Whom did it shelter? When were other rooms added? By whom? Is the original structure still good? Why or why not?

4. A ROPE OR CHAIN. What are the important links in the chain of democracy or the major fibers in the rope? What new links have been added? By whom? When? What parts of the rope have become frayed, or what links have been broken? When? What can be done to strengthen the rope or chain? These two ideas are similar, but only one should be used at a time.

5. AN EXPANDING CIRCLE. Draw a very small circle to represent the original concept of democracy in any given place and time. Draw larger circles around the original circle. Label them with dates, people, events, and ideas.

Each of these ideas lends itself to enlargement. Let the pupils do the thinking. Start a lesson with a drawing on the board. Label it: "a house–," "a highway–," "a rope–," "a tree–" "of democracy." Ask in what ways democracy is like "a . . . " Why?

You may want to have pupils discover the symbols of democracy, such as the ballot box, the robe of a judge, the Statue of Liberty, and others. Of course, these devices demonstrate other democracies as well as our own.

Democracy in the United States:
A Bibliography

Unfortunately , there is no one book for either adults or students that traces the development of democracy in the United States. The one volume that comes nearest to doing so is A. A. Ekirch's American Democratic Tradition listed in the bibliography below. Each of the other volumes treats only one or several aspects of this broad concept.

This list is primarily for teachers, although able students in high schools can profit by reading many of the books listed.

1. Beard, Charles and Mary. Rise of American Civilization. New York: Macmillan, 1933. 1689 pp. In large part, a history of democratic ideas, with a strong emphasis upon the economic interpretation of our national history.
2. Becker, Carl. L. Freedom and Responsibility in the American Way of Life. New York: Vintage, 1955. 135 pp. A paperback.
3. Becker, Carl L. Modern Democracy. New Haven, Conn.: Yale University Press, 1941. 100 pp.
4. Bode, Boyd H. Democracy As a Way of Life. New York: Macmillan, 1937. 114 pp. Deals primarily with education and democracy.
5. Cahn, Edmond. Predicament of Democratic Man. New York: Macmillan, 1961. 194 pp.
6. Commager, Henry Steele. The American Mind: An Interpretation of American Thought Since the 1880's. New Haven, Conn.: Yale University Press, 1950. 476 pp.
7. Commager, Henry Steele. Majority Rule and Minority Rights. New York: Oxford University Press, 1943. 92 pp.
8. Curti, Merle. The Growth of American Thought. New York: Harper, 1964 edition. 939 pp. An intellectual history of the United States.
9. de Tocqueville, Alexis. Democracy in America. New York: Oxford University Press, 1947. 513 pp. A classic commentary of the French traveler in the United States in the early 19th century. Still provocative.
10. Douglas, William O. Democracy's Manifesto. New York: Doubleday, 1962. 48 pp. A statement of the Supreme Court justice's belief that we can win the "cold war" if we are faithful to our ideals at home while we try to spread these ideas abroad.
11. Ekirch, Arthur A., Jr. The American Democratic Tradition: A History. New York: Macmillan, 1963. 338 pp. Also available as a paperback. Probably the best statement of the history of democracy in the United States currently available.
12. Frankel, Charles. The Democratic Prospect. New York: Harper,1962. 222 pp. An analysis of current criticisms of American democracy and a defense of the basic health of our society despite imperfections. Also available as a Harper Colophon paperback.
13. Gabriel, Ralph. The Course of American Democratic Thought. New York: Ronald, 1956. 508 pp. Another history of ideas in the United States.

14. Hartz, Louis. The Liberal Tradition in America: An Interpretation of American Political Thought Since the Revolution. New York: Harcourt, 1955. 329 pp.
15. Hofstadter, Richard. The Age of Reform: From Bryan to F.D.R. New York: Knopf, 1955. 328 pp.
16. Hofstadter, Richard. American Political Tradition, and the Men Who Made It. New York: Knopf, 1948. 341 pp. Also a Vintage paperback.
17. Kohn, Hans. American Nationalism: An Interpretive Essay. New York: Collier, 1961. 286 pp. A paperback.
18. Lilienthal, David E. This I Do Believe. New York: Harper, 1949. 208 pp. A beautifully worded, powerful, and often moving account of the tenets of democracy.
19. Lipson, Leslie. The Democratic Civilization. Berkeley, Calif.: University of California Press, 1964. 632 pp.
20. Padover, Saul K. The Meaning of Democracy: An Appraisal of the American Experience. New York: Praeger, 1963. 139 pp. An analysis and appraisal of democracy in the United States, followed by excerpts from speeches, letters, and other sources of some of the leading champions of democracy throughout our history.
21. Palmer, Robert Roswell. The Age of Democratic Revolutions: 1760-1800. Princeton, N.J.: Princeton University Press, 1959. 534 pp.
22. Parrington, Vernon L. Main Currents in American Thought: An Interpretation of American Literature from the Beginnings to 1920. New York: Harcourt, 1930. 1335 pp. Much broader than the title indicates. In reality, a classical history of ideas in the United States.
23. Rockefeller Panel Report. The Power of the Democratic Idea. Garden City: Doubleday, 1960. 75 pp.
24. Smith, Bradford. A Dangerous Freedom. Philadelphia: Lippincott, 1952. 383 pp. Also a Dell paperback. The role of private organizations in our democracy.
25. Smith, T. V. The Democratic Way of Life. Chicago: University of Chicago Press, 1939. 289 pp. Also available as a paperback.
26. Shotwell, James. The Long Road to Freedom. Indianapolis: Bobbs-Merrill, 1960. 639 pp. The summation of a lifetime of research on freedom in the Western world, by a prominent Columbia University professor.
27. Tyler, Alice Felt. Freedom's Ferment: Phases of American Social History from the Colonial Period to the Outbreak of the Civil War. New York: Harper, 1944. 608 pp. Originally printed by the University of Minnesota. Reprinted as a Harper Torchbook paperback.
28. Weyl, Walter E. The New Democracy: An Essay on Certain Political and Economic Tendencies in the United States. New York: Macmillan, 1912. 369 pp. Reprinted as a Harper Torchbook paperback.

The Growth of the United States

In a United States history course with a strictly chronological approach, events seem to move swiftly and smoothly. Consequently, one does not always see the enormous changes that take place over a period of 25 or 50 years.

Therefore, it is wise to stop from time to time and take a backward look, comparing several aspects of the national life at two dates separated by 25 or 50 years. Marcus Cunliffe has done that in his book The Nation Takes Shape: 1789-1837. (One of the series of books in the Chicago History of American Civilization. Available in both hardbound and paper edition. Chicago: University of Chicago Press, 1959. 223 pp.)

In his book, Cunliffe quotes from an article in the ''Democratic Review'' that summarized the advance of the United States over a period of 50 years.

In brief, during those years the territory of our nation tripled. The population quadrupled. The number of states doubled. But there were more changes than those striking ones. They are summarized here in tabular form for ease of teaching and to emphasize the contrasts.

CHANGES IN FIFTY YEARS

	1789-1790	1839-1840
	The United States was a small, struggling new nation.	The United States was a large, stable country.
Area	3,930,000 square miles	Territory tripled
Population	Less than 4 million	Approximately 16 million
States	11-13	26
National Revenue	$3-4 million	$20-30 million
Exports	$20 million	$80-100 million
Post offices	75	12,000
Canals	0	Around 2500 miles (including 363 miles in the Erie Canal)
Railroads	0	Around 1000 miles
Lighthouses	8-10	250

There are many ways in which you could present this material, depending upon your class and its needs.

For example, you can merely give students the topics and let them do the research necessary to complete the chart. This is probably the best method to use.

Or, you can put the material on the chalkboard as the basis for discussion, talking about why and how these changes took place.

You might like to have a student prepare a very large copy of the chart on oaktag and hang it somewhere in the classroom as a valuable reference for learning.

Or you might like to have students take separate items from the chart and report to the class in detail on them.

The chart would serve as a good review if you asked students to comment and enlarge upon the data it contains.

Whatever your method, the goal is to enlighten students about the far-reaching changes in this fifty-year period, the reasons for them, and their effects upon the nation.

Andrew Jackson:
Some Interpretations

In teaching about Andrew Jackson, it is important to remember that he is one of the most controversial persons in our history. Historians differ widely in their estimate of him.

Three major interpretations of Jackson are set forth by John William Ward in the chapter "The Age of the Common Man" in John Higham's Reconstruction of American History. One of these is the Turner interpretation of Jackson as the product of the moving frontier. A second is Arthur Schlesinger, Jr.'s thesis in The Age of Jackson, which portrays Jackson as the champion of the emerging groups (largely laborers and reformers) in the cities of the East. A third point of view comes from Richard Hofstadter's essay in The American Political Tradition and the Men Who Made It. This work sees Jackson as an "enterprising capitalist on the make."

James L. Bugg, Jr., in his pamphlet Jacksonian Democracy: Myth or Reality? calls attention to the variety of interpretations but categorizes them differently. He starts with James Parton's early works on Jackson, stressing the contradictory aspects: "a patriot and traitor"; a law-abiding, law-defying citizen; a democratic autocrat and an urbane savage. Bugg next refers to writers who castigated Jackson, yet conceded his nationalism. Later writers of the Progressive era, like John Spencer Bassett—a sympathetic yet critical representative—saw Jackson as an outstanding democrat. Vernon L. Parrington and Claude Bowers were much more partisan writers of the same school. Bugg next refers to Thomas P. Abernethy's appraisal of Jackson as an opportunist and politician. Interpretations like his reduced Jackson to the level of a vindictive schemer. The Age of Jackson by Schlesinger represents a return to praise for this controversial figure, but emphasizes the East rather than the West as the catalyst for his new ideas. Bugg calls the next group of writers the "entrepreneurial school" and cites Bray Hammond as its chief proponent. These historians pictured Jackson as hostile to the idea of including the emerging capitalists in the nation's new opportunities. Finally, John Ward and others see Jackson as a symbol, created by the people who needed an image of themselves as they wanted to be.

These varying viewpoints prove that Jackson is a difficult figure to present to students. He is a colorful but complex personality. You should mull over these dissident interpretations and decide how to use them best in your teaching. With your more able pupils, you may want to suggest all the conflicting opinions for discussion. With less able groups, you should probably concentrate on Jackson as a flamboyant character who came out of the West and yet was not typical of it.

SOME WAYS OF STUDYING JACKSON

There are, of course, many ways in which you can approach the study of Andrew Jackson with your students. Here are a few suggestions.

1. Assign a reading list for both homework and class reading. After a few days, ask the students to answer the question "Was Andrew Jackson a dangerous demagogue or a champion of democracy?" Or ask them to find supporting evidence for the following quotations:

   > Democracy was good talk with which to win the favor of the people and thereby accomplish ulterior objectives. Jackson never really championed the cause of the people; he only invited them to champion his. (Thomas P. Abernethy)

   > At last these Western forces of aggressive nationalism and democracy took possession of the government in the person of the man who best embodied them—Andrew Jackson. (Frederick Jackson Turner)

2. You may want to examine Jackson's cabinet and "Kitchen Cabinet" to see how they represented the different areas of the United States that supported him. See Van Deusen's The Jacksonian Era, (pp. 31 ff.), for the names and states of these cabinet members.

3. You may want to try the biographical approach. Have several students read about Adams, Calhoun, Clay, Webster, Jackson, and Van Buren; then discuss the major issues of the day as seen by these different men. For a summary on the chalkboard and in their notebooks, use a simple chart like this one.

	The Bank	Slavery	Internal Improvements	Expansion	Tariff	Indians
Clay						

4. Another approach to this period is to think of it in terms of the various regions of the country and their general attitudes on the leading issues. Again, a chart on the chalkboard and in student notebooks will help to clinch this learning. Or you may want to have the students role play the sections of the country on these important issues. At first, Jackson championed an uneasy alliance of the South, West, and parts of New York and Pennsylvania. Later, he gained the support of some of New England and lost much support in the South.

Background Readings
on Andrew Jackson and His Times

BOOKS ABOUT JACKSON
(For adults and good high school readers)

1. Benson, Lee. <u>The Concept of Jacksonian Democracy: New York as a Test</u> <u>Case</u>. Princeton, N.J.: Princeton University Press, 1961. 351 pp.
2. Bugg, James L., Jr. <u>Jacksonian Democracy: Myth or Reality?</u> New York: Holt, 1962. 122 pp. A paperback of readings.
3. Fish, Carl Russell. <u>The Rise of the Common Man 1830-1850</u>. New York: Macmillan, 1927. 391 pp. A volume in the American Life series.
4. Hofstadter, Richard. <u>The American Political Tradition and the Men Who</u> <u>Made It</u>. New York: Knopf, 1951. 378 pp. The common man as an enterprising capitalist on the make. Chapter on "Andrew Jackson and the Rise of Liberal Capitalism."
5. James, Marquis. <u>The Life of Andrew Jackson</u>. Indianapolis: Bobbs-Merrill, 1938. 972 pp. Two volumes in one book. Especially good on the Battle of New Orleans.
6. Meyers, Marvin. <u>The Jacksonian Persuasion: Politics and Belief</u>. Ann Arbor, Mich.: University of Michigan Press, 1957. 304 pp. Especially strong on his ideas and cohorts.
7. McCormick, R. P. "New Perspective on Jacksonian Politics." <u>American</u> <u>Historical Review</u>, January 1960. Pp. 288-301.
8. Rozwenc, Edwin C. <u>The Meaning of Jacksonian Democracy</u>. Boston: Heath, 1963. 124 pp. A paperback book of readings in the Problems of American Civilization series of Amherst College.
9. Schlesinger, Arthur M., Jr. <u>The Age of Jackson</u>. Boston: Little, 1950. 577 pp. Stresses the common-man ideology as provided by emerging labor groups and others in the East. Well written. Also available as a paperback.
10. Taylor, George Rogers. <u>Jackson Versus Biddle: The Struggles Over the</u> <u>Second Bank of the United States</u>. Boston: Heath, 1940. 118 pp. Another in the Amherst College series.
11. Van Deusen, Glyndon G. <u>The Jacksonian Era: 1828-1848</u>. New York: Harper, 1959. 290 pp. A volume in the New American Nation series.
12. Ward, John William. <u>Andrew Jackson: Symbol of an Age</u>. New York: Oxford University Press, 1955. 274 pp.
13. White, Leonard D. <u>The Jacksonians: A Study of Administrative History:</u> <u>1820-1851</u>. New York: Macmillan, 1954. 593 pp.

BOOKS FOR BOYS AND GIRLS

1. Andrist, Ralph, and Arthur Schlesinger, Jr. <u>Andrew Jackson</u>. New York: American Heritage, 1963, 153 pp. Grades 6-9.
2. Andrist, Ralph K. <u>Andrew Jackson, Soldier and Statesman</u>. New York: Harper, 1963. American Heritage Junior Library. Grades 6-9.
3. Coy, Harold. <u>Real Book About Andrew Jackson</u>. New York: Garden City, 1962. 192 pp. Grades 6-9.
4. Judson, Clara Ingram. <u>Andrew Jackson: Frontier Statesman</u>. Chicago: Follett, 1954. 224 pp. Grades 5-8.

135

5. Meadowcroft, Enid. The Story of Andrew Jackson. New York: Grosset, 1953. 182 pp. Grades 4-6. For very slow readers.
6. Parlin, John. Andrew Jackson. Champaign, Ill.: Garrard, 1962. 80 pp. Grades 5-8.
7. Remini, Robert U. The Election of Andrew Jackson. Philadelphia: Lippincott, 1963. 256 pp. Grades 6-9.
8. Wright, Frances F. Andrew Jackson: Fighting Frontiersman. Nashville, Tenn.: Abington, 1958. 128 pp. Grades 5-8.
9. Young, Stanley. Young Hickory. New York: Rinehart, 1940. 271 pp. Grades 6-9.

Dorothea Dix

To most social studies teachers and their students, Dorothea Dix is merely a reformer who worked to alleviate the poor conditions of prisoners and the insane. Most textbooks devote a line or two to this woman; a few give her as much as a paragraph.

How unfortunate that Dorothea Dix is treated so lightly. She certainly deserves more attention than that. Stewart H. Holbrook, in Dreamers of the American Dream, says that she was "one of the most effective reformers the United States—or the world—has known." He further states that "Dorothea Dix was one of the most distinguished, and surely remains to this day the most forgotten, outstanding woman America has produced in more than three hundred years."

Because she is so important, you and your students should know something about her. You may want to present her interesting life story in capsule form, or you may want a student to prepare an oral report about it.

> During her lifetime, Dorothea Dix was responsible for the building of mental hospitals in 30 states of the United States (plus several in Canada and in Europe) and for improving scores of city and county poorhouses, jails, and hospitals. This is quite a record for one person!
>
> Dorothea Dix was born in Hampden, Maine, in 1802. Very little is known about her family except that her father was a ne'er-do-well who alternated between drinking and selling religious tracts. In this latter work, he was helped from time to time by his daughter, Dorothea. The family lived in a log cabin in which not only money was lacking but even love and affection.
>
> At 12, she went to Boston to live with her grandmother, the wealthy widow of a doctor and druggist. Although the grandmother paid little attention to Dorothea, she did pay her tuition in a school for girls.
>
> At 14, Dorothea began to teach, a job in which she was unusually successful. She liked this work and wrote several books for children, as well as a volume entitled Conversations on Common Things, based on the questions her pupils asked and her replies. This book was published in 60 editions.
>
> In 1841, a young theological student, who was working in the jails in East Cambridge, Massachusetts, asked Dorothea Dix to teach a small group of women in the House of Correction. She agreed. When she visited the prison for the first time, she was shocked by conditions. The inmates, in rags and barefooted, were kept in a room with no heat and practically no light. She approached the responsible officials and brought about some improvement in conditions. But her interest, once aroused, did not stop there.
>
> She began to visit other institutions in Massachusetts and in nearby Rhode Island. She found prisoners in chains, in straw-covered stalls, in chicken coops, in cages. She found violent and nonviolent patients in the same room. She learned that most people felt that insane persons were born depraved—and that nothing could be done for them.

In the next four years, she visited 300 jails, 18 prisons, over 500 almshouses and other institutions. She traveled 10,000 miles by horseback, by steamboat, by railroad, and on foot.

Her first big sucess came in New Jersey in 1845 when the state legislature voted to construct a modern asylum (or what we would call today a "mental hospital"). Soon she was off to Indiana, Illinois, Kentucky, Tennessee, Missouri, Mississippi, Alabama, North and South Carolina, Maryland, and to Halifax, Nova Scotia, St. Johns, and Newfoundland in Canada. Everywhere she went, she studied local conditions, wrote for local newspapers, organized groups of citizens, and worked with legislators to improve conditions for the insane and for prisoners.

Then she tackled Congress. Pointing out that Congress had given millions of acres in land grants to railroads and to schools, she pled for gifts of land for work with the mentally ill. At first, she asked for 5,000,000 acres; later she raised the request to 12,225,000 acres, which could be sold with the proceeds used for her work. After five unsuccessful attempts, a land bill passed both houses of Congress. It was vetoed by President Pierce on the ground that it was unconstitutional and failed to pass over his veto. However, Congress did start St. Elizabeth's Hospital, a mental institution in the District of Columbia.

During the Civil War, Dorothea Dix was appointed superintendent of women nurses in the Union Army. Following the war, she went to England and the Continent, continuing her work in several countries there, with considerable success.

At the age of 85, she died and was buried in Mt. Auburn Cemetery in Cambridge, Massachusetts. Over her grave fly the American flag and the standard of the Corps of Army Nurses. On her tombstone, there is only her name—"Dorothea L. Dix."

BIBLIOGRAPHY

Two books for teachers and four references for pupils are all the information that is currently available on this famous American woman reformer.

1. Baker, Rachel. Angel of Mercy: The Story of Dorothea Dix. New York: Messner, 1955. 191 pp. Grades 6-9.
2. Fisher, Dorothy C. And Long Remember. New York: Whittlesey, 1959. 119 pp. Pp. 72-83. Grades 5-8.
3. Holbrook, Steward H. Dreamers of the American Dream. Garden City: Doubleday, 1957. 369 pp. See pages 227-237. Junior or senior high school pupils.
4. Marshall, Helen E. Dorothea Lynde Dix: Forgotten Samaritan. Chapel Hill, N.C.: University of North Carolina Press, 1937. 298 pp. For teachers.
5. Melin, Grace H. Dorothea Dix: Girl Reformer. Indianapolis: Bobbs-Merrill, 1963. 200 pp. Grades 5-8.
6. Tiffany, Francis. Life of Dorothea Lynde Dix. Boston: Houghton, 1918. 392 pp. The official biography. For teachers only.

---

*The Importance of Cities
in Early America*

No one doubts the importance of cities in our nation today; we are unquestionably an urban-centered country. But there is controversy over when the influence of cities began.

Until recently, most historians dated the importance of cities from the period after the Civil War. In the last few years, however, a new interpretation holds that a full-fledged and influential urban society existed well before the close of our first century and that the urban West, as well as the urban East, shaped United States history much more than has been assumed.

This theory adds a new dimension to American history—and challenges the frontier thesis of Turner and his followers. Two of its advocates are Carl Bridenbaugh and Richard C. Wade, whose works are cited here.

1. Bridenbaugh, Carl. <u>Cities in the Wilderness: The First Century of Urban Life in America 1625-1742</u>. New York: Capricorn, 1955. 500 pp. A paperback.
2. Bridenbaugh, Carl. <u>Cities in Revolt: Urban Life in America 1743-1776</u>. New York: Capricorn, 1960. 434 pp. A paperback.
3. Wade, Richard C. <u>The Urban Frontier: The Rise of Western Cities 1790-1830</u>. Chicago: University of Chicago Press, 1959. 360 pp. A paperback.

In <u>Cities in the Wilderness</u>, Bridenbaugh deals with the geography, economics, religion, and social life of Boston, Charles Town, Newport, New York, and Philadelphia, pointing out similarities. They were all harbor cities or cities on rivers; they had a fairly homogeneous population; they had a common heritage politically; and they early became commercial centers, with considerable specialization in labor.

He vividly presents some of the pressing problems of those early towns, including the building of streets and wharves, protection against vandalism and crime, fire prevention, water systems, sewage systems, subsurface drainage, and education. He points out that an aristocracy of merchants developed early and with it came the "emergence of a genuine colonial culture"—theaters, concerts, clubs, publishing firms, newspapers, and public education.

He also asserts:

> Commercial as well as agrarian interests dictated political if not also social revolution; most of the intellectual activity and much of the social and political advance of the eighteenth century depended upon an urban rather than a rural environment; certainly a large part of our radical thought came neither from farm nor forest but from the seaboard towns. I believe the colonial city, though it never embraced more than ten per cent of the population of the colonies, exercised a far more important influence on the life of early America than historians have previously recognized.

In Cities in Revolt, Bridenbaugh pushes the political thesis farther. He claims that the cities were the centers of radical activities and cites such events as the Stamp Act Riots and the "tea parties" as evidence.

Richard C. Wade presents similar ideas in his volume The Urban Frontier, using Pittsburgh, Cincinnati, Lexington, Louisville, and St. Louis as the case studies of frontier towns. He holds that the rise of such cities is a dominant theme in the development of the West—in the past overlooked by historians. He stresses the fact that these Western cities copied the Eastern cities, especially Philadelphia, in meeting pressing problems of space, crime, water, and illiteracy. He characterizes the struggle for power and primacy among these towns as one of the most persistent and striking points in their history. He claims that, by 1830, the towns in the West had developed ways and habits that contrasted sharply with those of the countryside.

Some historians think that this approach is a useful and important addition to our interpretations of life in early America, although they feel that the role of towns has been unduly magnified by recent interpreters. Richard Morris calls the Bridenbaugh books "seminal studies" that help "to correct the preoccupation of historians. . . with the role of the frontier and the rural image in early American life." But he questions the radical role of cities politically, citing the fact that John Adams, Washington, and Jefferson were not residents of cities and that the Tories lived primarily in the large towns.

Teachers who deal with the rise of towns in early American history and who want to extend this topic to more recent times may find the following data useful. It is taken from Winther and Cartwright's The Story of Our Heritage (Ginn). Similar data can be found in that volume or in reports of the census every ten years.

1790	1800	1810	1820
New York	New York	New York	New York
Philadelphia	Philadelphia	Philadelphia	Philadelphia
Boston	Baltimore	Baltimore	Baltimore
Charleston	Boston	Boston	Boston
Baltimore	Charleston	Charleston	New Orleans
Salem	Salem	New Orleans	Charleston
Newport	Providence	Salem	Salem
Providence	Norfolk	Albany	Washington
Marblehead	Richmond	Providence	Albany
Gloucester	Albany	Richmond	Richmond

1860	1890	1920	1960
New York	New York	New York	New York
Philadelphia	Chicago	Chicago	Chicago
Baltimore	Philadelphia	Philadelphia	Los Angeles
Boston	St. Louis	Detroit	Philadelphia
New Orleans	Boston	Cleveland	Detroit
Cincinnati	Baltimore	St. Louis	Baltimore
St. Louis	San Francisco	Boston	Houston
Chicago	Cincinnati	Baltimore	Cleveland
Buffalo	Cleveland	Pittsburgh	Washington
Newark	Buffalo	Los Angeles	St. Louis

The Reconstruction Era

SOME MISCONCEPTIONS

Both misinformation and myths about the Civil War and the Reconstruction period have been passed on to pupils through books, films, television programs, and other sources. A few of these are listed below in the hope that teachers will be alerted to them. A simple true-false test, given at the beginning of a study of this period, will show which misconceptions to work on. Here are some you may find in your classrooms.

1. ALL SOUTHERNERS WERE SLAVE HOLDERS. Actually, there were only 347,525 slaveholders in 1850. The largest number of these (105,683) owned only one to five slaves.

2. ALL NEGROES WERE SLAVES PRIOR TO THE EMANCIPATION PROCLAMA- TION. Actually, there were approximately 250,000 free Negroes in the United States at the beginning of the Civil War. Most of those were in the South. New Orleans was the primary center of free Negroes, having 18,000.

3. NEGROES COULD HAVE LEARNED TO READ PRIOR TO THE RECONSTRUC- TION PERIOD IF THEY HAD WANTED TO. Actually, some did learn to read, but there were laws against teaching Negroes in some states.

4. MOST OF THE WEALTH WAS IN THE NORTH PRIOR TO THE CIVIL WAR OR RECONSTRUCTION. Actually, much of the wealth of the United States was in the South. Louisiana was second in per capita wealth in 1860. (In 1880, it was thirty-seventh.) South Carolina was third in 1860. (In 1880 it was forty-fifth.) Mississippi was fifth in 1860. (In 1880, it was forty-sixth.)

5. ALL SOUTHERNERS WERE UNITED IN SUPPORT OF THE CONFEDERACY. Actually, most Southerners supported the Confederacy, but large segments of West Virginia, western North Carolina, eastern Tennessee, and some parts of Virginia did not. Some counties in Alabama, Mississippi, and Arkansas were pro-Union.

6. LINCOLN ALWAYS SUPPORTED THE FREEING OF THE SLAVES. Actually, Lincoln held several positions on the issue of freeing the slaves. Early in his political career, he supported the movement to assist Negroes to return to Africa. Later, he supported moves to limit the extension of slavery into free territory. Only much later did he support the freeing of all slaves.

7. THE NEGROES RULED IN THE SOUTH DURING THE RECONSTRUCTION ERA. Negroes were actually not dominant in any state. The nearest they came to domination was in South Carolina. Even where Negroes were in a majority in the lower house, the whites had control of the upper houses and were the governors.

8. THE RECONSTRUCTION PERIOD LASTED A LONG TIME. Only in Florida, South Carolina, and Louisiana was the reconstruction prolonged.

9. PRESIDENT JOHNSON WAS REMOVED FROM OFFICE. Actually, he was not. This error comes from a misinterpretation of the word impeachment.

SUGGESTED AIMS FOR TEACHING
ABOUT THE RECONSTRUCTION PERIOD

Since only a short time can be devoted to the Reconstruction period in most courses in United States history, you will need to be very clear on the points you want to stress. Here are a few important concepts.

1. DIFFICULTIES IN VIEWING THIS PERIOD OBJECTIVELY. Southerners tend to interpret this period as one of oppressive military rule, graft, and Negro domination. Northerners tend to be defensive about it without condoning all of the excesses. Some historians have seen the period as a triumph of industrialism over agrarianism and have soft-pedaled the issue of Negro rights. Recently, the issue of Negro rights has been reexamined. All students should be aware of the difficulties involved in dealing with the Reconstruction. Able students should read some of the conflicting interpretations.

2. THE RETURN OF THE SOUTH TO WHITE CONTROL POLITICALLY. After a brief interval, an oligarchy of whites in the South regained political control of the area. Only a few Negroes were able to vote. Rights were not "unalienable" but had to be granted. A single-party system, with the Democrats in control, developed at the local and state levels. The South became powerful in both the United States Senate (through seniority in committees) and in national conventions (through the unit rule of voting).

3. THE STATUS OF THE NEGRO WAS ONLY SLIGHTLY IMPROVED. Slavery was abolished legally; some Negroes began to obtain an education; a few rose economically. Nevertheless, the mass of Negroes remained disadvantaged persons economically, socially, educationally, and politically. Repressive measures were taken by the Klu Klux Klan and other organizations. Segregation even increased in some respects—as in public conveyances.

4. THE PSYCHOLOGICAL SCARS OF THE WAR AND RECONSTRUCTION WERE DEEP. Perhaps the most important aim for most pupils is that they understand the psychological scars of the Civil War and the Reconstruction period. The war defeat was bitter for Southerners; the humiliation of the Reconstruction compounded the bitterness. "For many, military occupation was worse than defeat in the field of battle" (Franklin). "The wounds remained unhealed, festering their poison of unforgiveness." Consequently, the old way of life was extolled by many Southerners and taught to later generations. Hostility to Yankees was acute. "The Confederacy was beaten, but it refused to die" (Franklin). And the high hopes of Negroes, raised by the Emancipation Proclamation, were dashed by postwar events.

5. THE SOUTH WAS IMPOVERISHED ECONOMICALLY. Some areas were almost totally destroyed. "Every index of wealth and culture revealed the South below the average of the Union" (Buck.) The economic system had to change radically after the war and reconstruction. The cost of public education and of government skyrocketed. The South became a major economic problem for the entire United States for a long, long period—perhaps even today.

The Reconstruction Era and Negroes:
Bibliographies

THE RECONSTRUCTION ERA

It is difficult to select only a few books on the Reconstruction era because of its many inter-pretations. However, the books listed below are an attempt to give readers titles that represent a variety of viewpoints, are highly readable, and include recent interpretations of the Recon-struction.

Some readers may want to supplement the list below with books by writers such as Rhodes, Dunning, Bowers, Burgess, and Milton. Teachers who are interested in an interpretation of the period as a struggle between agricultural and industrial orders, should see the writings of Charles Beard.

1. Bentley, George. A History of the Freedman's Bureau. Philadelphia: University of Pennsylvania Press, 1955. 298 pp.
2. Buck, Paul H. The Road to Reunion 1865-1900. New York: Random, 1932. 320 pp. Also available as a paperback in the Vintage series. A fairly neutral interpretation, although optimistic about efforts at reconciliation.
3. Carter, Hodding. The Angry Scar: The Story of Reconstruction. New York: Doubleday, 1959. 425 pp. Written by a Southern liberal. Favorable to the South but not blatantly so. Includes several biographical sketches of leaders of the period.
4. Cox, L. and J. Politics, Principles and Prejudice: 1865-1866: Dilemma of Reconstruction America. Glencoe, Ill.: Free Press, 1963. 294 pp.
5. Franklin, John Hope. Reconstruction After the Civil War. Chicago: University of Chicago Press. 1961. 258 pp. A very balanced account.
6. Krug, Mark M. "For a Fair Deal in the Teaching of Reconstruction." Social Education. January 1965. Pp. 7-14, 56.
7. McKitrick, Eric L. Andrew Johnson and Reconstruction. Chicago: University of Chicago Press, 1960. 533 pp.
8. Nevins, Allan. The Emergence of Modern America: 1865-1878. New York: Macmillan, 1927. A volume in the American Nation series.
9. Rozwenc, Edwin C. Reconstruction in the South. Boston: Heath, 1952. 109 pp. A book of readings suitable for senior high school pupils.
10. Simkins, Francis B., and Robert A. Woody. South Carolina During Reconstruc-tion. Chapel Hill, N.C.: University of North Carolina Press, 1932. 610 pp.
11. Woodward, C. Vann. Reunion and Reaction: The Compromise of 1877 and the End of Reconstruction. New York: Doubleday, 1956. 297 pp. Available also as a Doubleday Anchor paperback. Sees the election of Hayes as a triumph of Northern industrialists. See also Woodward's Strange Career of Jim Crow.

SOME BOOKS ON NEGROES AND NEGRO HISTORY
(For boys and girls)

Several of the books listed in the bibliography below are relatively easy and are intended for slow readers. Most of these books have been used in the BRIDGE project of Queens College of the City University of New York in an integrated junior high school.

1. Bontemps, Arna. Frederick Douglass: Slave, Fighter, Freeman. New York: Knopf, 1959. 177 pp.
2. Bontemps, Arna. The Story of the Negro. New York: Knopf, 1960. 243 pp. A very good general account of Negro history.
3. Epstein, Sam and Beryl. George Washington Carver. New York: Grosset, 1960. 79 pp. For pupils below the fifth grade reading level.
4. Graham, Shirley. Booker T. Washington. New York: Messner, 1955. 192 pp. For advanced readers only.
5. Graham, Shirley. The Story of Phyllis Wheatley. New York: Messner, 1949. 176 pp. The story of a young slave in a Boston family at the time of the Revolution. Educated by the family and became an internationally known poetess. Her life ended in hardships.
6. Hughes, Langston. The First Book of Negroes. New York: Watts, 1952. 69 pp. Third or fourth grade reading level. General summary, with the emphasis, however, on the present.
7. Kugelmass, J. Alvin. Ralph Bunche: Fighter for Peace. New York: Messner, 1962. 178 pp. The story of a Negro who rose from the slums of Detroit to a high post in the United Nations and who received the Nobel Prize for peace. More difficult reading than most of the books on this list. Grades 7-10.
8. Meadowcroft, Enid. My Secret Railway. New York: Scholastic, 1963. 220 pp. Exciting reading about a white boy and his relationship with an ex-slave his own age. Grades 4-6.
9. Rollins, Charlemae H. They Showed the Way: 40 American Negro Leaders. New York: Crowell, 1964. 165 pp.
10. Shapiro, Milton J. Jackie Robinson. New York: Messner, 1960. 190 pp. Story of the player who broke the color barrier in Big League baseball.
11. Sterling, Dorothy. Freedom Train: The Story of Harriet Tubman. New York: Doubleday, 1954. 191 pp. An illiterate Negro aids hundreds of her people to escape to freedom on the underground railway.
12. Sterne, Emma G. The Long Black Schooner. New York: Scholastic, 1961. 188 pp. Fiction based on the actual capture of a ship by 50 Negroes, illegally enslaved. Insights into slave trading and slave traders. The time is 1839-1840. Grades 7-10.
13. Stratton, Madeline R. Negroes Who Helped Build America. Boston: Ginn, 1965. 166 pp. Grades 7-10.
14. White, Anne Terry. George Washington Carver. New York: Scholastic, 1953. 182 pp. Grades 6-9.
15. Yates, Elizabeth. Amos Fortune: Free Man. New York: Aladdin, 1960. 181 pp. The story of a slave in the 18th century in a New England village who finally gains his freedom and remains in that community. Grades 6-9.

Important Inventors and Inventions in the United States

The Industrial Revolution in the United States is one of the major events that shaped both our history as a nation and the history of the world. For that reason, the inventions and inventors of the period merit attention. Boys, particularly those of junior high school age, find the subject fascinating.

The list of inventors and inventions that follows is too long for intensive study, however you can use it for background or mimeograph it for student reference. Dates vary from source book to source book, depending, in some cases, upon the time of the invention—in others, upon the time when it was patented. Sometimes the name of more than one inventor appears.

Invention	Date	Inventor
Steamboat	1787	John Fitch (see Fulton)
Cotton gin	1793	Eli Whitney
Iron plow	1798	Charles Newbold
Steamboat	1831 or 1834	Robert Fulton
Reaper and mower	1834	Cyrus McCormick
Light steel plow	1837	John Deere
Screw propeller	1837	John Ericsson
Telegraph	1837 or 1844	Samuel F. B. Morse
Vulcanizing of rubber	1844	Charles Goodyear
Sewing machine	1846	Elias Howe
Elevator	1852	Elisha Otis
Shoe sewer	1862	Gordan McKay
Typewriter	1868	Sholes and Gidden
Atlantic cable	1866	Cyrus Field
Railroad air brake	1869	George Westinghouse
Telephone	1876	Alexander Graham Bell
Phonograph	1877	Thomas A. Edison
Incandescent lamp	1879	Thomas A. Edison
Linotype	1880	Ottmar Mergenthaler
Aluminum extractor	1885 or 1889	Charles Hall
Movie projector	1893	
Airplane	1903	Wilbur and Orville Wright
Plastics (bakelite)	1907	Leo Baekeland
Televison	1926–1934	Baird, Farnsworth, and Zworykin
Mechanical cotton picker	1927	Rust brothers
Nylon	1937	
Atomic bomb	1945	
Polio vaccine	1954	Jonas Salk and others

OTHER DATES TO ADD

There are many ways in which you may treat these inventors and their inventions. Among them are the following:

1. Individual reports, in chronological order.
2. A small unit on inventors and their inventions.
3. Production of a time-line with drawings or pictures of the inventors and/or inventions at the appropriate dates.
4. A dramatic presentation with individuals representing each of several inventors ("My name is . . . and I . . . .").

A BRIEF BIBLIOGRAPHY

Collective Biographies

1. Blow, Michael. Men of Science and Invention. New York: American Heritage, 1961. 153 pp. By the editors of the American Heritage magazine. Grades 8-12.
2. Burlingame, Roger. Inventors Behind the Inventor. New York: Harcourt, 1947. 211 pp. Grades 7-10.
3. Fanning, Leonard M. Fathers of Industries. Philadelphia: Lippincott, 1962. 256 pp. Grades 8-12. Twenty-four leaders.
4. Manchester, Harland. Trail Blazers of Technology: The Story of Nine Inventors. New York: Scribner's, 1962. 256 pp. Grades 7-12. Stories of Diesel, Goodyear, Nobel, Lake, Mwxim, Tesla, De Forest, Sikorsky.

Individual Biographies

Bell:
1. Burlingame, Roger. Out of Silence Into Sound: The Life of Alexander Graham Bell. New York: Macmillan, 1964. 146 pp. Grades 6-9.
2. Shippen, Katherine B. Mr. Bell Invents the Telephone. New York: Random House, 1952. 183 pp. Grades 6-9. A Landmark book.
3. Stevenson, O. J. The Talking Wire: The Story of Alexander Graham Bell. New York: Messner, 1960. 207 pp. Grades 7-10.

Edison:
4. Garbedian, H. Gordon. Thomas Alva Edison: Builder of Civilization. New York: Messner. 1960. 231 pp. Grades 7-10.
5. North, Sterling. Young Thomas Edison. Boston: Houghton, 1958. 182 pp. Grades 7-10.

Field:
6. Latham, Jean Lee. Young Man in a Hurry: The Story of Cyrus W. Field. New York: Harper, 1958. 238 pp. Grades 6-9.

Ford:
7. Gilbert, Miriam. Henry Ford: Maker of the Model T. Boston: Houghton, 1962. 192 pp. Grades 8-12.
8. Neyhart, Louise A. Henry Ford: Engineer. Boston: Houghton, 1950. 210 pp.

Fulton:
9. Judson, C. I. Boat Builder: The Story of Robert Fulton. New York: Scribner's, 1944. 121 pp. Grades 7-10.

Korn:
10. Korn, Terry and Elizabeth P. Trailblazer to Television: The Story of Arthur Korn. New York: Scribner's, 1950. 144 pp. Grades 7-10.

McCormick:
11. Judson, Clara I. Reaper Man: The Story of Cyrus Hall McCormick. Chicago: Follett, 1959. 156 pp. Grades 5-8.

The Agricultural Revolution in the United States

Despite a rapidly growing population that demands more and better food than it did in the past, the number of farms in the United States is diminishing rapidly as indicated by the graph below:

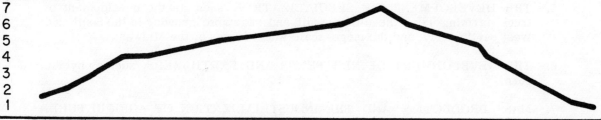

Number of Farms in the U.S.A.

1860	1880	1900	1920	1935	1965	1980 (Est.)
2,044,000	4,009,000	5,737,000	6,448,000	6,800,000	3,700,000	1,000,000

Why is the number of farms decreasing? Is this decline likely to continue? Is it a dangerous trend? In the light of the facts illustrated by the chart above, how can we explain the surplus of food in the United States today?

These are questions that should be raised in courses in United States history and contemporary problems and should be studied by all social studies students in our secondary schools today.

Unfortunately, existing textbooks contain only partial answers to those questions. Furthermore, the answers are hard to find, for they are scattered throughout the books with only a sentence or two of explanation for each. The agricultural revolution has been woefully neglected, despite its importance in explaining our high standard of living, despite its usefulness in determining types of foreign aid, and despite the problems of price supports, consumer prices, and allied difficulties that our surplus food supply raises.

It is almost impossible to date the beginning of our revolution in farming and livestock raising. Perhaps it started with the introduction of the steel plow in the 1830s; certainly it was well under way by the Civil War and was rolling along by 1900. In successive decades, our agricultural revolution gained momentum. Here are some of the factors students should consider.

1. INVENTIONS, such as the McCormick mechanical reaper, the Marsh harvester (which cut reaping time in half), Appleby's self-knotting binder (with its eight-fold increase in the speed of harvesting), the steel-toothed cultivator, the plow with a steel moldboard, and the introduction of gas-powered implements—the tractor, the combine, the thresher, and other modern equipment.

147

2. AGRICULTURAL EDUCATION, with the establishment of land-grant colleges by the Morrill Act of 1862. Experimentation in seeds, farming methods, demonstration plots, and public education of the farmers. The development of a Department of Agriculture in the federal government in 1862, by the Morrill Act. Later, the Smith-Lever Act (1914) provided for the distribution of agricultural literature, and the Smith-Hughes Act (1917) granted federal financial aid for agricultural education in rural public schools. The work of various farm organizations, such as the Grange and the Farm Bureau.

3. THE EXPANSION OF RAILROADS AND OTHER TRANSPORTATION FACILITIES including eventually the introduction of refrigerated cars—today, the use of airplanes for combating insects by spraying.

4. AN EXPANDING MARKET, with the increase of population in the United States.

5. THE DEVELOPMENT OF SPECIALIZATION, such as the development of truck farming near the cities, fruit and vegetable growing in the South and West particularly, and the large-scale wheat farms of the Midwest.

6. THE DEVELOPMENT OF NEW SEEDS AND FERTILIZERS, such as hybrid corn.

7. MASS PRODUCTION AND THE INDUSTRIALIZATION OF AGRICULTURE.

8. CONTOUR FARMING, which improved crops and saved much of our soil.

9. IRRIGATION, which opened up vast areas for farming, especially in the Southwest and West.

10. THE REMARKABLE GROWTH OF ANIMAL BREEDING, especially in the field of poultry raising; the scientific methods used in this and other areas.

11. THE WIDESPREAD USE OF FERTILIZERS, making the present time a chemical age in farming.

These and other factors have caused tremendous changes in farming and livestock raising in the United States in recent years, and more changes certainly lie ahead. Here are a few facts culled from the Twentieth Century Fund's study of farming as reported in Farms and Farmers in an Urban Age (New York: Macmillan, 1963. 163 pp. Edited by Edward Higbee).

Tractors, 1917—51,000; 1960—5,000,000.
Horses and mules, 1917—27,000,000; 1960—3,000,000.
Average corn yield per acre, 1949—38 bushels; 1961—67 bushels.
Food produced by one farmer in 1940 for 11 persons, in 1960 for 26 persons.
Farms in 1930 with 1000 acres or more: 28 per cent of the land cultivated;
in 1959, 49 per cent of the land cultivated.

Today, farming has become a big business. The top 3 per cent of farms produce more than the bottom 78 per cent. The 100,000 "top-drawer" farms produce 31.5 per cent of all crops and livestock. A single mechanical cotton picker can do the work of 40 pairs of human hands. A self-propelled lettuce picker (which costs $20,000) can pick and pack 600 boxes of lettuce in an hour in the field. Machines can now prune and pick fruit that formerly could be processed only by hand. These are just a few of the illustrations you and your students will find as you explore the agricultural revolution in our nation. This ought to be a fascinating study for all of you.

The Revolution in Health in the United States

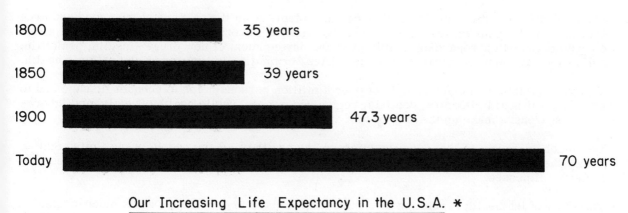

1800	35 years
1850	39 years
1900	47.3 years
Today	70 years

Our Increasing Life Expectancy in the U.S.A. *

This chart is taken from Winther and Cartwright's The Story of Our Heritage (Ginn and Company, P.743) and is reprinted with the permission of the publisher.

These four bars represent one of the most astounding and significant changes in the history of the United States. One might refer to these changes as "the revolution in health" or as "the sanitary revolution."

Even though the lengthening of life is important, there is very little mention of it in social studies textbooks. Despite the lack of textbook material, teachers should emphasize the importance of improved health as an outstanding feature of our national history and refer to it occasionally throughout American history courses. Placing the bar graphs shown above on the chalkboard and asking students to determine how this great change took place in our country is one way to handle the topic. Another approach is to ask students to do some element-ary research on the health revolution, reporting back to the class with some visualization of their findings. These researchers could be students who are especially interested in medicine, public health, and nursing, although any students may be selected for this assignment. A third way to treat the topic is to ask all members of the class to search for materials on the health revolution and then "pool" their finds for a summary report to other classes.

All students need to know the great toll of life that various diseases took in the early days of our history. They need to know about the deaths of immigrants on shipboard, about the deaths upon arrival in this part of the world, about the high rate of infant mortality—and mothers who died in childbirth.

Gradually, however, health conditions improved in the United States. Small towns and cities passed public health laws. Doctors and nurses were educated. Inoculations against diseases were found and used; for example, as early as 1796 smallpox was discovered. Pure milk and water, as well as improved sanitary conditions in hospitals, saved many babies and their mothers.

The first half of the 19th century saw important strides in medicine, especially in surgery. In 1809, Dr. Ephraim McDowell performed the first internal surgery in this country. A few years later, in the Massachusetts General Hospital in 1846, Dr. W. T. G. Morton performed the first operation using anesthesia.

The greatest gains in public health and in conquering disease have occurred in the past 60 to 70 years. As Dr. Harry J. Johnson recently pointed out in a Public Affairs pamphlet on Your Health Is Your Business, "In the twentieth century more advances in medicine have been made than in all the centuries before."

By now, a good many diseases have been eliminated or greatly reduced: typhoid fever, diphtheria, measles, smallpox, and whooping cough. Infantile paralysis has recently been eliminated, largely as a result of team research.

Much of the progress made in this century stems from the passage of pure food and drug laws in local communities, states, and the federal government, coupled with an emphasis on public education regarding health. And the development of new drugs—insulin, penicillin, sulfa—and of new surgical techniques have dramatically improved the nation's health.

Today, a veritable "health army" of over a million persons helps to conquer disease and to protect good health. Doctors, dentists, registered nurses, public health officials, and laboratory researchers make up the bulk of this army.

Yet much remains to be done to improve the health of all the people of the United States. Today there is concern over the increase in cancer, in alcoholism, in coronary diseases, and in mental illnesses.

The story of the health revolution is an important chapter in our history and a much-neglected part of our teaching. Here is a wide-open field for you and your students to explore together.

Theodore Roosevelt:
A Bibliography

In any course in United States history, you will want to study about Teddy Roosevelt. There is a great deal of material about him at every reading level. The following bibliography contains a sampling of these books.

BOOKS FOR TEACHERS AND SENIOR HIGH SCHOOL STUDENTS

1. Beale, Howard K. Theodore Roosevelt and the Rise of America to World Power. Baltimore: Johns Hopkins, 1956. 600 pp.
2. Busch, Noel F. TR-The Story of Theodore Roosevelt and His Influence On Our Times. New York: Reynal, 1963. 346 pp. There is also an excerpt from this book in the Reader's Digest for July 1963.
3. Hagedorn, Hermann, ed. The Free Citizen: A Summons to Service of the Democratic Ideal. New York: Macmillan, 1956. 238 pp. A selection of writings.
4. Hagedorn, Hermann. Theodore Roosevelt Treasury: A Self Portrait from His Writings. New York: Putnam, 1957. 342 pp.
5. Hofstadter, Richard. American Political Traditions. New York: Vintage, 1948. 378 pp.
6. Mowry, George E. The Era of Theodore Roosevelt and the Birth of Modern America: 1900-1918. New York: Harper, 1962. 320 pp. A volume in the New American Nation series. Available also as a Harper paperback.
7. Padover, Saul K. The Genius of America. New York: McGraw-Hill, 1960. 369 pp. See pages 286-303 on T. Roosevelt. This volume is a collection of brief essays on famous Americans.
8. Pringle, H. F. Theodore Roosevelt. New York: Harcourt, 1956. 435 pp.
9. Roosevelt, Theodore. Theodore Roosevelt: An Autobiography. New York: Scribner's, 1927. 597 pp.
10. Rozwenc, Edwin C., and A. Wesley Roehm. The Status Revolution and the Progressive Movement. Boston: Heath, 1963. 66 pp. Source materials suitable for high school students.

BOOKS FOR JUNIOR HIGH AND ELEMENTARY SCHOOL PUPILS

1. Beard, Charles A. Presidents in American History. New York: Messner, 1957 revision, 177 pp. See pages 105-106, 172-173 on Roosevelt. Grades 7-9.
2. Castor, Henry. Teddy Roosevelt and the Rough Riders. New York: Random, 1954. 192 pp. Grades 5-7. A Landmark book.
3. Cavannah, Frances. Adventure in Courage: The Story of Theodore Roosevelt. New York: Rand, 1961. 111 pp. Grades 6-9.
4. Considine, Bob. The Panama Canal. New York: Random, 1951. 192 pp. Grades 6-9. A Landmark book.

5. Cook, Fred J. Theodore Roosevelt: Rallying a Free People. Chicago: Encyclopedia Britannica, 1961. 192 pp. Grades 6-9.

6. Coy, Harold. First Book of Presidents. New York: Watts, 1952. 68 pp. See pages 52-53 on Roosevelt. Grades 4-6.

7. Foster, Genevieve. Roosevelt: An Initial Biography. New York: Scribner's, 1954. 106 pp. Grades 5-8.

8. Hagedorn, Hermann. Boy's Life of Theodore Roosevelt. New York: Harper, 1957. 374 pp. Grades 5-8.

9. Harlow, Alvin F. Theodore Roosevelt: Strenuous American. New York: Messner, 1943. 302 pp. Grades 5-8.

10. Judson, Clara I. Theodore Roosevelt: Fighting Patriot. Chicago: Follett, 1953. 222 pp. Grades 6-9.

11. Kane, J. N. Facts About the Presidents. New York: Wilson, 1959. 348 pp. See pages 172-178 on Roosevelt.

12. Lawson, Robert. Watchword of Liberty. Boston: Little, 1957. 115 pp. See pages 96-99 on Roosevelt. Grades 4-6.

13. KcKown, Robin. Roosevelt's America. New York: Grosset, 1962. 92 pp. Grades 6-9.

14. Mexer, E. P. Champions of Peace. Boston: Little, 1959, 216 pp. Grades 7-9.

15. Morgan, J. Our Presidents. New York: Macmillan, 1958. 470 pp. Grades 6-9. See pages 251-262, 267-270.

16. Neilson, Winthrop. The Story of Theodore Roosevelt. New York: Grosset, 1953. 179 pp. Grades 5-8.

17. Parks, Edd Winfield. Teddy Roosevelt: All Around Boy. Indianapolis: Bobbs-Merrill, 1953. 192 pp. Grades 5-8.

18. Petersham, Maud and Miska. Story of the Presidents of the U.S. New York: Macmillan, 1953. 80 pp. See pages 58-60 on Roosevelt.

19. Thomas, Henry. Theodore Roosevelt. New York: Putnam, 1959. 128 pp. Grades 5-8. In the Lives to Remember series.

Mary McLeod Bethune

One of the really great women in the history of the United States was Mary McLeod Bethune. Her name does not appear in the textbooks, but you and your students should know about her. Negro children should recognize her as a person who brought distinction to their race; white children should acknowledge her as a remarkable individual who achieved greatness in the face of seemingly insurmountable obstacles. All Americans should be proud of her as an outstanding citizen.

Mary Jane McLeod was born in Mayesville, South Carolina, on July 10, 1875. She was the fifteenth of 17 children of Samuel and Patsy McLeod. Her parents were both slaves and all the children before Mary Jane were born into slavery. Their home was a log cabin with a fireplace for a cookstove and with straw-filled sacks for mattresses. In the home was one book—the Bible—but none of the McLeods could read.

At the age of six, Mary Jane picked up a book in the playhouse of a little white girl and was intrigued by its contents. She was told "Put down that book; you can't read." Probably, at that point, her life's ambition began—to learn to read and write, and eventually to teach others to become literate.

Her opportunity came within a few months. A Miss Wilson appeared in Mayesville as a representative of the mission board of the Presbyterian church. She started the first school for Negro children, and Mary Jane McLeod, who had to walk five miles back and forth to school each day, was one of her first pupils.

When she had completed all the work in that school, Mary Jane McLeod went on to Scotia Seminary in Concord, North Carolina (now Barber-Scotia College). The tithing of a Quaker dressmaker in Denver, Colorado, built up a small scholarship fund available through Miss Wilson. At Scotia, Mary Jane McLeod was an outstanding student, a good public speaker and debater, and a soloist in the school choir. She spent seven years in Scotia Seminary, completing the high school course and taking some advanced work.

From there, she went to Moody Bible Institute in Chicago, hoping to prepare herself for work as a missionary in Africa. But there were no jobs for Negroes as missionaries in those days and, upon the completion of her work, she began to teach in her old school in Mayesville and, later, in several other parts of the South.

In 1904, at the age of 29, she started her own school in Daytona, Florida, with a down-payment of 50 cents on a charge of $11 a month for a broken-down house. Charred wood splinters served as pencils, crushed elderberries as ink, packing boxes as furniture. Mrs. Bethune earned extra money for food and supplies by baking and selling sweet-potato pies.

But the school grew and grew and grew. Within two years, she had 250 pupils. Eventually a new school was built on the city dump heap, known as "Hell's Hole." In its early days, the school was called the Daytona Educational and Industrial Training School for Negro Girls. Today, it is Bethune-Cookman College, a highly respected coeducational institution.

The success of this school was due to Mrs. Bethune's determination, industry, and ingenuity, and the many friends she made (including John N. Gamble of the Proctor and Gamble Company of Cincinnati, Thomas H. White, a sewing machine magnate in Cleveland, and, in later years, Eleanor Roosevelt).

Mrs. Bethune's prominence in education brought her to the attention of people all over the country. She became President of the National Association of Colored Women and, in 1935, the founder and president of the National Council of Negro Women. She also served as vice-president of both the National Association for the Advancement of Colored People (the NAACP) and the National Urban League.

President Coolidge and President Hoover both appointed her as a member of the National Child Welfare Commission; and, in the days of the Great Depression, she served under President Roosevelt as special adviser on minority affairs in the National Youth Division and later as director of the division of Negro affairs in the National Youth Administration. During World War II, she held several posts in the federal government.

The crowning point in her career occurred in 1945 when she was a member of the United States delegation to San Francisco for the formation of the United Nations. In 1952, she was a member of the United States delegation to the inauguration of the President of Liberia in Africa.

Throughout her lifetime, many institutions presented Mrs. Bethune with honorary degrees. Among the ten colleges that honored her and themselves in this manner were Howard University, Wilberforce, Tuskegee, and Lincoln. In 1935, she received the Spingarn Award of the NAACP, given "for the highest or noblest achievement by an American Negro during the preceding year or years."

Mrs. Bethune died on May 18, 1955, in her home in Daytona Beach, Florida, leaving this country a better place for her incredibly full life.

Students and teachers will find more details about her life in the following references:

1. Holt, Rackham. Mary McLeod Bethune: A Biography. New York: Doubleday, 1964. 306 pp. Grades 9-12. For better readers. Stresses the later part of her life. Excellent summary at the end of the book.
2. Nathan, Dorothy. Woman of Courage. New York: Random House, 1964. 188 pp. See pages 74-116. Grades 6-9. A very good brief account.
3. Peare, Catherine O. Mary McLeod Bethune. New York: Vanguard, 1952. 220 pp. Grades 6-9. A highly readable account.
4. Sterne, Emma G. Mary McLeod Bethune. New York: Knopf, 1957. 268 pp. Grades 6-9.

The United States in the 1920s

The period of the 1920s is one of the saddest chapters in the entire history of the United States. James Shotwell calls it "The Dark Era of American Liberalism." Ekirch terms it a period of "disillusionment and prosperity." Leuchtenburg summarizes it as a period of "materialism, political corruption, and cultural vulgarity."

It was the period of the "Red scare," with the deportation of aliens, the raids on radical organizations, and the Sacco-Vanzetti case in Boston. It was a period of hatred against Catholics, Jews, Negroes, immigrants, and liberals. (The Ku Klux Klan had 4 million members and tremendous power.) It was a period of restrictions on immigration, of race riots in large cities, and of lynchings. It was a period of graft in government. (Four of the top administrative officers in the Harding administration were imprisoned.) It was a period of tough times for labor unions. And it was the time of the Scopes trial – the famous "monkey trial" in Tennessee. Leuchtenburg speaks of this decade as the period of "tired liberals."

Yet, progressive events that changed the United States radically took place in the '20s too. The automobile age and mass production of cars was really ushered in during the '20s. The airplane age began in this period, with the famous solo flight of Charles Lindbergh across the Atlantic. Radio came into its own and brought music for everyone. In 1900, a child had only one chance in ten of going to high school; in the '20s, he had one chance in two. A second Industrial Revolution took place and the work week dropped from 60 to 48 hours. The United States began its rapid shift from a nation of villages and small towns to a nation of urban centers.

One writer has gone so far as to say that "the period was one of amazing vitality, of social invention, and change. And perhaps it is not too much to say that the Twenties were really the formative years of modern American society."

How are you – as a social studies teacher – going to handle this period with boys and girls in secondary schools?

One way is to approach the years through the use of quotations like those contained in the foregoing paragraphs. The statement that it was "one of the saddest chapters in the entire history of the United States" could be contrasted with that from George E. Mowry's The Twenties that "the period was one of amazing vitality, of social invention, and change." Ask students which quotation they support and why.

Another approach is to present the dark picture of the period and analyze the students' reasons for our unsavory record as a democracy. Undoubtedly, they will find one explanation in the economic expansion and prosperity of the 1920s. They will probably find another in the "let-down" after World War I – the demoralization that came with the end of the war and the disillusionment of realizing that the world had not been made safe for democracy.

Having explored these and other reasons for the slump in the political and moral "tone" of this period, ask your students what aspects of the period represent a more optimistic appraisal of our nation's history. (These are listed on the reverse page.)

A slightly different approach would be to draw up a balance sheet of democracy in the 1920s.

Little has been written on this period for junior high school pupils. Students in high schools and teachers will find many answers to their questions about the '20s in the following references:

1. Allen, Frederick Lewis. Only Yesterday. New York: Harper, 1931. 270 pp. Includes an entire chapter on "The Red Scare." Probably the best account of this period. Also a Bantam paperback.
2. Chitwood, O. P., and others. The American People: A History. Vol. II. Princeton, N.J.: Princeton University Press, 1937. 585 pp.
3. Dumond, Dwight L. Roosevelt to Roosevelt: The United States in the Twentieth Century. New York: Holt, 1937. 585 pp.
4. Ekirch, Arthur A., Jr. The American Democratic Tradition: A History. New York: Macmillan, 1963. 338 pp. A paperback.
5. Galbraith, John K. The Great Crash: 1929. Boston: Houghton, 1961. 199 pp.
6. Goldman, Eric F. Rendezvous with Destiny. New York: Knopf, 1956. 372 pp. Also a Vintage paperback.
7. Leuchtenburg, William E. The Perils of Prosperity. Chicago: University of Chicago Press, 1958. 313 pp. In the Chicago History of American Civilization series.
8. Morison, Samuel E., and Henry S. Commager. The Growth of the American Republic. Vol. II. New York: Oxford, 1937. 695 pp.
9. Leighton, Isabel. The Aspirin Age 1919-1941. New York: Simon, 1963. 491 pp. Also a paperback.
10. Mowry, George E. The Twenties: Fords, Flappers, and Fanatics. Englewood Cliffs, N.J.: Prentice-Hall, 1963. 186 pp. A paperback.
11. Schlesinger, Arthur M., Jr. The Crisis of the Old Order: 1919-1933. Boston: Houghton, 1957. 557 pp.
12. Slosson, Preston. The Great Crusade and After: 1914-1928. New York: Macmillan, 1931. 486 pp.
13. Sullivan, Mark. Our Times. New York: Scribner's, 1936. Six volumes.

Franklin D. Roosevelt

The year 1933 is one of the great watersheds in American history. It was in that year that the Great Depression occurred and that Franklin D. Roosevelt became President.

Estimates of Franklin Roosevelt, as a person and as a President, are tremendously varied. Allan Nevins, in the preface of <u>Nothing to Fear</u> (a collection of the speeches of Roosevelt), refers to his "effective greatness" as consisting of "his power of imaginatively timing an impressive measure to meet a desperate need"; "his ability to indicate the American method of pragmatic experiment"; and "his ability to imbue Americans, and to some extent citizens of other lands, with a new spiritual strength."

Max Lerner, ordinarily a champion of Roosevelt, writes in <u>America as a Civilization</u> that there is "little question that Roosevelt used imaginative daring and pugnacity along with the cunning of maneuvering" in his role as President.

Oliver Wendell Holmes is quoted as saying that Roosevelt had "a second-class intellect but a first-class temperament."

Sherwood calls him a complex and contradictory character, and James Burns, in <u>Roosevelt: The Lion and the Fox,</u> shows his strength and his cunning, stating that he was "a complex man because he was a deeply divided man."

A more favorable portrait is drawn by Oscar Handlin in <u>The Americans</u>, where he says, "The New Deal was the culmination of four decades of the Progressive Movement . . . " According to Handlin, "The New Deal provided Americans with an escape from collectivism."

In <u>The American Story</u>, Frank Friedel calls Roosevelt "The most controversial figure to occupy the White House since Lincoln . . . "

Pupils need to find a variety of opinions themselves and consider why outstanding authorities differ in their estimates of Franklin D. Roosevelt.

One way to handle the Roosevelt era is to give students two statements such as these:

> Franklin D. Roosevelt saved the United States from collectivism and saved this country for capitalism.

> Franklin D. Roosevelt led the United States down the road to state socialism.

Students should then read about Roosevelt, organizing their notes around these two themes. A class discussion, lasting two or three days, can be based on their reading and their tentative conclusions.

Another technique is to divide the students into interest groups and let them see what Roosevelt did to win or to alienate each group. Role playing could be used effectively.

A third method is to list the problems of the United States in 1933 and to see what Roosevelt did about each problem.

There are already scores of books on Roosevelt and the New Deal. These are just a few of the volumes you could consult.

1. Burns, James M. Roosevelt: The Lion and the Fox. New York: Harcourt, 1956. 553 pp. A very good one-volume account, stressing Roosevelt's tactics.
2. Franklin D. Roosevelt and the Supreme Court. Boston: Heath, 1952. 109 pp. A source book in the Amherst series.
3. Freidel, Frank, ed. The New Deal and the American People. Englewood Cliffs, N.J.: Prentice-Hall, 1964. 151 pp. Accounts by several individuals. For a very full account, see the three volumes by Freidel in a projected nine-volume series on Roosevelt.
4. Gunther, John. Roosevelt in Retrospect. New York: Harper, 1950. 410 pp.
5. The New Deal: Revolution or Evolution? Boston: Heath, 1959. 113 pp. Another in the Amherst Problems in American Civilization series.
6. Perkins, Dexter. The New Age of Franklin Roosevelt: 1932-1945. Chicago: University of Chicago Press, 1957. 194 pp. A volume in the Chicago History of American Civilization. As good a brief account as is now available.
7. Perkins, Frances. The Roosevelt I Knew. New York: Viking, 1946. 408 pp.
8. Roosevelt, Eleanor. This I Remember. New York: Harper, 1949. 387 pp.
9. Rosenman, Samuel. Working with Roosevelt. New York: Harper, 1952. 560 pp.
10. Rozwenc, Edwin C., and Thomas T. Lyons. Presidential Power in the New Deal. Boston: Heath, 1963. 66 pp. Source materials in the Amherst series.
11. Schlesinger, Arthur M., Jr. The Age of Roosevelt series of three volumes: The Crisis of the Old Order, The Coming of the New Deal, and The Politics of Upheaval. Boston: Houghton, 1958-60.
12. Zevin, Ben D. Franklin D. Roosevelt—Nothing to Fear. New York: Popular Library, 1956. 476 pp. A paperback of speeches.

BOOKS FOR YOUNG READERS

1. Hickock, Loren A. The Road to the White House. New York: Chilton, 1962. 145 pp. Grades 6-9.
2. Kleeman, Rita H. Young Franklin Roosevelt. New York: Messner, 1948. 188 pp. Grades 5-8.
3. Merriam, Eve. The Real Book about Franklin D. Roosevelt. Garden City: Doubleday, 1952. 191 pp. Grades 6-9.
4. Peare, Catherine O. The FDR Story. New York: Crowell, 1962. 245 pp. Grades 7-9.
5. Weil, Ann. Franklin Roosevelt: Boy of the Four Freedoms. Indianapolis: Bobbs-Merrill, 1947. 200 pp. Grades 5-8.
6. Weingast, David E. Franklin D. Roosevelt: Man of Destiny. New York: Messner, 1952. 184 pp. Grades 9-12.

The Tennessee Valley Authority

Few Americans realize the importance of the Tennessee Valley Authority project to the United States and to the world. In this country, it has been responsible for tremendous gains in a stricken area. In the world, TVA has become the prototype or model for the development of river valleys. The map below shows the area affected directly by the TVA.

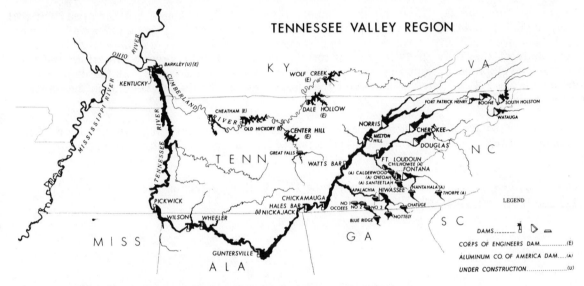

TENNESSEE VALLEY REGION

Here are four aims to keep in mind in teaching about the TVA.
1. To show the poverty of the Tennessee Valley area in the 1930s.
2. To discover the problems that arose from this poverty.
3. To determine how the TVA met these problems.
4. To study some of the geography of this area.

In a class of able students, you may want to compare the concept of the TVA to the type of aid being given to economically underdeveloped areas today or ask how it is similar to "foreign aid." You could debate the question of whether or not the federal government should engage in such enterprises as the TVA. And you could tell the students about the hundreds of foreign officials who have visited the project and ask why people in other countries are interested in it.

In a class of less able students, you may want to say "We're going to visit the home of John and Jane Jones—sharecroppers in the Tennessee Valley in the 1930s," and quickly draw a shack on the chalkboard. Ask the students how the Jones cabin looked, what furniture it had, and some of the problems of the family. You can discuss the school the children attended, the farm their father worked, the tools he used, etc. As you discuss the Jones family, list their problems on the board. The class can then read aloud about the TVA, searching for ways in which it affected the Jones family.

159

Your board work might look something like this:

Problems	How the TVA tried to solve these problems
1. Poor income.	1. Improved land, helped with seed, reduced power costs. Greatly increased income.
2. Poor schools.	2. Consolidated schools, better roads made school buses possible. Better income and better schools.
3. Poor land: floods. poor soil. no fertilizers.	3. Land improved in many ways: Floods controlled. Officials taught crop rotation, use of fertilizers, such as nitrates made in TVA project.
4. Poor community life or none.	4. Model town of Norris built. General improvement of communities.
5. Poor recreation.	5. Fishing, boating on the lakes of the TVA project.
6. Little or no contact with outside world.	6. More people coming into this area, better roads, more income to travel.

A summary question is "How did the Joneses feel about the changes in their area?" It will be important to point out that they might not have welcomed all these changes—and why.

In any study of the TVA, it is important to keep in mind that the agency has attempted total resource development, including soil, water, forests and minerals, as the basis for the economy of the region. Having achieved that goal, the emphasis has been upon the development of the human resources.

Two weeks or so before this lesson, you may want to write to the Public Information Office, Tennessee Valley Authority, Knoxville, Tennessee, for background information, pictures, and maps.

Probably the best single account available of the TVA is the paperback book by David Lilienthal on T.V.A on the March (Pocket Books).

United States History and Music

The story of American music is a dimension of United States history that is sadly neglected in most schools. By including it, you can arouse interest, provide special opportunities for students with an interest in music, and instill the feeling of a period or place.

There are many ways to bring music into history classes. You may want to include some music in several classes during a term or to devote a day in each of several units to the music of the period. You may want to have a short unit on music at the end of the year as a special musical review of our nation's history. You can handle this part of the course yourself with student help or turn it over to a group of students. Certainly the people in charge of music in your school will be anxious to help. Records and tape recordings, instrumental music and singing, will all enhance your course in United States history.

If you plan to start chronologically with the music of the Indians, a warning is in order: most students find Indian music difficult to understand. The adaptation of Indian songs, in such selections as MacDowell's "Love Song" (Indian Suite) or Lieurance's "By the Waters of Minnetonka," is a good way to lead into authentic Indian music. An album on "Songs from the Iroquois Longhouse" represents the music of some East coast Indians, and "American Indian Songs and Dances" contains songs of Western Indians.

Next, you will undoubtedly want to talk about the Puritans' interest in sacred music. Their famous Bay Psalm Book, published in 1640, contains many hymns (such as "Old Hundred") that the class might like to sing.

As you study the immigrant groups, you can show how each brought its own music to the New World, providing a wealth of music in the colonial times and early days of our republic. "Barbara Allen," "The Three Ra'ens," and "The Lass from the Low Countree" are in the English tradition; there are also Creole songs of New Orleans and eastern Louisiana and many Dutch ones.

A student who is especially interested in music might report on the musical contributions of the Moravians, and several students could discover the special contributions of the Germans in music.

Many ballads, including "Yankee Doodle," represent the American Revolution period. Perhaps you could learn a new song of the Revolution in class. "Johnny Has Gone for a Soldier" appears on some of today's albums. And there is a wealth of music from the days of the canals, the railroads, and the cattle era: "The Erie Canal," "The Old Chisholm Trail," "The Dying Cowboy," and "John Henry."

No history of the United States would be complete without some attention to the songs of Stephen Foster. "Old Folks At Home," "O Susanna," and "My Old Kentucky Home" have become part of our musical heritage.

Nor will you want to overlook the beauty and the pathos of the Negro spirituals. The familiar songs—"Swing Low, Sweet Chariot," "Ezekiel Saw the Wheel," and "Nobody Knows the Trouble I've Seen"—have enriched all our lives.

The Civil War provided music from both the North and South, as a glance at the volume by Professor Glass in the bibliography below will show. You know some of them, such as "John Brown's Body," "The Battle Hymn of the Republic," and "Tenting Tonight on the Old Camp Ground." Do your students know these stirring tunes?

Around the turn of the century, band music became popular and John Philip Sousa rose to fame. Why not play a good recording of "Semper Fidelis" or "The Stars and Stripes Forever" when you talk about this period in our history?

Then there are the songs of World War I, the '20s, and into the Depression. How could you give your students a better insight into the feeling of the Depression than by playing or singing together "Brother, Can You Spare a Dime?"

But where does one stop? There is the music of Ferde Grofé and the music of Aaron Copland, the songs of Irving Berlin and those of Rodgers and Hammerstein. "Oklahoma," "Carousel," and "South Pacific" give us rollicking glimpses of different periods in American history. "West Side Story" is a musical social document. And the protest songs of the civil-rights movement have carried its emotional appeal into many hearts.

This is the barest outline, but it does suggest some of the possibilities for exploring United States history through music. This should be fun. Does fun rule out learning?

As background for you and your students, here are a few references on music in United States history. In addition to these and other volumes, you will want to refer to the latest catalogues of companies like Decca, Folkway Records, Columbia, and RCA-Victor, paying special attention to their collections of songs for history classes.

1. Boni, Margaret B. Fireside Book of Folk Songs. New York: Simon, 1947. 323 pp.
2. Glass, Paul. The Spirit of the Sixties: A History of the Civil War in Song. St. Louis: Educational Publishers, 1965. 285 pp.
3. Johnson, James Weldon and Rosamond. The Books of American Negro Spirituals. New York: Viking, 1944. 189 pp.
4. Landeck, Beatrice. Echoes of Africa in Folk Songs of the Americas. New York: McKay, 1961. 184 pp.
5. Lomax, Alan. The Folk Songs of North America. Garden City: Doubleday, 1960. 623 pp. A stupendous volume with just about everything in it!
6. Seeger, Ruth C. American Folk Songs for Children. Garden City: Doubleday, 1948. 190 pp.
7. Sandburg, Carl. American Song Bag. New York: Harcourt, 1929.
8. The Cooperative Recreation Service (Delaware, Ohio) has three pocket-size songbooks that may be of value to you: "One More Tune," "Songs of All Time" (songs of the Appalachian South), and "Look Away" (56 Negro folk songs). Each book is 25¢.

Some Leading Economists

Below are thumbnail sketches of nine of the world's leading economists. Although they provide a quick review, teachers are urged to read or reread the original works of these and other economists, as well as to utilize the brief bibliography at the end of this Background Paper.

1. ADAM SMITH (1723-1790) is often called "The Father of Political Economy." Contrary to the accepted beliefs of his day, he espoused free trade among nations (as opposed to the prevailing policy of mercantilism) and the pursuance of private business without government interference. Living in the early part of the Industrial Revolution, he saw earlier than others the advantages of division of labor, and he believed that labor was "the ultimate and real standard by which the value of all commodities can . . .be estimated and compared." His principles appear in his famous book on The Wealth of Nations, published in 1776.

2. THOMAS MALTHUS (1776-1834) has been called "The Pessimistic Parson" because of his predictions that, unless the birthrate was drastically reduced, the world's food supply could not sustain the exploding population. He set forth these ideas in his famous "Essay on the Principles of Population as It Affects the Future Improvement of Society." This essay is being reread with interest today, even though many economists point out that his predictions have not come true in the Western world because he did not foresee improvements in farming techniques and soil conservation, and because the population of this part of the world has not increased as rapidly as he predicted.

3. ROBERT OWEN (1771-1858) was a successful textile manufacturer who was shocked by the conditions in the factories he had acquired and by the health of his workers. He felt that industrialists had a social responsibility and acted upon that conviction by introducing such reforms as reduced working hours, higher wages, the abolition of child labor for children under ten years of age, better housing conditions, insurance funds, and recreational facilities. His greatest interest was in cooperative associations; the Rochdale Society, based on his ideas, is considered the beginning of the worldwide cooperative movement. He is one of the leading Utopian socialists.

4. JOHN STUART MILL (1806-1873) was a brilliant thinker, philosopher, writer, and economist. As a boy, he was profoundly influenced by his father, James Mill, and by Jeremy Bentham. Before he was 20, he had done considerable writing, including a three-volume work on the writings of Bentham. But he soon rebelled against the gloomy thinking of his elders, championing a more optimistic view of man and man's ability to reform the world along socialistic lines. Mill's greatest discovery in the field of economics was that the true province of economics is production rather than distribution. His famous two-volume book on Principles of Political Economy appeared in 1848 and his famous essay On Liberty in 1859.

5. KARL MARX (1806-1873) was a German political exile in Britain who wrote two earthshaking books—The Communist Manifesto (with Friedrich Engels) and Das Kapital—maintaining that history has been a continuous struggle between the workers (or proletariat) and their rulers. Eventually, he foresaw the overthrow of capitalism and the inauguration of a classless society in which the labor theory of value would be substituted for the capitalist theory of supply and demand. His ideas of historical materialism or economic determination today range in interpretation from the British Labor party to the Communist party of the Soviet Union and China.

6. HENRY GEORGE (1839-1897) held that the land, like the air and sunlight, belonged to all the people. Nevertheless he believed in private property, maintaining that those who did own land should be taxed heavily. In fact, his idea was that the land tax should be "the single tax." Although this idea has not been accepted, his belief that surplus wealth should be taxed has been. His basic beliefs are spelled out in his famous book Progress and Poverty (1880).

7. THORSTEIN VEBLEN (1857-1929), an American of Norwegian background, was an outspoken and merciless critic of the society of his day, especially the upper-class merchants. In The Theory of the Leisure Class, The Theory of Business Enterprise, The Higher Learning in America, and other books, he ruthlessly dissected society, forecasting a time when engineers, interested in the production of goods, would replace capitalists, interested merely in making money.

8. JOHN MAYNARD KEYNES (1883-1946), English economist and professor at the London School of Economics, has had a more profound influence upon the economic policies of governments in recent times than any person except Karl Marx. In the 1930s, he held that the worldwide depression would not automatically right itself and that cutting prices and lowering wages would not reestablish "equilibrium." He maintained that, in such times, government spending must be employed to stimulate the economy and take up the slack caused by the decline of private investments. His policies, outlined in 1936 in a book on The General Theory of Employment, Interest, and Money, have been incorporated by many governments in recent years, including the United States.

9. WESLEY CLAIR MITCHELL (1874-1948), an American economist who taught many years at Columbia University, contributed primarily to economic theory through his investigation of the cyclical nature of business fluctuations, as outlined chiefly in Measuring Business Cycles (written with Arthur Burns). His further contributions were largely as director of the research work in the Bureau of Economic Research and in the field of economic sociology.

A SELECTED BIBLIOGRAPHY OF PAPERBACKS

1. Heilbroner, Robert L. The Worldly Philosophers: The Lives, Times and Ideas of the Great Economic Thinkers. New York: Simon, 1953. 342 pp.
2. Kapp, K. William and Lore L. History of Economic Thought: A Book of Readings. New York: Barnes, 1962 edition. 444 pp.
3. Schumpeter, Joseph A. Ten Great Economists: From Marx to Keynes. New York: Oxford University Press, 1965. 305 pp.
4. Soule, George. Ideas of the Great Economists. New York: Mentor, 1963. 160 pp.
5. Spiegel, H. W., ed. The Development of Economic Thought: Great Economists in Perspective. New York: Wiley, 1964. 486 pp.

Source Materials
for Students on Economics

There are now scores of pamphlets and books (including many paperbacks) suitable for use with students in teaching economic concepts. Most of the items listed here are relatively easy to read and popular in nature. Teachers interested in more difficult materials should turn to the bibliographies in economics textbooks or to one of these excellent bibliographies:

Sayre, J. Woodrow. Paperbound Books in Economics: An Annotated Bibliography. Albany, New York: New York State Council on Economic Education, 1964. 55 pp.

Suggestions for a Basic Economics Library. New York: Joint Council on Economic Education, 1965. 64 pp.

The following popular books and booklets should prove stimulating to students who are being introduced to economic concepts and economics as a field of study.

1. Alexander, Albert. Economics. New York: Watts, 1963. 66 pp. Grades 8-10.
2. Gambs, John S. Man, Money and Goods. New York: Columbia University Press, 1962. (A paperback.) 339 pp.
3. Heilbroner, Robert L. The World of Economics. New York: Public Affairs Committee, 1963. 33 pp. An excellent pamphlet for good readers in grades 10-12, and for teachers.
4. Shackle, G. L. S. Economics for Pleasure. New York: Cambridge University Press, 1962. 257 pp. Grades 10-12.
5. Soule, George. Economics for Living. New York: Abelard, 1961. 159 pp. Grades 7-10.

Two books that should arouse the interest of students in economics as related to the United States are

6. Barach, Arnold B. U.S.A. and Its Economic Future. New York: Macmillan, 1964. 148 pp. Based largely on charts and graphs in color.
7. Heckman, Harry W. The Economics of American Living. Chicago: Rand McNally, 1959. 168 pp. Includes several charts.

An excellent and inexpensive pamphlet filled with case studies of economic problems is

8. Today's Economics: Case Studies for Student Understanding. Columbus, Ohio: American Education Publications, Education Center, 1965. 64 pp.

Several publishers have recently brought out pamphlets on economics. Among them are the following: (Teachers should write for titles and prices.)

1. Bureau of Business and Economic Research, College of Business Administration, State University of Iowa, Iowa City, Iowa. A Primer of Economics series.
2. Committee for Economic Development, 711 Fifth Avenue, New York, N.Y. 10022. Statements of National Policy by the Research and Policy Committee.

3. Council for Advancement of Secondary Education. Order from Webster-McGraw-Hill Book Co., 1154 Reco Ave., St. Louis, Mo. 63126.
4. Council on Consumer Information, Colorado State College, Greeley, Colo.
5. Federal Reserve Bank, Philadelphia, Pa. Series for Economic Education.
6. Holt, Rinehart and Winston, 383 Madison Ave., New York, N. Y. 10017. American Problems series, and Select Problems in Historical Interpretation.
7. Institute of Life Insurance, 277 Park Ave, New York, N.Y. 10017.
8. National Association of Manufacturers, 2 East 48th St., New York, N. Y. 10017. Industry and the American Economy series.
9. National Council for the Social Studies, 1201 16th St. N. W., Washington, D.C. Economic Life series.
10. National Industrial Conference Board, 460 Park Ave., New York, N.Y. 10022.
11. Oxford Book Company, 71 Fifth Ave., New York, N. Y. 10003.
12. Public Affairs Committee, 22 East 38th St., New York, N. Y. 10016.
13. Rand McNally and Company, Box 7600, Chicago, Ill. 60680. Resources for the Future series, Policy Background series.
14. Scott, Foresman and Company, 433 East Erie Street, Chicago, Ill. 60611. Area Studies in Economic Progress (World); Economic Forces in American History series (by periods of United States history); Studies in Economic Issues series.

Here are a few of the many books in the field of economics that students should enjoy.

1. Calder, Ritchie. After the Seventh Day: The World Man Created. New York: New American Library, 1961. 339 pp. A history of technology; very well written.
2. Carr, Edward H. The New Society. Boston: Beacon, 1957. 119 pp. The transition from a competitive to a planned society.
3. Galbraith, John K. The Affluent Society. New York: New American Library, 1958. 286 pp. Fairly heavy.
4. Galbraith, John K. American Capitalism: The Concept of Countervailing Power. Boston: Houghton, 1956. 208 pp. Heavier than most items here.
5. Hansen, Alvin H. The American Economy. New York: McGraw- Hill, 1957. 199 pp.
6. Hansen, Alvin H. Economic Issues of the 1960's. New York: McGraw-Hill, 1960. 177 pp. Fairly heavy reading.
7. Heilbroner, Robert L. The Great Ascent: The Struggle for Economic Development in Our Time. New York: Harper, 1963. 160 pp.
8. Lens, Sidney. Working Men: The Story of Labor. New York: Putnam, 1960. 191 pp. For grades 8-10 or slow readers in high schools.
9. Litwack, Leon. The American Labor Movement. Englewood Cliffs, N.J.: Prentice-Hall, 1962. 176 pp.
10. Neal, Harry E. From Spinning Wheel to Spacecraft: The Story of the Industrial Revolution. New York: Messner, 1964. 191 pp.
11. Perry, John. 17 Million Jobs: The Story of Industry in Action. New York: McGraw-Hill, 1958. 236 pp.
12. Shippen, Katherine B. Miracle in Motion: The Story of America's Industry. New York: Harper, 1955. 150 pp.
13. Shippen, Katherine B. This Union Cause: The Growth of Organized Labor in America. New York: Harper, 1958. 180 pp.
14. Sterling, Dorothy. Wall Street. New York: Doubleday, 1955. 128 pp. The Stock Exchange and how it works.

Wealth

Ask the average student or citizen to define wealth, and he will probably say that it means "being rich." In common parlance, that explanation is generally accepted.

Economists, however, are much more precise in their use of the term "wealth." By wealth, they mean all the goods and services that have economic value.

Some economists go farther, adding the qualifying phrase "that contribute to human welfare." Thus they eliminate items such as opium (unless used for medicinal purposes) and gambling machines.

Another way of defining wealth is to say that it includes any economic goods that can command something in exchange. This includes any item that is useful, material, transferable, and owned by an individual or a group of individuals.

Wealth is often divided into three categories: land, labor, capital. Thus, the wealth of a farmer may include his land (if he owns it), plus the value of his harvested crops, his livestock, his tractor and other tools, and his automobile. The wealth of a worker may include his home (if he owns it), the value of his house furnishings, and his automobile. The wealth of a student may include his bicycle, his camera, his record player, his wristwatch, and other items of value.

Items such as health, education, and good character are not considered wealth. They are useful, but they are neither material nor transferable.

Inasmuch as property is merely a legal relationship of persons to goods and services, items like bonds, contracts, licenses, and mortgages are not considered wealth. And money, which is termed a claim to—or a measure of—wealth, does not itself constitute wealth.

In traditional societies, the factors of land, labor, and capital were not sold or exchanged. People who owned land held on to it. Labor was not "sold" for a price or wage. Capital, as we know it today, did not exist and is a new form of social wealth. Although some of these traditional societies still exist in the world, their number is dwindling rapidly.

Our "market society" is based on new approaches to land and labor and on the accumulation of capital for many uses.

In our economy, some wealth is private or individual, for example, the material goods owned by individuals, partners, and corporations. Private wealth is often interpreted to include various types of valuable claims, such as ownership interest in firms and creditor claims against corporations or governments.

Other wealth is public: public libraries, playgrounds, streets and highways, postoffices, and schools.

When combined, these two forms of wealth are called "national wealth." The Gross National Product or GNP of a nation is its annual production.

In our society, the advent of the corporation has radically changed the nature of wealth. Now, most real wealth used in production is owned by corporations and governments rather than by individuals. These funds are sometimes referred to as "active wealth."

The claims of individuals against corporations and governments, stocks and bonds, for example, are often called "passive wealth."

Another way to approach the definition of wealth is to think in terms of the factors that contribute to its production.

The first factor is land, including all the natural resources of our planet. Perhaps, sometime in the future, it will even include the resources of our solar system!

The second factor is labor, which converts the raw materials of the land into wealth. "Labor" is a broad term, including mental as well as physical effort.

The third factor is tools. This term includes everything from plows to computers. Taken altogether, the tools of production are referred to as "capital."

These different aspects of the term "wealth" may be difficult at first for students because they tend to think of wealth in a narrow and popular sense. But if they are to understand our economic society, students must grasp the economist's meaning of wealth.

Money

"Money? Of course I know what it is," the student usually responds to a question about his understanding of money. "It's what you use to buy things," he will add. "It's pennies and nickels and dimes and quarters and half-dollars—and paper bills."

Pressed on this point, some students will add that there are other currencies in the world—the English pound and the Russian ruble.

But is money just that? After World War II soldiers in many countries learned through experience that money was cigarettes and candy. They bought the things they wanted with those commodities, rather than with money as such.

And in ancient times, as well as in a few places today, other items have been money—cattle, beaver skins, sea shells, coconuts, fish hooks, arrowheads, strings of beads, stone wheels, and salt, for example. (The Roman soldiers were paid in blocks of salt, hence the expression "worth your salt." Our word "salary" comes from the Latin word for salt.)

These media of exchange became cumbersome as society developed the idea of division of labor, and money, as we know it, was the result.

What, then, is money? In brief, it is
    1. A medium of exchange—something used because almost everyone accepts it in exchange for something else.
    2. A measure of value.
    3. A store of value—a value stored for future use.

Students usually wonder why gold and silver were used for so long to back up coins and paper money. There are at least four reasons.
    1. They were considered valuable.
    2. Chemists could tell how pure they were.
    3. They did not wear out or spoil with time.
    4. They had psychological value to people.

In his popular little volume on Money to Grow On, Stuart Chase asserts that children and young people (and he might have added adults) need to think on three conceptual levels about money:
    1. The popular concept of money.
    2. The device of money as it is handled today.
    3. The mystique of money as power, control, status.

Most students still believe our money is supported by gold and silver, and many of them think that they could obtain these metals for their paper money if they requested an exchange. They need to be dissuaded of this notion. The United States went off the gold standard in 1933 and, fairly recently, withdrew the silver behind "silver certificates." As Professor Samuelson, the well-known and highly respected Harvard economist, has said in his widely used textbook on Economics, "Today, all American currency is essentially 'fiat' money. It is money because the government decrees it is money, and because we all accept it." This public faith in money is the characteristic that makes it valuable as a means of exchange of goods and services.

In recent times we have moved into an era in which money has become largely a paper transaction in the form of checking-account and bank-deposit money. The coins we use amount to only about one-thirteenth of the community's cash. Paper money constitutes a larger percentage. The paper transactions done by banks account for about 90 per cent of the exchange of money.

Some economists say that we are rapidly moving into an era in which currency, as we know it today, will become obsolete and where credit cards and computer systems will be the common means of exchange. Some students should believe this fact from the amount of cash and the number of cards their fathers carry in their wallets!

When students understand these elementary concepts, teachers should be able to delve more deeply into the intricacies of money and banking as it is carried on today, handling more advanced ideas: the flow of money, the place of the Federal Reserve System, how banks "create" money, the role of the federal government in controlling money and credit, and the controversial question of tax cuts and other devices to accelerate economic growth.

The following list of pamphlets and books includes reading materials that range from simple to complex, in order to meet a variety of teacher and student needs.

1. Burr, Susan S. Money Grows Up in American History. Washington: Service Center for Teachers of History, 1962. 36 pp.
2. Chase, Stuart. Money to Grow On. New York: Harper, 1964. 171 pp. A popular account of money. A paperback.
3. Commission on Money and Credit. Money and Credit: Their Influences on Jobs, Prices, and Growth. Englewood Cliffs, N.J.: Prentice-Hall, 1961. 285 pp. Fairly difficult reading.
4. Daugherty, James S. Money and Credit: Impact and Control. Englewood Cliffs, N.J.: Prentice-Hall. 1964. 117 pp. Fairly difficult.
5. Neisser, Edith G. The Many Faces of Money. New York: Human Relations Aids, 1958. 29 pp. Brief and very popular.
6. Lindholm, Richard W. Money and Banking: An Introduction. Ames, Iowa: Littlefield, 1958. 227 pp.
7. Robertson, D. H. Money. Chicago: University of Chicago Press, 1959. 187 pp. A paperback. Fairly difficult.
8. Samuelson, Paul A. Economics: Introductory Analysis. New York: McGraw-Hill, 1964. 838 pp. Chapter 14, "Prices and Money." A classic textbook.
9. Soule, George. Economics for Living. New York: Abelard, 1961. 159 pp. Very simple introduction; highly readable.
10. Waage, Thomas O. A Teachers Guide to Money, Banking and Credit. Washington: National Council for the Social Studies, 1955. 99 pp.
11. Welfling, Weldon. Money and Banking in the American Economy. Washington: Council for the Advancement of Secondary Education, 1960. 104 pp. For high school students.

The United States:
An Affluent Society

Students in the social studies are constantly examining local, national, and world problems. They should be. Often they are confronted with what seem to be insoluble problems. That, too, should happen to them.

But occasionally they ought to realize that they are lucky individuals because of the land their ancestors chose as a homeland and the efforts of millions of their forebearers.

Here are some of the facts of life in the United States and in a few other countries, as presented by Nation's Business magazine.

COUNTRIES	Gross National Product (per capita)	Infant Mortality Rate (per 1,000 births)	Food Supply (calories per day)	Energy (tons of coal equivalent)
UNITED STATES	$3,100	25	3,120	8.6
U.S.S.R.	$1,100	32	NO DATA	3.1
ARGENTINA	$600	61	2,950	1.2
AUSTRALIA	$1,600	20	3,160	4.2
BRAZIL	$375	170	2,680	0.4
CANADA	$2,100	27	3,100	6.0
EGYPT (U.A.R.)	$180	110	2,530	0.3.
FRANCE	$1,450	26	2,990	2.7
WEST GERMANY	$1,450	29	2,950	4.1
INDIA	$80	87	1,990	0.2
ITALY	$750	41	2,740	1.3
JAPAN	$500	29	2,240	1.4
MEXICO	$330	70	2,440	1.0
TURKEY	$200	165	2,830	0.2
UNITED KINGDOM	1,500	22	3,270	5.4

These figures are only a few that can be assembled to show that the standard of living in the United States today is the highest it has ever been for any people at any time in the history of the world.

With only 6 per cent of the world's population and 7 per cent of its land, the United States
1. Produces one-third of the world's goods and services.
2. Uses one-third of the energy consumed in the world.
3. Has half of the world's telephones and television sets.
4. Owns 60 per cent of the world's passenger cars.
5. Has more food to eat than almost any nation in the world.
6. Has health facilities that permit long life, compared to almost all other nations.

And our Gross National Product is increasing each year. "GNP," as economists call it, is a scorecard of our annual production in goods and services. It is the total market value of all the goods and services produced in a country during a single year. Here are the figures for a few years, adjusted to 1950 prices.

1929	$ 157.8 billion
1932	$ 113.6 billion
1959	$ 480. billion
1964	$ 624. billion

Pupils should be encouraged to seek the reasons for such wealth rather than simply being told about them. Among the factors they may discover, with the help of competent teachers, are the following. Perhaps you will want to add to or rearrange this list.

A unified country.

Lack of trade barriers.

Good transportation.

Good communication.

Excellent resources, especially coal, iron, and petroleum.

Skilled manpower.

High educational standards.

A large population.

Health facilities.

Friendly neighbors.

Agricultural productivity.

Industrialization.

Large amounts of capital.

Stable government.

Leadership.

Trade with other nations.

A system of revised capitalism, with controlled competition and many incentives.

Students should also delve into the "pockets of poverty" in our country (see Background Paper No. 167) and into the other problems of our economy that mar an otherwise outstanding record.

And they should look into the responsibility of an affluent society towards other nations (see Background Paper No. 110) from the standpoint of national self-interest as well as moral obligation.

Finally, weighing our assets against our failures and our responsibilities, they should consider the future of this affluent society in achieving its goal of an even higher standard of living for all people.

Poverty in the United States

Despite the affluence of the United States, this nation is the scene of a painful paradox. There is hunger in the midst of abundance, illiteracy in a highly literate populace, unemployment at a time of astonishing production, and poverty in spite of unprecedented prosperity.

COMPARISON OF FAMILY INCOMES IN THE UNITED STATES

0 - $3,000   18.6%
$3,000 - $6,000   28.8%
$6,000 - $10,000   32.6%
$10,000 - $15,000   14.5%
$15,000 AND OVER   5.5%

KERMIT JOHNSON AND GEORGE JEENS

WHO ARE THE POOR? There are many different definitions of poverty in the United States. The chart above (from Weekly News Review, January 11, 1965, by permission) shows that almost 19 per cent of our families earn less than $3000 a year (a figure sometimes used as the poverty level).

Other writers place "poverty" income elsewhere. In 1964, there were 30 million people in the United States who lived in families earning less than $2000 annually plus 3 million single individuals who earned less than $1500 a year. Four-fifths of these persons were whites; one-fifth were Negroes or members of other minority groups. Many were farmers eking out a bare existence on small farms or impoverished land. Many were migrant workers—fruit and vegetable pickers. Some were old people—lonely and isolated. Some were young people. (Three out of every ten unemployed people are under 25 years of age.) A large percentage of them had little education. Most of them made the mistake, as Michael Harrington points out in The Other America, of being born to the wrong parents, in the wrong section of the country, in the wrong racial or ethnic group.

About half of these impoverished people live in urban areas. New York City has nearly one million of the poor, "the forgotten Americans." The other 50 per cent live in rural areas, with large numbers in Appalachia.

In the 1960s "pockets of poverty" were discovered in the midst of plenty. Books and articles were written about them; political leaders as well as other people began to talk about them.

WHAT IS BEING DONE ABOUT POVERTY? Economists generally agree that poverty need not exist in the United States today. There will always be some persons who are unemployed and some who are unemployable (the seriously ill and the mentally retarded). But this country need not and should not have large numbers of citizens who live at the deprivation or poverty level.

The Kennedy administration launched a war against poverty. President Johnson has continued and enlarged that program greatly. Its particulars can be found by able students doing research on this topic. But the broad outlines of the administration's war on poverty (and that of other interested groups) include the following:

1. Improved educational facilities for disadvantaged children and youth; classes for preschool children who have been handicapped educationally by their home background; literacy classes for adult illiterates.
2. More low-cost housing.
3. Medical care for disadvantaged persons. Health insurance, as part of the Social Security program, for older people.
4. Job training for the unemployed, especially young people and persons thrown out of work by shifts in industry.
5. Aid to farmers over a period of years to improve their land, crops, and buildings.
6. Aid to needy college students for continuing their education.
7. Establishment of a Domestic Peace Corps to work with persons in poverty areas.
8. Loans to small businesses.
9. Extension of Social Security to more persons.
10. A broad program to improve economic conditions in Appalachia (the area extending from Pennslyvania through Alabama), which is the largest single area of poverty in the country. These measures include: the improvement of forest and pasture areas, stream purification, flood control, revitalization of the declining coal industry, and the attraction of tourists to the region.

These and other measures of local, state, and federal government units and private groups are calculated to improve the lot of millions of Americans and, in the long run, benefit everyone in the United States.

A SELECTED BIBLIOGRAPHY

1. Bagdikian, Ben H. In the Midst of Plenty: A New Report on the Poor in America. New York: Signet, 1964. 160 pp. A paperback.
2. Distressed Areas in a Growing Economy. Washington: Committee for Economic Development, 1961. 74 pp.
3. Harrington, Michael. The Other America: Poverty in the United States. Baltimore: Penguin, 1962. 203 pp. A paperback.
4. Humphrey, Hubert. War on Poverty. New York: McGraw-Hill, 1965. 206 pp.
5. May, Edgar. The Wasted Americans. New York: Harper, 1964. 227 pp.
6. Miller, Herman P. Rich Man, Poor Man: The Distribution of Income in America. New York: Crowell, 1964. 260 pp.
7. Pomfret, John D. New Opportunities for Depressed Areas. New York: Public Affairs Committee, 1963. 27 pp. A pamphlet.
8. Poverty and Deprivation in the United States: The Plight of Two-Fifths of a Nation. Washington: Conference on Economic Progress, 1962. 97 pp. Profusely illustrated with charts and graphs.
9. Stewart, Maxwell S. The Poor Among Us — Challenge and Opportunity. New York: Public Affairs Committee, 1964. 20 pp. A pamphlet.

Economic Growth

Nearly all nations today are interested in economic growth. Like individuals, they want more goods and more services. They want a larger Gross National Product, and in most cases, a wider distribution of goods and services to the people.

In the United States, we, too, are concerned with economic growth for a variety of reasons. We want to maintain our high standard of living in the face of an increasing population and, if possible, to raise it still higher. We want to reduce the amount of unemployment and the amount of poverty in our midst. We want more services, such as education and medical care, from our government. In addition, we want to keep our lead over the Soviet Union (which is growing economically at a faster rate than we are), and to meet the challenge of the European Common Market, of Japan, and of other nations and combinations of nations.

To do all this, we must use our present resources wisely and increase our production of goods and services in the nation as a whole and as individuals. "Economic growth means the progressive rise over a long period of time of a nation's total output and its output per person" (Marion Daugherty in Understanding Economic Growth).

Historically, our average rate of growth has been 3 per cent a year for the 90 years from 1870 to 1960. Actually, we have not had that amount of growth each year, but the average comes to that figure. In the same period, our population expanded but not so rapidly as our production. Annual per capita output has skyrocketed as follows:

1880	$ 494	1920	$1350
1900	$1048	1940	$1784
1960	$2793		

The growth, however, has slowed down in recent years. From 1946 to 1957, our real GNP per capita (adjusted for price increases) was only 2 per cent. After 1957, it dropped below 1 per cent. In the meantime, other nations have made remarkable gains, especially Japan, France, West Germany, and Italy. Thus, many people in the United States are concerned about our economic growth.

In a pamphlet on The Mystery of Economic Growth, the Federal Reserve of Philadelphia simplified this concept by describing two ways in which an economy grows. The writer compared the growth of a national economy with the growth of a person, an analogy that teachers can use in working with students on this major economic concept.

> ANALOGY ONE. The economy is "underweight." Factories are closed or not producing up to capacity. Unemployment is high. What is needed is to "gain weight," to put people back to work and thus to produce more goods and services. This can be done in several ways: (1) increased government spending, (2) increased business spending, and (3) increased consumer demand and spending—through devices such as tax cuts and/or easier and cheaper borrowing (by rulings of the Federal Reserve).

175

ANALOGY TWO.   Encourage the economy to grow "taller" by

1. Assisting workers through greater education and skill; improved attitudes, such as incentives and taxes that are not too high; discovery of new and better ideas, products, and processes; and more and better machinery.

2. Assisting businesses through special tax credits for spending on plants and equipment; more recognition of depreciation of factories and equipment; increased consumer spending, without bringing on inflation; a tax structure that does not unduly interfere with the investment for business growth.

These and other suggestions (from economists, business leaders, union officials, government leaders, and others) all presuppose federal planning. They also assume a delicate balance among the factors affecting growth.

W. W. Rostow has added a new dimension to this subject of economic growth in his book <u>The Stages of Economic Growth: A Non-Communist Manifesto.</u> In that provocative volume, he indicates that all or almost all nations pass through five stages: the traditional society, the preconditions for take-off, the take-off, the drive to maturity, the age of mass-consumption.

Students in American history, in world history, and in economics should find this approach stimulating. Here is a chart of several societies and their positions in these five stages.

STAGES OF ECONOMIC GROWTH FOR SELECTED COUNTRIES

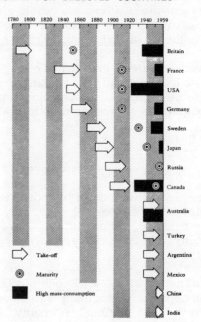

Source: W. W. Rostow, *The Stages of Economic Growth*, The University Press, Cambridge, Mass., 1960. (By courtesy of the Economist.)

176

Corporations

Corporations loom large on the economic horizon of the United States and of other parts of the world. In a recent year, there were 700,000 corporate organizations in the United States, and though they represented only 6 per cent of the firms in the country, they did a majority of the business.

The chart below indicates the ten largest companies in the United States and in Europe (reprinted by permission from <u>American Observer</u>, April 30, 1962):

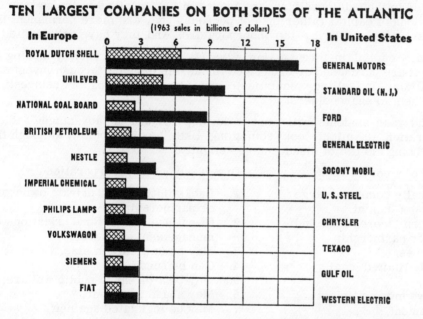

TEN LARGEST COMPANIES ON BOTH SIDES OF THE ATLANTIC

(1963 sales in billions of dollars)

You may notice that the largest corporation of them all, in one sense, is omitted—the American Telephone and Telegraph Company, which owns, operates, and services 83 per cent of the nation's telephones, has a labor force of 733,000, and an annual revenue of over $10 billion (more than the combined income of 30 states). It is not listed because it sells services rather than manufactures products.

Here is another way of presenting the largest corporations in the United States. The table comes from an article in The American Observer in 1963:

Company	Assets in Billions	Number of Employees	Number of Stockholders
American Telephone and Telegraph	22.6	735,766	1,911,484
Standard Oil of New Jersey	10.1	140,000	655,000
General Motors	8.6	595,151	867,000
U. S. Steel	4.8	225,081	336,000
Ford Motor Company	4.0	160,181	232,010
Gulf Oil	3.8	47,400	118,099
Texaco	3.6	56,658	145,425
Socony Mobil	3.5	69,000	234,300
DuPont	3.1	88,514	226,919
Standard Oil of Indiana	2.9	42,638	160,099
Pennsylvania Railroad	2.9	74,969	120,088
Standard Oil of California	2.8	37,677	169,646

After learning about the size of corporations, students should be anxious to discover how they are formed. Corporations are chartered in most states with a minimum of three persons to act as a legal entity. They must have a specific purpose (although this is often broad), must not be opposed to the public welfare, and must limit themselves to the powers specified. They are associations of capital rather than of persons. They are more permanent than other forms of business, often outliving the incorporators. And they have only limited liability.

Corporations obtain capital in three major ways: (1) by borrowing; (2) by issuing shares of stock or bonds that are purchased or exchanged for assets (usually through investment banking firms specializing in selling securities); and (3) by retaining and reinvesting profits instead of paying them to shareholders.

Eventually you and your students will want to develop a list of the advantages and disadvantages of incorporation. It might look something like the chart below, although the author confesses to stretching his list of disadvantages slightly.

Advantages of a corporation

1. Can usually command large amounts of capital.
2. Can earn more than individual or partnership businesses.
3. Has only limited legal liability.
4. Can have more efficient management.
5. Can have lower costs of production.
6. Distributes risks more widely.
7. Has credit available more easily.
8. Can sue.
9. More permanent.
10. Can have considerable political power.

Disadvantages of a corporation

1. Lacks initiative of private ownership or partnership.
2. Often has impersonal relations between management and labor.
3. May be unwieldy in size.
4. Can be sued.
5. May be a threat to public welfare.
6. May abuse its power.
7. May be legislated against.

In an economics class, you may want to set up a corporation or discuss whether to form a corporation or some other kind of business to produce zippers, cars, steel, or the latest game. In classes in United States history, you will certainly want to stress the development of corporations, the abuses of corporations around the turn of the century, and the moves of the federal government to curb corporate excesses.

Inflation

All students need to know about inflation. It is a basic economic concept that underlies an understanding of many parts of our own history as well as many parts of world history. It is one of the unsolved economic problems of our times, affecting young as well as older people.

One way to introduce this concept is to display a German postage stamp of the 1920s, like the one pictured above. You or one of your students may have such a stamp. Failing this, you can draw a picture of this stamp on the chalkboard. Your students should be intrigued with the idea that a little stamp, issued for 40 reichsmarks, could soon cost five thousand reichsmarks. Their interest should lead into a discussion of what this price change would mean to the purchaser and to the government. If a stamp can rise in cost so sharply and so quickly, what would happen to other prices? Who would be hit hardest? How could such inflation occur?

The German stamp shifted values in the disastrous inflation that came to Germany after World War I. Another way to handle this same inflationary period in Germany would be with samples of the paper money used there after World War I. The author has bills marked 50 million marks and 200,000,000 marks that were worth next to nothing in Germany. A wheelbarrow of these bills often bought only a week's supply of groceries. People spent their money as quickly as they could, for fear that it would purchase less in a few hours.

A dramatic way to introduce inflation is to cut a piece of "toy money" in half in front of the class, as a graphic example of what happened to the purchasing power of the dollar in a short time during inflation.

You should then come quickly to the main point of the lesson—that inflation occurs when there is too much money and too few goods or when there is an <u>overall</u> rise in the price of goods and services. It is important to stress that a general trend toward higher prices is usual; the rise of a few prices does not mean that inflation has occurred. Phrased differently, inflation occurs when there is a <u>disproportionate</u> increase in purchasing power in relation to the available supply of goods and services. When developing this idea, it is essential to emphasize the fact that purchasing power includes both money <u>and</u> credit, including bank deposits.

Inflation during wartime is an easy example with which to start. Wartime production emphasizes guns, ammunition, ships, uniforms, and similar items, rather than goods that are sold. There are fewer consumer goods so their prices rise. If the government does not intervene, inflation ensues. Nowadays, governments step in with price controls, rationing, and the sale of government bonds (not only to aid the war effort but to absorb the expansion of money). If, after a war, controls are lifted before equilibrium has been attained, inflation may become a problem then.

This is the classic explanation of inflation and is sometimes called the "demand-pull" process. In it, the government bids against the civilian economy for available goods.

A more recent explanation concerns the "cost-push" inflation. There, certain groups acquire and wield sufficient power to push up costs and prices without experiencing the pressure of demand upon supply. One example is the power of labor groups in wage demands.

Any discussion of inflation should also stress who loses and who profits by inflation. Debtors, of course, profit most. A person who owes $1000 can pay it back much more easily when money is "cheap." Throughout our history, there are numerous examples of demands for "cheap" money by debtor groups.

People who live on fixed incomes are hurt by inflation. This group includes all the professional people on fixed wages or salaries, pensioners, investors in bonds and other fixed-income obligations, and hospitals, private schools and colleges, and other endowed institutions.

The next topic of discussion should be the control of inflation. It is important for students to realize that economic controls are relatively new in our national life. In the past, people either objected to controls or thought that inflation had to run its course. Today, most people are willing, even anxious, for controls against inflation. There are many of these. For example, some labor contracts contain "escalator" clauses that guarantee rising wages when prices rise. The government sponsors others: spurs to productivity, price control, and regulation of interest rates charged by banks and other financial institutions.

With some pupils, you may also want to discuss a currently popular but controversial theory that some inflation is inevitable—that we must choose between inflation and unemployment.

Taxes

Teaching about taxes is an important part of any social studies program in secondary schools. It may be done in an economics class, a civics class, a United States history class, or in all of them. The place where it falls in the curriculum does not matter greatly; the topic and the teaching methods do. An economically literate citizen in a democracy needs a knowledge of taxes and a good attitude toward them.

From the standpoint of interest, the best time to teach about taxes is in late March or early April, when the students' parents (and, in some cases, the students themselves) are making out their federal income tax reports. But if the teacher is emotionally involved in his own tax report, he might be wiser to discuss the topic at some other point in the term.

The subject will be richer if students bring specific tax questions to class as well as charts, graphs, and articles from current newspapers and magazines. Current events magazines usually run articles on the subject in March or April and, if pertinent, these articles will add to your discussion.

Make large charts and graphs of the material students bring in as well as the charts shown below. You can enlarge many of these materials through overhead and opaque projectors.

In any study of taxes, the federal government's sources of income and expenses are important. Each year, the Bureau of the Budget prepares charts similar to the ones reproduced here. They are an excellent way to point out the budgetary needs that control annual taxes.

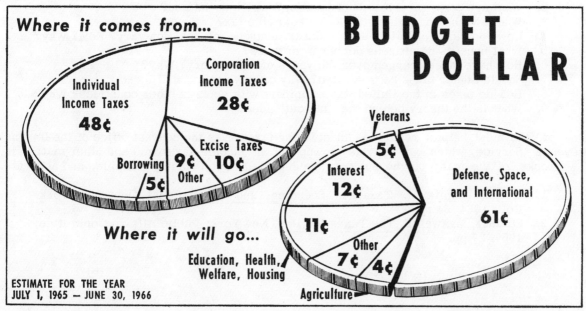

ADAPTED FROM BUREAU OF THE BUDGET CHART

If the class is also studying state and local taxes, you should make or obtain similar charts for those units of government.

In studies of taxation, commentators often stress the large increase in taxes over the last few years. Show that this is caused by a number of factors: the large percentage spent for defense (including past wars), for space exploration, and for increased services to citizens. Remind students that the people have voted for these increases through their representatives. The total amount spent by our federal government should be seen in relation to Gross National Product, as shown in the bar graph below:

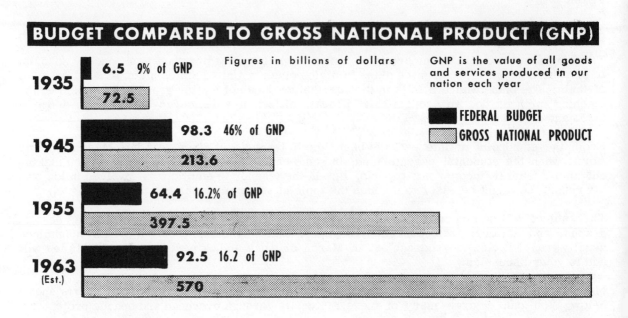

Each teacher will want to develop his own outline for handling taxes. Here are some of the items you may want to include in a series of lessons or a unit on taxation.

1. Why taxes?
2. What are some theories about taxation? Which do we use?
3. What are the characteristics of an equitable tax?
4. How do local, state, and federal sources of taxation vary? How? Why?
5. What benefits do citizens derive from taxes?
6. How have taxes changed over the years of our history? Why?
7. Should higher taxes be prevented? Why or why not?
8. How do taxes in the United States compare with taxes in other countries? Why?
9. What is the theory behind the "tax cut" idea?

One of the most helpful resources in studying taxation is the nearest office of the Internal Revenue Service, which can provide blowups of the income-tax forms and other materials. Two books, of the many on the subject, are especially good—brief, readable, and accurate.

1. Kreps, Juanita M. Taxation, Spending, and the National Debt. New York: Holt, 1964. 64 pp.
2. Stewart, Maxwell S. The Taxes We Pay. New York: Public Affairs Committee, 1959. 27 pp.

Hamilton and the Financial Problems
in Our Early History

Many students (and some teachers, too) find it difficult to understand the complex and confusing financial situation in our country during the Revolutionary War under the Articles of Confederation, and in the early republic.

During those periods, many people used the barter system, especially in the "back country" and in the West. After 1764, no paper money could be printed, but some still circulated from previous periods. British, French, and Spanish coins were, of course, in demand. In Virginia, tobacco warehouse receipts often served as money and other colonies used similar means.

During the Revolutionary War, the Continental Congress issued some paper money. Citizens selling "material" to the army or rendering special services were given promissory notes, and the soldiers were often paid in IOUs. Furthermore, Europeans held notes for their aid to the revolutionary cause.

To complicate the picture still further, each of the states issued its own paper money under the Articles of Confederation government.

You may be able to make the financial situation clearer if you have your students actually handle different kinds of money and face some of the problems that people faced in those days. Have some students represent the wealthy merchants during the Revolutionary War and others represent the soldiers who received IOUs. Designate a few others (perhaps in the back of the room) as the Europeans holding promissory notes. Pay these groups with "play money" (index cards marked "IOU" or "promise to pay").

Then move to the period of the Articles of Confederation when each state printed its own money. Hand out cards for the money of Massachusetts, Pennsylvania, Virginia, and Georgia (each a different color).

By the time you have distributed some of all these "monies," the class should see what a complicated financial situation existed. If you want to make the confusion more apparent, have some pupils move West and try to use their money in a Kentucky store. The storekeeper will be baffled by the various kinds of money, much of which was worth very little in 1789. Throughout the entire demonstration, you would be wise to reiterate the problems, illustrating them by manipulating the students and their funds. By now you should be ready to introduce Alexander Hamilton. You may either decide to play the role and tell a little about him yourself, or ask a good student to be Hamilton and to tell about his ideas of government and finance. If the role is skillfully played, the students should see the problems that faced Hamilton and Congress. Among them were the following:

1. What shall we do with the debts of previous governments?
   a. The foreign debt of about $12,000,000.
   b. The domestic debt of about $44,000,000, incurred during the Revolution and the critical period following it.
   c. The state debts of about $25,000,000.
2. How can we find money to run our new government?
3. How can we strengthen the credit of our new government?

Hamilton and some members of Congress were further concerned about how to strengthen the central government and how to win support for it among the wealthier people.

There was little objection to the payment of the foreign debt and, despite opposition, Congress adopted Hamilton's plan to pay the domestic debt in full. The big battle came over the assumption of the states' debts.

The pros and cons of that issue can, again, be illustrated by referring to the "money" held by students. For example, Georgia had only a small debt and Virginia had paid most of its debts. They did not favor the assumption by the federal government of the debts of states, partly because of this economic situation and partly because they preferred a weak central government. Massachusetts, on the other hand, had large unpaid debts. It wanted the federal government to assume these debts, of course. It also supported a strong central government.

You can then describe the "deal" made to win support for the assumption cause. Explain that Hamilton won this issue by supporting the elements that wanted to move the capital to Washington—an early example of "logrolling."

You may want to refer to the "money" cards again to dramatize the scene in Congress at the time of the vote on assumption of state debts. Two or three boys can become "speculators" and gather up IOUs and notes, as well as paper money printed by the states, realizing some profits in the process.

Throughout any study of this problem of finances, you should stress the part played by Alexander Hamilton. Experts differ in their evaluation of him, but most authorities credit him with putting the new government on a strong financial basis. Nevins and Commager call him "the greatest finance minister in American history."

Economic Geography
of the Steel Industry

One of the reasons many people dislike geography is because it is taught as a parroting of places and products. And one reason people retain so little of what they have studied about geography is because they have merely memorized facts.

Students retain geographical knowledge when they discover facts for themselves and see the relationships between them.

For example, consider the relationship between geography and economics in the location of steel plants in the United States. Pupils at almost any grade level can work out the relationships involved if they can discover the basic facts with which to work.

One of these, of course, is the need for the major ingredients used in making steel: iron, coal, and limestone. (The limestone is the least important of the three, but it is needed to help remove the impurities from the iron.)

These three materials are seldom found in the same place, so the next important factor is getting them together—the problem of inexpensive transportation.

Faced with the basic considerations, students can begin to work out the places where plants might be located. One solution would be near the coal deposits. Another would be near the iron deposits. A third would be at some point between the sources of the two main raw products or somewhere between all three—including the limestone.

In the past, most of our iron in the United States has come from the Mesabi Range in Minnesota; most of our coal has come from Pennsylvania, Ohio, and West Virginia. The limestone deposits are chiefly in the Ohio river area.

Students can mark these areas on the map and then figure out how to move the minerals inexpensively. Eventually, they should discover that steel mills might be built near the coal deposits in West Virginia, western Pennsylvania, and eastern Ohio; near the iron deposits in Minnesota; or somewhere between those points, and on the Great Lakes—in northern Illinois, northern Indiana, or northern Ohio.

After students have thought about these relationships, they can be shown the places where the large steel plants have been located in the past: Pittsburgh, Wheeling, Gary, Hammond, and Chicago.

But a new factor has entered the picture in recent years—the depletion of the rich deposits of iron ore in the Mesabi Range. As a result, steel plants are now being built in different cities.

Some have sprung up in the South, near Birmingham, Alabama, because coal and iron are both nearby.

More recently, we have begun to import iron from Labrador, Canada, and Venezuela and to build new steel plants near Baltimore and Philadelphia. The reasons for those locations include additional economic factors—the availability of manpower, capital, and transportation, as well as the ready access to markets—that your students can add to their basic considerations of materials and transportation.

The map below, reprinted with the permission of the Civic Education Service, shows the chief centers of steel mills in the United States.

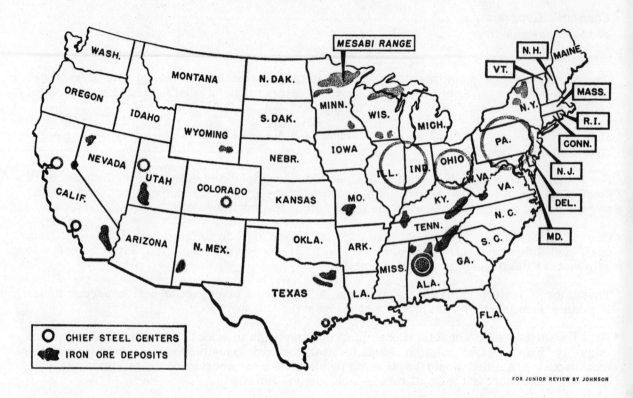

FOR JUNIOR REVIEW BY JOHNSON

Teachers can obtain some free materials about the steel industry from the following sources:

1. American Iron and Steel Institute, 150 East 42nd Street, New York 17, N.Y.
2. Inland Steel Company, Public Relations Department, 30 West Monroe Street, Chicago 3, Ill.
3. United States Steel Corporation—Public Relations Department, 71 Broadway, New York 6, N.Y.

Economic Dependence
of American Industry
on the Rest of the World

Many students, like their parents, think that because the United States is very rich it is self-sufficient. They ask, naively, "Why should we concern ourselves with the rest of the world?"

These students need to discover the economic interdependence of the world, including the economic dependence of people in the United States upon the rest of the world. One of the most effective examples of this economic dependence is the need of our industry for raw materials from all over the world. The automobile industry is a good case to use.

The American Manufacturers Association (New Center Building, Detroit 2, Michigan) has a large map entitled "The World Makes An Automobile." The map is large, but there is too much material on it for the entire class to see it at a distance; so individuals or a committee should study it in detail, then report to the class. Teachers will find it useful as background material.

It points out that over 300 products from 50 countries are used in the manufacture of automobiles in the United States. Without these products, we would not have cars. Men would not have jobs in auto plants. Car dealers would not exist. Filling stations would close. The petroleum business would be curtailed. One could show effects on the entire economy of the United States if these foreign products were cut off.

Here are some of the products from abroad that go into the manufacture of autos.

> RUBBER. We now use some synthetic rubber that is made in this country, but much of our rubber still comes from Indonesia, Malaysia, Ceylon, and parts of what was once Indochina.

> LEAD, COPPER AND ZINC. The lead for auto batteries comes in large part from Mexico. The zinc door handles come from materials from Canada and Mexico. Much of the copper for automobile electrical systems comes from Chile.

> TEXTILES. Cotton, wool, leather, and nylon are used in the interior sidewalls, the upholstery, the head lining, seat padding, and other parts of cars. Sisal comes from the Yucatan peninsula of Mexico, jute from East Pakistan, wool from Turkey and South Africa. The leather comes chiefly from the United States, but some of it comes from Canada and some from the Argentine pampas. The cotton in automobiles originates in Egypt and the Sudan.

Students will find many other products from all over the world that are necessary in automobile production.

187

MATERIALS FROM ABROAD FOR TELEPHONES

In a sense, every telephone is a little United Nations. There are 475 parts on each phone; there are 75 parts in the handpiece alone. The parts are made from 62 materials ranging from A to Z (aluminum to zinc) and coming from many parts of the world.

Some of them are listed in a recent publication on "How the Telephone Works," published by the American Telephone and Telegraph Company.

Aluminum	From the United States, British Guiana, and Jamaica
Asphalt	From the United States, Venezuela, and the British West Indies
Beryllium	From Brazil, Argentina, India, South Africa, and Australia
Carbon (coal)	From the United States
Chromium	From Turkey and South Africa
Cobalt	From the Republic of the Congo and Canada
Copper	From the United States
Cotton	From the United States
Gold	From the United States, Canada, South Africa, and Australia
Lacquer	From the United States
Lead	From the United States and Mexico
Molybdenum	From the United States
Nickel	From Canada and Norway
Nylon	From the United States
Palladium	From Canada and South Africa
Paper	From Canada and Sweden
Phosphorus	From the United States
Plastics	From the United States
Rayon	From the United States
Rubber	From Indonesia and Malaysia
Steel	From the United States
Tin	From Indonesia and Malaysia
Vanadium	From the United States
Wax	From the United States
Zinc	From the United States

Petroleum in the World Economy

The relationship between resources and politics is intricate and important. As George Cressey has pointed out, "If we wish to measure the economic potential of nations in the twentieth century or understand international political relations or weigh the prospective welfare of different people, we must first have an inventory of the world's mineral wealth."

His point can be made over and over again. Many nations have been interested in the petroleum of the Middle East, and the world politics of that area is closely tied to the importance of petroleum. The wealth of Southeast Asia is certainly one of the reasons for the interest of China—and of the United States—in that region. The difficulties of the Katanga province of the Congo are closely related to the valuable copper deposits there. Perhaps you and your students can find other examples of the interrelated nature of economics and politics on the world scene. You may want to chart the basic resources of the world and make an overlay map of the political difficulties that have arisen over the control of these resources.

All over the world today, engineers are searching for oil. As a result, oil has been found in several parts of the world where it was not known to exist: Libya and Nigeria in Africa; Australia; India and Japan.

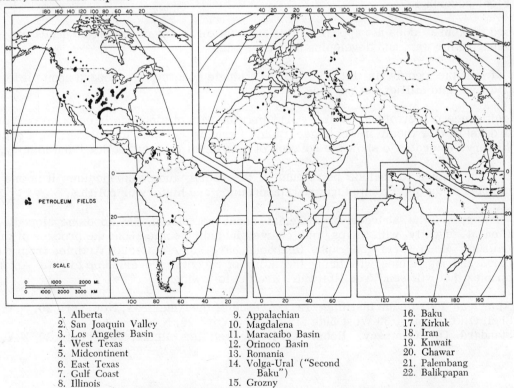

1. Alberta	9. Appalachian	16. Baku
2. San Joaquin Valley	10. Magdalena	17. Kirkuk
3. Los Angeles Basin	11. Maracaibo Basin	18. Iran
4. West Texas	12. Orinoco Basin	19. Kuwait
5. Midcontinent	13. Romania	20. Ghawar
6. East Texas	14. Volga-Ural ("Second	21. Palembang
7. Gulf Coast	Baku")	22. Balikpapan
8. Illinois	15. Grozny	

From <u>World Economic Geography</u> by C. Langdon White, Paul F. Griffin, and Tom L. McKnight. ©1964 by Wadsworth Publishing Company, Inc., Belmont, California. By permission.

The world map on the preceding page shows the principal parts of the world in which petroleum is now found. The largest producer is still the United States, with the U.S.S.R. in second place and Venezuela in third place. Of the four billion barrels of oil the United States needs annually, we produce only 2.7 billion barrels per year. We import the rest from Venezuela and the Middle East primarily.

In studying the importance of petroleum in the world economy, you may want to start with a list made by your students of all the uses of oil they can discover. This can be either a class or a homework assignment. The statement "Today oil is king of the world," followed by "What does that statement mean?" will lead you naturally into the many uses of oil.

A partial list, culled from a publication of the American Petroleum Institute, includes the following uses:

Liquefied petroleum gas	Fuels for ranges, space heaters, incubators
Aviation gasoline	Illuminants
Automotive gasoline	Home-heating oils
Tractor fuels	Diesel fuels
Heavy industrial fuels	Lubricating oils and greases
Dry-cleaning fluids	Coating paper
Lighter fluids	Printer's inks
Commercial solvents	Detergents
Thinners for paints and enamels	Medicinal oils
	Bases for cosmetics
Oils for dipping sheep and cattle	Spraying oils for trees
	Weed killers
Cutting oils	Insecticides and fungicides
Rust preventatives	Wood preservatives
Plastics	Waxes for candles
Roofing materials	
Floor coverings	

The word "defense" does not appear on this list, but oil is one of the major needs for waging war, preparing for war, and developing defense systems.

A list of all the people in the world (or in a single country) who depend upon oil for their livelihood runs into millions of persons.

The significance of petroleum to the world may be part of a course in economics. You may want to develop this theme in world geography. Perhaps you want to include it in a course in world history, in order to show the relation of petroleum to world politics and history.

Wherever you decide to include petroleum in the social studies curriculum, it is one of the best examples of the interrelated nature of economics and history or politics.

There are many fine sources of material about petroleum. Any good encyclopedia has a section on it, usually with maps and charts, including some about the process of drilling for petroleum. Most world geography textbooks have some material. Articles from current newspapers and magazines will bring the story of recent discoveries up to date. Among the oil companies that will send free literature are the following:

American Petroleum Institute, 1271 Avenue of the Americas, New York 20, N.Y.
Shell Oil Company, 50 West 50th Street, New York 20, N.Y.
Standard Oil Company, Room 1626, Rockefeller Plaza, New York 20, N.Y.

Political Science: Key Ideas

Teachers and teachers-to-be may find helpful several statements of the key concepts in political science or government. The briefest list is one prepared by the Wisconsin Social Studies Committee for the publication on "A Conceptual Framework in Social Studies for Wisconsin Schools." The five ideas listed are as follows:

1. Every society creates laws. Some laws are designed to promote the common good; other laws protect special interests or groups. Penalties and sanctions are provided for violations of law.
2. Governments are established by men. In some situations people delegate authority to government; in others, authority is imposed.
3. Democracy is a form of government in which decision making is in the hands of the people, who make their desires known through voting, political parties, and pressure groups. Democracy seeks to protect the rights of the individuals and minority groups.
4. Citizenship involves active participation in the process of governing.
5. All levels of government are interrelated. There is a division of responsibility and an interdependence among all levels of government. At the world level, all nations are interdependent.

The author of this book, working with a group of social science teachers, developed a slightly longer list of major concepts. It includes the following:

1. People live in groups and establish goals and rules—written and unwritten— for those groups.
2. Communities and larger units are organized as governments.
3. The world is composed of many nations with different forms of government.
4. All governmental units are interrelated.
5. Governments have some common functions and characteristics, such as symbols, leadership, courts, costs, and services.
6. In every unit of government, persons have some responsibilities and some rights; these differ in different types of government.
7. The United States is a democracy and a republic.
8. Decision making is an important aspect of government, but methods vary radically; decision making in a democracy is closer to the people and their representatives.
9. All governments have problems.
10. Nations of the world are increasingly interdependent; regional and international organizations are developing.

A third approach has been developed by Professor David Easton and Mr. David Collier of the University of Chicago and Professor Lawrence Senash of Purdue University for the Social Science Education Consortium, West Lafayette, Indiana. They point out that recent research indicates that children first learn about politics in the family as their basic attitudes toward authority develop; that, as early as second grade, children identify with political parties and are aware of such political authorities as policemen and the President of the

United States. Consequently, they suggest that political learning should begin very early in the school lives of children, even as early as the primary grades.

They emphasize the fact that political learning is a term that applies to all aspects of political life in society. The purpose of political life is to settle differences or to regulate activities of society that cannot be managed by the private efforts of members of society. Speaking in more technical language, they refer to "the authoritative allocation of valued things for the society." Such functions, they point out, are carried on in a wide variety of patterns—through voting, parties, interest groups, administration, judiciary, and legislatures. All these patterns take place within the wider environment of society.

From this overall approach they develop a chart or scheme that includes demands, one of the two major inputs from the environment into the political system; outputs, the decisions made by the authorities; support for the political system, the other major input; and feedback, a concept that unifies their whole analysis.

They further differentiate between the wants of a society and demands. When wants are agreed upon by society, they become political demands—such as care for the aged, guarantees of civil rights, control of decent housing, equal educational opportunities for all, and assurance of income for the unemployed. In the process of shifting from wants to political demands, these researchers refer to gatekeepers: interest groups, opinion leaders, business organizations, newspapers, political parties, legislators. Other researchers might call them the opinion makers or decision makers. Sometimes "the people" also serve as gatekeepers.

In the process of arriving at political decisions, cleavages may appear. Where these are deep, the political system may undergo considerable strain. Ways have been developed—such as appeals to national unity or to the public interest—to reduce such cleavages.

The decisions of the authorities are the outputs affecting the environment. These may include legislation, court decisions, regulations by governmental agencies, actions by the Justice Department or Post Offices, or even orders by policemen.

Support is another important factor, indicating the degree of approval of the system. Support may be expressed in many forms and range from support of particular people to a general administration.

Division of authority differs from one political system to another.

Any political system needs a fairly high level of support most of the time. To work, any political system must also be self-regulating. The term for this concept is "feedback." Those in authority must be responsive to the demands of the governed. Thus, a political system is a vast conversion process that regulates itself in order to persist.

* * *

Are there ideas in the above which you can apply in your teaching?
Are there ideas here which you can develop with your students?

Books on Government
for Boys and Girls

No textbook can possibly deal in detail with the various parts of our government. "Trade books" or supplementary books should be used along with texts. The list that follows includes some books for slow readers in junior high school classes; the grade level is noted on them.

1. Acheson, Patricia C. Our Federal Government: How It Works. New York: Dodd, 1962. 168 pp. Grades 6-9.
2. Beard, Charles A. The Presidents in American History. New York: Messner, 1962. 182 pp. Grades 8-10.
3. Botter, David. Politicians and What They Do. New York: Watts, 1960. 213 pp. Grades 7-10.
4. Bradley, Duane. Electing a President. Princeton, N.J.: Van Nostrand, 1963. 156 pp. Illustrations from many campaigns.
5. Cavanah, Frances, and Elizabeth L. Crandall. Meet the Presidents. Philadelphia: Macrae, 1962. 352 pp. Grades 6-9.
6. Commager, Henry Steele. The Great Constitution. New York: Bobbs-Merrill, 1961. 128 pp. Grades 5-8.
7. Cooke, David C. How Money Is Made. New York: Dodd, 1962. 64 pp. Grades 4-6. How the government mints and prints money.
8. Coy, Harold. The First Book of Presidents. New York: Watts, 1961. 69 pp. Grades 5-7. Brief introduction and one page on each President.
9. Coy, Harold. The First Book of Congress. New York: Watts, 1956. 59 pp. Grades 4-6.
10. Coy, Harold. The First Book of the Supreme Court. New York: Watts, 1958. 59 pp. Grades 5-8.
11. Davidson, Bill. President Kennedy Selects Six Brave Presidents. New York: Harper, 1962. 96 pp. Grades 6-8. Washington, John Quincy Adams, Lincoln, Johnson, Arthur, and Teddy Roosevelt.
12. Eskie, Sunny. A Land Full of Freedom. New York: Friendly House, 1963. 27 pp. Grades 4-5.
13. Fribourg, Marjorie G. Ports of Entry: U.S.A. Boston: Little, 1962. 240 pp. Grades 7-10. The U.S. Customs Service.
14. Galloway, George B. History of the House of Representatives. New York: Crowell, 1962. 216 pp. Grades 8-10.
15. Gray, Lee L. How We Choose a President: The Election Year. New York: St. Martin's, 1964. 144 pp.
16. Hemphill, Josephine. Fruitcake and Arsenic. Boston: Little, 1962. 144 pp. Grades 6-9. The story of the Food and Drug Administration.
17. Holisher, Desider, and Graham Beckel. Capitol Hill. New York: Abelard, 1952. 143 pp. Grades 6-9.
18. Johnson, Gerald W. The Congress. New York: Morrow, 1963. 128 pp. Grades 5-8.
19. Johnson, Gerald W. The Presidency. New York: Morrow, 1962. 128 pp. Grades 5-8.
20. Johnson, Gerald W. The Supreme Court. New York: Morrow, 1962. 127 pp. Grades 5-7.
21. Knapp, G. L. Uncle Sam's Government at Washington. New York: Dodd, 1933. 283 pp.

193

22. Kutner, Nanette. The White House Saga. New York: Atheneum, 1962. 119 pp.
23. Lincoln Filene Center. Practical Political Action: A Guide for Young Citizens. Boston: Houghton, 1962. 197 pp. Grades 5-8.
24. McCarthy, Eugene J. The Crescent Dictionary of American Politics. New York: Macmillan, 1963. 195 pp. Grades 6-9.
25. Morris, Richard. The First Book of the Constitution. New York: Watts, 1958. 69 pp. Grades 5-7.
26. Neal, Harry E. Diary of Democracy: The Story of Political Parties in America. New York: Messner, 1963. 191 pp. Grades 6-9.
27. Newman, Shirlee P. and Diana F. About People Who Run Your City. Chicago: Melmont, 1963. 48 pp. Grades 5-7.
28. Petersham, Maud and Miska. Story of the Presidents of the United States of America. New York: Macmillan, 1962. 80 pp. Grades 5-8.
29. Rosenfield, Bernard. Let's Go to the Capitol. New York: Putnam, 1959. 47 pp. Grades 5-7.
30. Rosenfield, Bernard. Let's Go to the U.S. Mint. New York: Putnam, 1960. 48 pp. Grades 5-8. A very detailed account of the Philadelphia mint.
31. Ross, George E. Know Your Government. New York: Rand, 1959. 72 pp. Grades 5-8.
32. Spingarn, Natalie D. To Save Your Life. Boston: Little, 1963. 213 pp. Grades 7-10. The work of the U.S. Public Health Service.
33. Urell, Catherine, and Elizabeth Vreeken. Big City Government. Chicago: Follett, 1957. 96 pp. Grades 4-6.
34. Weingast, David E. We Elect a President. New York: Messner, 1962. 190 pp. Grades 8-10.
35. Wolfe, Louis. Let's Go to a City Hall. New York: Putnam, 1958. 48 pp. Grades 4-7.

Teaching about the Constitution
and the Federal Government

One of the most difficult topics to teach in any course in civics or United States history is the Constitution and the power and functions of our federal government. This is especially true in dealing with students who are average or below average in either ability or motivation.

Often we try to teach too much; sometimes we teach solely with word symbols. Very often we analyze the Constitution section by section or even line by line. Perhaps this can be done successfully with superior students; it is not likely to stimulate interest or learning with average or slower students.

Here are a few suggestions and illustrations for teaching about the Constitution and the federal government to less than talented students.

1. Compare the forming of our government to the organization of a club and the Constitution to the club rules.

2. Compare the choice of governments that faced the colonists with the choice of roads that confront travelers.

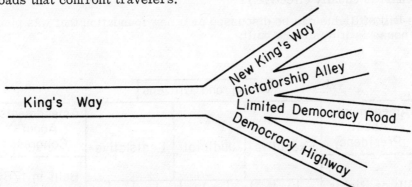

Many students will not realize that the colonists had any choice and that they chose the road of "limited democracy" for many years, before transferring to the broader road of "democracy." You may want to draw a narrow road marked "Democracy Road" that broadens later into a wide highway.

3. Read aloud excerpts from accounts of the Constitutional Convention. The personal accounts of the men present or the biographies of Franklin, Jefferson, and Madison illuminate the proceedings especially well.

4. Have the students discuss the preamble to the Constitution; then have them individually, or as a class, rewrite this section in their own words. Post their rewrites on the bulletin board, perhaps with names signed.

5. Role play a meeting of the Constitutional Convention. If it is to be well done, this exercise takes time, but the results justify the expense.

6. Have the students discuss the preamble to the Constitution. Then have small groups or committees prepare large murals on each phrase of it, such as "We the people . . . to form a more perfect union . . . establish justice . . . insure domestic tranquility . . . provide for the common defense . . . promote the general welfare." Hang the murals in the order they occur in the preamble and leave them on exhibit for several days or weeks.

7. Develop choral speaking on the preamble of the Constitution. Students who do not take part easily in discussion are likely to participate when they can join with others in a group recital.

8. Discuss with students why people often buy old houses rather than new ones, bringing out the fact that old houses often are structurally sound, needing only some interior changes, additions, and rearrangement of furniture to make them livable. Then discuss our Constitution as framed in 1789 as an "old house" that has lasted until today, with very few changes.

   To dramatize this analogy, draw a house with three rooms—for the President and his helpers, for the Senators and Representatives and their helpers, and for the Supreme Court Justices and their helpers. Add new rooms to represent the constitutional amendments, attaching them to the part of the house with which they dealt:

   Presidency: 12, 20, 22.
   Congress: 14, 17, 20.
   Citizenship and voting: 14, 15, 19, 23, 24.
   Economic and social issues: 13, 16, 19, 21. (The 11th amendment seems relatively unimportant for this purpose.)

   You can draw the changes on the chalkboard as shown below, or you can tape pieces of colored paper to the original house. (Of course, a flannelboard or chart is equally effective.)

   The Bill of Rights can be discussed as a new foundation that was placed under the house as it was being built:

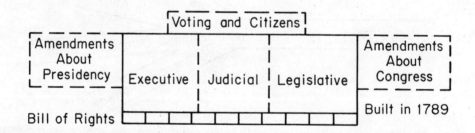

9. Consult with your audio-visual department on films and filmstrips to use with your study of the Constitution and the federal government.

10. Develop a diagram like the one below on the chalkboard or flannelboard showing the separation of powers between the states and federal government. If you use a flannelboard, you can show that the overlapping sections have changed from time to time.

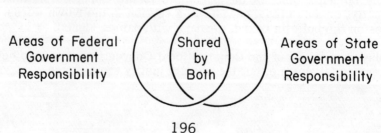

196

The Presidency

The Presidency of the United States is the biggest and most important job in the world today. As Richard E. Neustadt says in his book on Presidential Power, "His office has become the focal point of politics and policy in our political system." Moreover, it is also the focal point of most world politics today.

Every student in our secondary schools needs a detailed knowledge of the Presidency as a part of his preparation for effective citizenship. The particular aspects of the Presidency that should be emphasized must be determined by teachers according to the age level and abilities of their students and the scope of the course. Here are a few approaches to consider, according to the groups with which you are working:

1. THE POWERS OF THE PRESIDENT. This is probably the focus for most studies of the Presidency. For younger and less able students, you may want to present this theme in terms of the "different hats" the President wears. Remember, however, that the public expects him to "wear all of his hats at one and the same time in a manner superior to anyone else's," as Francis Heller points out. The chart below pictures the powers and duties of the President:

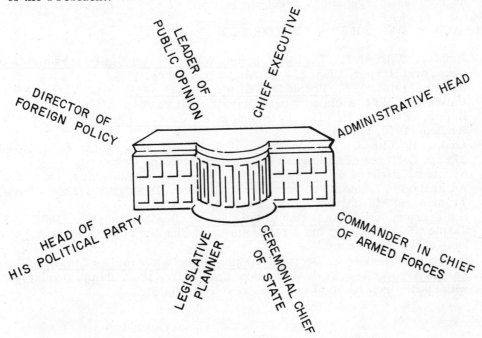

2. A DAY IN THE LIFE OF THE PRESIDENT. This method can be used with any students, but is especially satisfying with the younger and less able. A great deal of good material on former President Kennedy has been presented in this manner.

3. EARLY IDEAS ON THE PRESIDENCY. Some students should study in depth the dilemma of the colonists in developing the institution of the Presidency, examining, for instance, the idea that the Presidency was considered at first as an "elected monarchy," as Chancellor Kent describes it.

4. HOW THE PRESIDENT IS ELECTED. All students should certainly study the process by which a President is elected. This can be done with the most meaning in an election year, but it should not be left solely to that special time.

5. HOW THE PRESIDENCY HAS CHANGED. Through history, the Presidency has undergone many changes, especially in recent years. All students should know something of these changes; a few students should consider the specific changes created in the Acts of 1921, 1937, and more recent years.

6. PRESIDENTIAL HELPERS. All students should know something about the chief officers in the executive branch of the government; some students should study the problem of organization of this branch.

7. HOW THE PRESIDENT GATHERS INFORMATION AND OBTAINS COUNSEL. In varying degrees of depth, this aspect of the work of a President should be studied by all students.

8. AN EVALUATION OF OUR PRESIDENTS. Almost all students will enjoy "rating" our Presidents. In this connection, a recent poll of 75 historians will interest the students (see Schlesinger's Paths to the Present). Lincoln, Washington, Franklin Roosevelt, Wilson, and Jefferson ranked as the outstanding Presidents, in that order.

9. SUGGESTED CHANGES IN THE PRESIDENCY. All students should know about some of the suggested changes in the Presidency; some of them should analyze these suggestions in detail.

PAPERBACKS ON THE PRESIDENCY

1. Binkley, Wilfred E. The Man in the White House: His Powers and Duties. New York: Harper, 1958. 274 pp. Also a paperback, 1964.
2. Corwin, Edward S. President: Office and Powers. New York: New York University, 1964. A classic, but fairly difficult reading. 519 pp.
3. Heller, Francis H. The Presidency: A Modern Perspective. New York: Random, 1960. 114 pp.
4. Laski, Harold J. The American Presidency. New York: Grosset, 1940. 278 pp. Lectures of an English economist at Indiana University.
5. Neustadt, Richard E. Presidential Power. New York: Wiley, 1964. 219 pp. An analysis of how a President wins influence. Illustrations largely from the Truman and Eisenhower administrations.
6. Schlesinger, Arthur W. Paths to the Present. Boston: Houghton, 1964. 293 pp. Chapter 6 on "Rating the Presidents" and Chapter 7 on "Persisting Problems of the Presidency."
7. Sorensen, Theodore C. Decision-Making in the White House: The Olive Branch or the Arrow. New York: Columbia University, 1963. 94 pp. Decion making with special reference to the late President Kennedy.

Agencies of the Federal Government

Almost all textbooks, and probably most teachers, say that our federal government is composed of three branches – the executive, the legislative, and the judicial.

In one sense, that statement is true. Historically, it is certainly correct. But in another sense, our federal government today has four divisions or branches.

"The fourth branch of government" is a term that is increasingly used to describe federal bureaus, boards, agencies, commissions, and corporations. A few of the better known of these are the Atomic Energy Commission, the Bureau of the Budget, the Civil Aeronautics Board, the Federal Reserve System, the Interstate Commerce Commission, and the Veterans Administration.

Scores of other independent or semi-independent agencies have been created in recent years. In a manual about the federal government issued as an official document recently, 470 pages were devoted to administrative agencies and the general work of the executive branch as compared with 30 pages each to the legislative and judicial branches.

As John D. Weaver pointed out in his recent book on The Great Experiment, every citizen is affected directly or indirectly by some government agencies daily. Weaver says, "He (the average citizen) is involved with this 'fourth branch of government' whenever he picks up a phone, turns on a television set, pays a gas bill, buys a widely advertised headache remedy, entrusts his savings to a stockholder or his life to a plane, bus, or train." He could have added many more examples.

Many of these agencies are as large or larger than the departments that compose the President's Cabinet. Most of the boards and commissions – for example, the Federal Trade Commission, the Interstate Commerce Commission, and the Federal Communications Commission – are charged with regulating some aspect of our economic life. Some were set up by Congress; others have been established by the President.

In many, the President appoints the head or heads of the agencies with the consent of the Senate. And often this chairman cannot be removed from office until his term expires.

Most of the bureaus, commissions, or agencies are either independent or semi-independent. Some are really publicly owned corporations, controlled by a board of directors. Other groups are headed by a single individual.

Although most agencies are connected with the executive branch and are often described as executive agencies, many perform functions that are legislative or judicial in nature. They may make rules or regulations interpreting statutes and thus become quasi-legislative agencies. They may also hand down decisions and impose penalties, thus becoming quasi-judicial.

Historically, this proliferation of our government began with the establishment of the Interstate Commerce Commission by act of Congress in 1877, based upon the "commerce" clause (Art. I, Section 8, paragraph 3) of the Constitution. Under President Wilson, the Federal Trade Commission and the Federal Power Commission were established. The New Deal set up the Securities and Exchange Commission, the Civil Aeronautics Board, and the National Labor Relations Board as well as many more. In more recent years, scores of other independent agencies have been created.

Among the most important agencies working directly with the President today are these:

Bureau of the Budget
Central Intelligence Agency
National Security Council

Council of Economic Advisers
National Aeronautics and Space
   Council

The more independent agencies include:

Atomic Energy Commission
Civil Aeronautics Board
Farm Credit Administration
Federal Communications
   Commission
Federal Deposit Insurance
   Corporation
Federal Reserve System

Federal Trade Commission
Interstate Commerce Commission
National Labor Relations Board
National Science Foundation
Securities and Exchange Commission
Selective Service Commission
U. S. Civil Service Commission
Veterans Administration

Students should be urged to read about and discuss the importance of these independent agencies. You may want to discuss their place in our present government, the reasons for their rise, and some of their work. Point out the need for coordination between agencies and the recommendations of the Hoover Commission and other more recent bodies to that end.

You may also want to encourage students to explore the work of some bureau, agency, commission, or corporation in detail. Brief resumés of their findings may then be given to the other students.

You may be interested in exploring some of the general suggestions as to ways in which to gear these organizations into the general framework of the three branches of federal government.

Congress

Almost everyone agrees that a study of Congress should be one of the central topics of any course in civics or government and a basic part of any course in United States history. But everyone does not agree upon how these studies should be taught.

This writer contends that studies of Congress are often worthless to prospective citizens because they stress structure rather than function and emphasize theory rather than practice.

It is difficult to balance theory and practice, but one should try to do it. Students need to know how the Constitution defines the powers of Congress, but they also need to know how the lines separating congressional and presidential powers have blurred in recent years. They need to know how Senators and Representatives are elected, but they also need to recognize the place of seniority in Congress as it affects power in both houses.

If your class studies Congress while the House and Senate are in session, textbook material can be blended with information from current newspapers and magazines. When students can trace a current bill from its introduction to its finalization as law, they learn a great deal about a working legislature.

Your class is likely to have a realistic view of Congress if the students can be divided into "the Senate" and "the House" and then divided again to represent the committees of each house. As they organize themselves and discuss the real issues before the current Congress, they are likely to learn both the theory and the practices of our legislature.

After using one or all of these teaching techniques, you can take your class back into history to see how the founders of our republic decided on the powers and functions of Congress. Describe how those powers and functions have changed through the years. Two examples of change are the Senate's growth in power as the United States has become more and more involved in world affairs; and the House's swing from primarily representing rural and small town areas to its present urban-suburban representation.

1. THE POWERS AND DUTIES OF THE HOUSE AND SENATE. As stated in the Constitution and as developed over a long period of time.

2. RELATIONS WITH PRESIDENTS AND THE SUPREME COURT. With emphasis upon the shifts of power among the three branches of government, depending upon the period of history and the relative strength of the three branches at any given time.

3. THE ORGANIZATION OF THE SENATE AND THE HOUSE.

4. THE CONCEPT OF CONGRESS AS THE FOUNDERS OF OUR REPUBLIC SAW IT.

5. THE IMPORTANT ROLE OF COMMITTEES IN THE HOUSE AND SENATE, emphasizing a few central, important committees like the powerful Rules Committee in the House.

201

6. "CONTROL" BY SPEAKERS OF THE HOUSE AND A FEW CONGRESSMEN, stressing the role of seniority and its effect upon influence in the House and Senate. See, for example, "Nine Men Who Control Congress" (Atlantic Monthly, April 1964).

7. THE POWER OF LOBBIES.

8. CONGRESSIONAL HELPERS, with special reference to the research done for Congressmen.

9. CONGRESSIONAL INVESTIGATIONS.

10. HOW BILLS ARE INTRODUCED AND HOW THEY DEVELOP, showing that only a very limited number of bills, out of the thousands introduced, actually are passed.

12. SOME SUGGESTED REFORMS OF CONGRESS, including four-year terms for Representatives, modification of the seniority rule and the filibuster, retirement at full pay at the age of 70, etc. (See the American Assembly's volume on The Congress and America's Future, Columbia University Press.)

A SELECTED BIBLIOGRAPHY ON CONGRESS

1. Berman, D. M. In Congress Assembled. New York: Macmillan, 1964. 432 pp.
2. Binkley, Wilfred E. The President and the Congress. New York: Knopf, 1962. 403 pp.
3. Bolling, Richard. House Out of Order. New York: Dutton, 1965. 253 pp. A Representative from Missouri comments on the House, with special reference to needed reforms.
4. Clapp, Charles L. The Congressman: His Work as He Sees It. Washington: Brookings Institution, 1964. 452 pp. Discussions of a cross section of 36 members of Congress evaluating their experiences.
5. Clark, Joseph S. Congress: The Sapless Branch. New York: Harper, 1964. 268 pp. Emphasizes suggestions for reform.
6. Drury, Allen. A Senate Journal: 1943-1945. New York: McGraw-Hill, 1963. 489 pp. The human drama of the Senate by a veteran Washington correspondent, the author of Advise and Consent.
7. MacNeil, Neil. Forge of Democracy. New York: McKay, 1963. 496 pp. Some of the dramatic decisions made in the Congress since Washington's time. More favorable in its treatment of the House than some of the other books.
8. Mathews, Donald R. U.S. Senators and Their World. Chapel Hill, N.C.: 1960. Also a Vintage paperback. 303 pp.
9. White, William S. Citadel: The Story of the U.S. Senate. New York: Harper, 1957. 274 pp.
10. White, William S. Home Place: The Story of the U.S. House of Representatives. Boston: Houghton, 1965. 175 pp. A popular account, fairly well balanced.

SOCIAL STUDIES BACKGROUND PAPER
NO. 102
FILE: GOVERNMENT, CIVICS, OR U.S.
HISTORY

Considering Bills in Congress

At some point in high school every student should be confronted with the study of how bills are considered in Congress. This process is essential to the general knowledge of all citizens in a democracy.

Students are likely to remember the steps of this process best if they actually take part in tracing a bill's progress through Congress. Probably the best way to clinch this learning is to have students role play the consideration of a bill. Do not assume that students, even those in honors class, will find this easy, but they will all find it worthwhile.

Students in bright classes can prepare a bill as homework, selecting a topic they think important and one in which they are interested. Or, have them prepare a letter to a Congressman or Senator, suggesting legislation about a certain problem. In classes of less able students, you should select a topic and write the suggested bill together in the classroom. This is a good time to discuss how bills or ideas for bills originate: the work of organizations, the ideas of individual citizens, the reports of committees, the thinking of Representatives and Senators, and the suggestions of the President or other members of the executive branch.

Our classroom bill should then be marked S or HR to represent the part of Congress in which it originates. Remember that theoretically revenue bills originate only in the House; in actual practice, only <u>appropriation</u> bills (not <u>authorization</u> measures) originate exclusively in the House.

The class can then be assigned roles. Don't take the time to let students select their own roles. A small part of the class should represent the Senate. A larger part should act as the House of Representatives. A few students may play the roles of interested citizens, members of pressure groups, and members of the executive branch. You may want to play the role of the President or, perhaps, you could ask a student to do this.

One student should then present the bill; it should be read and referred to the proper committee. A few students representing that committee may meet briefly in the front of the room in order to show the importance of this part of the work. Two or three citizens or members of pressure groups may appear before the committee. A vote can then be taken in the committee. Play the situation first of the bill's defeat; then replay the vote so that the bill passes and is returned to the house of Congress where it originated.

Discuss the bill briefly on the floor of that chamber. You can have the bill rejected, in order to illustrate what happens in that situation, and then replay the vote to have it passed and sent to the other house.

Go through the same procedure again with the second house.

As you go, trace these various steps: actually pass the piece of paper with S or HR on it from the deliberative body to the committee, back to the lawmaking body, and then on to the other house of Congress. Seeing this process and handling the bill fixes the process in students' minds and helps them remember it.

You may want to have a joint committee of the Senate and House rewrite minor parts of the bill in order to show this revision process.

A "clerk" should then take the bill to the White House. You, or the student playing the role of the President, can think out loud about whether or not to sign the bill, perhaps giving the reasons.

Probably you will want to sign the bill first, because signing it demonstrates the easiest process.

Then replay the situation and veto the bill to show how Congress either upholds or overrides a Presidential veto.

Finally, perhaps the next day, review the entire process on the chalkboard, giving students a chance to take notes on a pictorial representation.

You may want to point out that a similar process takes place in state legislatures, except in Nebraska where the one-house legislature simplifies the procedure.

The Supreme Court:
Today and Yesterday

In the early days of our republic, the Supreme Court was considered so insignificant that men like Alexander Hamilton and Patrick Henry refused to serve on it and men like Chief Justices John Jay and Oliver Ellsworth resigned after short periods of service.

Throughout much of our history, the Supreme Court has been a staid body of judges with relatively little power or a group that did not exercise the power it possessed. Of course, this was not true under the leadership of men like John Marshall and Roger Taney who made the Court a center of controversy—a history shattering and a history making body.

Today, the Supreme Court is again a storm center. It is interpreting its powers broadly rather than narrowly. It is leading rather than following the trends of the times. It is expanding its power, moving into new fields, tackling basic economic, social, and political issues. Its impact upon our society is tremendous. Here are a few of the areas in which its decisions are fortifying liberal movements in the United States.

1. In the field of education, the 1954 decision on segregated schools has caused radical shifts in some parts of the country already and will undoubtedly call for changes in other sections eventually.

2. Its directive to the state legislatures that they must henceforth select members of both houses on the basis of population has broken the traditional hold of rural areas and has given urban areas control in many states—a larger share in state governments elsewhere.

3. In antitrust cases, the Court has strengthened the government's hand in extending the scope of antitrust laws.

4. On freedom of the press, by passing on the legality of a Kansas law permitting book seizure on grounds of obscenity and on an Ohio case involving obscenity in a French film. Thus the Supreme Court has broadened the interpretations of freedom of the press.

5. In several civil-rights cases, the Court has strengthened the case for civil rights, directing the Alabama Supreme Court to take all steps necessary for the operation of the National Association for the Advancement of Colored People in that state and clearing persons convicted for trespassing in privately owned segregated restaurants.

6. It has widened the provisions of the Fifth Amendment by extending its protection into state and local courts, permitting individuals to refuse to testify against themselves on grounds of self-incrimination.

7. It has protected individuals further by stating that states should provide free lawyers for all indigent defendants rather than just those in exceptional circumstances.

8. It has reaffirmed the separation of state and church by ruling against officially prepared prayers and required reading from the Bible. This decision has changed the practices in hundreds of schools.

9. It has ruled against misleading advertising, thus fortifying the hand of several governmental bodies in examining the truthfulness of radio and television advertisements.

These and other leading decisions of the Supreme Court are making history. They are changing our society, shaping a future for this country that is different from its present; therefore, they should be discussed in high school social studies classes, whatever the course name. Current court decisions should be related, too, to the powers of other branches of government and should be placed in the framework of the Court's history.

It is important that you deal with the explosive ideas of today's Court decisions as calmly and objectively as possible. These are issues that require more light than heat—an emphasis that is not always possible with adult citizens and that is not always predominant in the press.

Students should learn about the Justices themselves—as human beings and as judges. They should learn both the arguments in favor of recent Supreme Court decisions and the arguments against them. In some cases, at least, they should read excerpts from the arguments presented to the Court and the majority and minority opinions. They may be encouraged to interview local persons who have studied some of these decisions. They may even role play one or more of the cases after studying them in depth.

All this is a part of the realistic preparation for citizenship in our democracy. It is an essential part of education for democracy.

SOME PAPERBACKS ON THE SUPREME COURT

1. Abraham, Henry J. The Judicial Process. New York: Oxford University Press, 1962. 381 pp.
2. Freund, Paul A. The Supreme Court of the United States: Its Business, Purposes, and Performance. Cleveland: World, 1962. 224 pp.
3. Jackson, Robert H. The Struggle for Judicial Supremacy: A Study of a Crisis in American Power Politics. New York: Random, 1962. 353 pp.
4. James, Leonard F. The Supreme Court in American Life. Chicago: Scott, 1964. 159 pp.
5. Konefsky, Samuel J. The Legacy of Holmes and Brandeis: A Study in the Influence of Ideas. New York: Collier, 1961. 288 pp.
6. McCloskey, Robert G. The American Supreme Court. Chicago: University of Chicago Press, 1960. 260 pp.
7. Westin, Alan F., ed. The Supreme Court: Views from Inside. New York: Norton, 1961. 192 pp. Source materials.

FILMSTRIP ON THE SUPREME COURT

"The Supreme Court: Justice under Law." New York Times. Black and white. 55 frames.

The Urban Revolution

The headlines fairly scream! "Boy Stabs Girl in Subway...Sees Summer Water Shortage... Building Collapses; Twenty Killed...Tax Increases Seen Inevitable...Double Session for Schools...Suburban Trains May Terminate...Smog Covers City Again."

In smaller type, the inside pages carry more optimistic reports: "Federal Government Grants More Aid...Campus Plan Proposals Aired...Sales Tax Gains Reported...Urban Renewal Plan Gains...Cultural Center First Concert...New Housing Plans Proposed."

People read the screaming headlines and ask, "What is happening to our city?" Fewer people read and comment about the less spectacular news of changes and gains in sprawling metropolitan centers.

But the social studies teacher needs to keep both sides of the coin in mind when presenting one of the most pressing, confusing, and challenging issues of our times — the revolution in our cities.

Many of our large cities are barely holding their own in population. Some cities, such as Chicago and New York, are actually losing population within the city limits. But that is only part of the story, for as the stampede to the suburbs continues, the urban sprawl widens.

Cities are no longer limited to their political boundaries. They spread out for miles, sometimes into other states. And cities that were once separated by miles are now connected as parts of a larger metropolitan area, which Jean Gottman has called "megalopolis." There are many examples of these metropolitan areas — the 17 million people in the Greater New York area, the giant city that stretches from Boston to Norfolk, the Los Angeles-San Diego complex, the Chicago-Milwaukee-strip city, and the Pittsburgh-Youngstown-Canton-Akron-Cleveland megalopolis. Every day an estimated 3000 acres of country is bulldozed and transformed into suburbs. And this process will continue for years to come, sustained by the population explosion and the "push" and "pull" of the cities and adjacent areas.

These changes multiply the basic problems of city government. Inadequate facilities are overcrowded and new facilities are badly needed, yet tax revenues often decrease because industries have fled and residents have stampeded to the suburbs. The increased need for government assistance by the groups who remain in the city puts additional strain on city finances. Municipal problems are compounded by the overlapping and often ill-defined maze of governments within a metropolitan area. In the New York metropolitan area, for example, there are 1400 separate units of government. No wonder people refer to this as the "urban jungle."

Among the cities' biggest problems today are the following: housing, transportation, schools, water, safety and health, recreational facilities, minority-majority group relations, and fiscal solvency.

Problems are apparent and easy to pinpoint. Solutions are more intricate. Here is a thumb-nail sketch of the general proposals made by Senator Clark of Pennsylvania for all cities: (1) better schools, (2) reorganization of local governments, (3) break-up of local political machines, (4) taxes based on income instead of primarily on real estate, (5) isolation of problems by civic leaders and government officials and joint work on their solution, (6) urban renewal plans, (7) master transit plans, (8) safeguarding water supplies, and (9) honestly facing the question of race relations.

Luther Gulick, a long-time expert on city governments, has suggested four alternatives on the more specific problem of governmental arrangements for the new metropolitan areas as follows: (1) creation in each state of a Department of Local Affairs; (2) reconstruction of county governments so that they include an entire metropolitan area; (3) creation of a new, limited-purpose state agency for metropolitan problems of planning, land use, and transportation; or (4) development of a new layer of governments between the present city governments and states, to be called "metropolitan councils."

Other leaders propose more federal aid and the establishment of a Cabinet office on urban affairs, federal control or ownership of railroads, accelerated emphasis on metropolitan area planning, and the hiring of more city managers and others trained in public administration.

Some students may think all these suggestions are "pipe dreams." They are not. The new governmental set-up in Dade County, Florida, and in Toronto, Canada, the interstate agencies (like the Port Authority in New York and the transit plans of San Francisco and Philadelphia), and scores of similar advances made in recent years, prove that progress is possible.

Here are a few books that should help you and your students investigate the problems and progress of today's cities.

1. Christensen, David E. Urban Development. New York: Holt, 1964. 95 pp. A pamphlet for students in the American Problems series. Compact.
2. Editors of Fortune. The Exploding Metropolis. New York: Doubleday, 1958. 177 pp.
3. Elias, C. E., Jr., and others. Metropolis: Values in Conflict. Belmont, Calif.: Wadsworth, 1964. 326 pp. A series of articles.
4. Fiser, Webb S. Mastery of the Metropolis. Englewood Cliffs, N.J.: Prentice-Hall, 1962. 168 pp.
5. Geen, Elizabeth, and others. Man and the Modern City. Pittsburg: University of Pittsburgh Press, 1963. 134 pp.
6. Hoover, Edgar M. and Raymond Vernon. Anatomy of a Metropolis. New York: Doubleday, 1962. 338 pp.
7. MacKaye, Benton. The New Exploration: A Philosophy of Regional Planning. Urbana, Ill.: University of Illinois Press, 1962. 243 pp.
8. Munzer, Martha E. Planning Our Town: An Introduction to City and Regional Planning. New York: Knopf, 1964. 179 pp. For secondary school students.
9. Vernon, Raymond. Metropolis: 1985. New York: Doubleday, 1960. 319 pp. On the New York city area.
10. Wood, Robert C. 1400 Governments. New York: Doubleday, 1961. 297 pp. On governments in the New York metropolitan area.

Council-Manager Governments

Slowly, but consistently, the council-manager form of government is gaining favor in the United States and Canada. By 1965, over 2000 cities and counties in those two countries had that form of local government. And each year, for the past several years, an average of 75 new localities have joined the list of council-manager governments. Today over 40 million persons in the United States and Canada live under this relatively new form of local administration.

Of the total of 2027 cities and counties with the council-manager form of government in 1965, 73 were in Canada, one was in Puerto Rico, 32 were county units, and the remaining 1921 were cities in the United States.

Although many small towns have council-manager administration, this movement has grown strongest in the larger towns and cities. Today, council-managers run more than half of the cities of over 25,000 and 40 per cent of those over 10,000.

Council-manager governments are located in almost every state, but they are especially popular in these states: California has 250; Texas comes next with 161; Michigan follows with 150; next are Maine with 147, Pennsylvania with 134, Florida with 100, and Virginia with 80.

This movement is not confined to the United States and Canada. Over 1700 communities in Finland, West Germany, Ireland, Norway, and Sweden have council-manager governments.

The reasons for the growth of this form of government are varied and differ from locality to locality. In the main, however, they have appeared because of the growth of cities and the complexity of administration. The management of a city or a county today is a much more complex task than it was formerly; it takes more training and experience than it formerly did. A mayor can no longer work part time at his community job and part time at his vocation. The same is true of councilmen. In many places, the council-manager form of local government was introduced when graft and corruption were revealed and citizens' groups demanded a more honest and efficient type of government.

Historically, the council-manager form of government began around the turn of the century. After the tidal wave in Galveston, Texas, in 1901, the commission plan of government was introduced to insure "more business in government." The Galveston government was said to be analogous to a business corporation—the citizens representing the stockholders—the elected commission, the board of directors. For a time, that form of government was popular. Citizens soon discovered, however, that the men they elected as commissioners were not necessarily qualified to run technical departments. Furthermore, since the commissioners ran the government as a group, there was no centralized administration.

Consequently, the council-manager form of government developed. Some claim that the first city to use this form was Staunton, Virginia; others give the credit to Sumter, South Carolina. The first large city to adopt the plan was Dayton, Ohio, following a devastating flood in 1913.

As the hyphenated title of this paper indicates, there are two major parts to this relatively new form of local government. The council is an elected body, thus the people share directly in their own choice of representatives. (In the majority of cities and counties, council members are now selected on a nonpartisan ballot.) Those elected representatives then hire a city manager. The city manager is usually chosen from another part of the country (so that he is not involved in local politics) and usually serves for an unlimited term.

Who are the men ordinarily selected as city managers? Like men in other jobs, they represent a wide variety of human beings. Usually, they are men who have had some government experience previous to their selection as city managers. Most of them are college graduates and many have advanced degrees. Ordinarily they are quite young. At the present time, the city managers in cities of 25,000 or less are in their 30s; those in cities of 25,000 and over are usually in their 40s.

Increasingly, city managers are men who have studied public administration in college or in graduate school. They have then served an internship in government just as a doctor serves an internship in a hospital. Several colleges and universities now specialize in public administration, including the training of city managers. Among these are the University of Pennsylvania, the University of Southern California, Syracuse University, New York University, and the state universities of Kansas, Michigan, Minnesota, and California (Berkeley and Los Angeles).

In evaluating candidates for city-manager appointments, councils usually look for an interest in good government and the courage to work for it; the ability to analyze priorities among local needs; the initiative to develop new ideas and approaches; organizational leadership; a sense of public relations; honesty; and technical proficiency.

Originally, city managers were often engineers by training, but today's cities demand broader training in the man who must cope with a variety of problems.

Students in social studies classes in our secondary schools should be conversant with the different forms of city government now in existence in our country and should examine analytically the rise of the council-manager form of government. In order to help teachers and students, two organizations provide both free and inexpensive materials on this movement.

The International City Managers' Association, 1313 East 60th Street, Chicago, Ill. 60637.
The National Municipal League, 47 East 68th Street, New York, N.Y. 10021.

Studying Any Community

Sometime during high school, most students take a course in civics or government. Usually this course if given in the 7th or 9th grades, although the placement differs from school system to school system. Such courses usually study the local community. Sometimes the students also study other communities in the United States or in foreign countries.

Students will gain more from a study of their community if it is organized around a few concepts or features common to all communities. The chart below suggests some of those "basics."

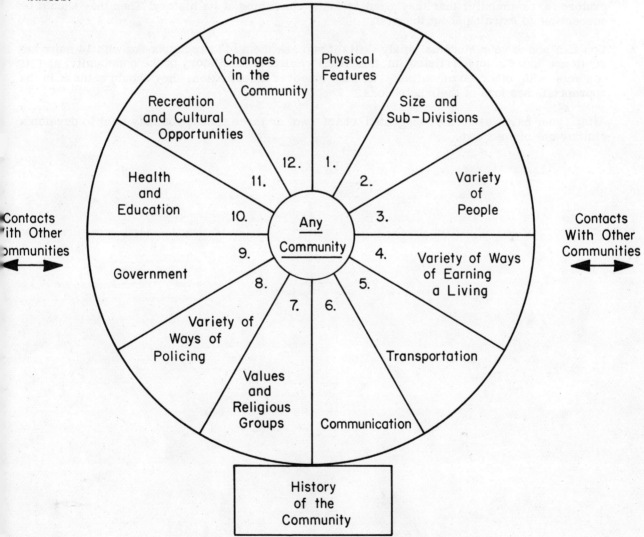

It should be helpful to students to have a large reproduction of this chart posted somewhere in the classroom where it can be seen by everyone in the class. If it is used frequently, students will actually learn the basic concepts therein, instead of merely memorizing the words.

Although you may not want to be bound by this chart and follow it point by point, it might serve as a general outline for studying your own or other communities.

Wherever possible, students should discover the relationships between the segments of this chart. For example, the physical features of your community affect its size and shape, the ways of earning a living, the transportation, the communication, and possibly other features.

Similarly, the values and religious groups in the community may help to determine the ways of living in your community and others.

As you explore the subject, you will undoubtedly find many more relationships or inter-relationships.

It is sound teaching practice (from a psychological rather than a logical standpoint) to begin studying your local community as it now exists. Because students recognize the present-day aspects of their hometown, they find it an exciting topic. They will find, however, as they explore a community, that they need to know something of its history. Then they should be susceptible to learning about the past.

You can add to your students' study skills if you ask them to keep notebooks with 14 separate sections: the 12 topics listed in the chart's circle, the history of the community, and its contacts with other communities. As they discover information, they should enter it in the appropriate sections of their notebooks.

After you have used the suggested chart two or three times, you may want to develop a similar one of your own.

Governments and Economies
of the World

In almost any high school social studies course, students need to wrestle with the topics of governments and economies in different parts of the world and in different periods of history. These two topics are interrelated and are highly important to an understanding of any place or any period.

Many students find the topics difficult. The difficulties may arise from misuse of terms or from the shades of differences between various forms of government and economy. Or perhaps students find it hard to accept governmental organization that is foreign to them, because they have been taught only the framework of their own.

Students should learn that over the centuries men have organized their societies in different ways in order to achieve what they considered "the good life." They have settled upon particular forms of economy and government because of their history, their religion, their geography and other factors. And your students must realize that the why of that structure is just as important as its what or how.

The basic concepts of government and economy are so complicated that they cannot be dealt with adequately in one or two lessons. They need to be examined several times in the hope that meaningful repetition will bring about better learning. Therefore, a unit of a few days duration is the most helpful approach to these two themes.

In discussing forms of government and economy, teachers will find visualizations extremely helpful. Although visual aids do not guarantee understanding, they are likely to promote learning.

Here are two simple diagrams that may be useful to you in teaching about governments and economies around the world. You may want to change the descriptive terms in the charts or rearrange the order of the categories, but the basic plans should help you and your students.

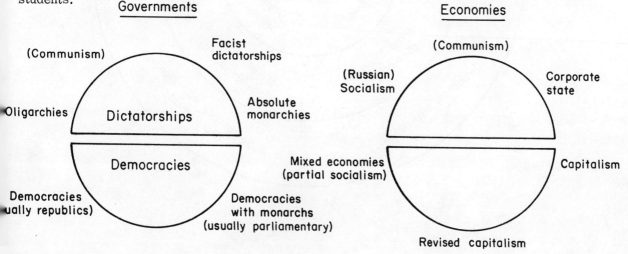

The term "communism" appears in parentheses on both charts on the previous page because there is actually no communist government or communist economy, in the correct sense of those terms, in the world today. The Russian economy is actually socialistic; the government is at least a partial dictatorship. Students who have heard the term "communist" bandied about will find this difficult to believe, but they should discover the difference between complete communism and the present setup in the U.S.S.R.

The suggestions presented in this Background Paper do not imply our approval of all these different economies or forms of government. Nor do they suggest that we want to adopt them for ourselves. But they do indicate the variety of economies and governments in the world today and yesterday. Students should learn how our own concepts of democracy and of capitalism have changed over the period of our national history. They should discover, too, that democracy and capitalism take different forms today in Great Britain, Sweden, and the United States. They should also delve into some of the reasons for the development of "mixed economies" (or "partnership economies" as some countries call them) in most of today's nations.

Perhaps the following chart, which combines forms of government with forms of economies, will be useful to you and your students. It might be copied and hung on the wall of your class-room, with whatever variations you want to make. If possible, the various circles should be made on separate pieces of different-colored cardboard so they can turn. By manipulating the circles, students can learn which forms of government and economy belong to each of the countries included on the chart.

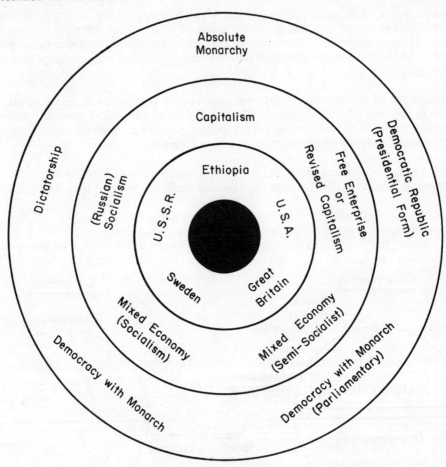

Arms Control and Disarmament

Would you like to be alive tomorrow—a year from now—ten years from now—fifty years from now? Would you like to enjoy a higher standard of living, made possible by drastic cuts in federal expenses for defense and wars?

These are basic questions that should be asked of all students during their secondary school days. With missiles capable of killing millions of persons within minutes after they are launched and with bacteriological and chemical warfare strong possibilities in the future, war is Public Enemy Number One in today's world.

Survival is the first question we have to solve; therefore, arms control or disarmament becomes the most crucial problem of the people on our planet. Every student needs to confront it, needs time and materials to study it in depth. Certainly no topic in the entire social studies program cries out for a more searching examination or for better critical thinking.

Here are some key questions you may want to consider as the basis of your study of arms control. They are merely suggestions. The urgency of the topic suggests that each class should work out an individualized list.

1. What is the nature of war today? What weapons are now available? What weapons are possibilities in the near future?
2. What nations have the most powerful weapons today? What nations may have them within a short time?
3. How do these facts alter past thinking about wars and international relations?
4. What is meant by "arms control"? By "disarmament"?
5. Why are the people of the world all concerned with arms control, even though they differ drastically in their suggestions for controlling arms?
6. How does the problem of arms control affect you, your family, and your friends?
7. What percentage of our national budget goes for defense and wars—past, present, and future—including interest on debts incurred by wars, defense, and veterans' payments?
8. What discussions have been going on for years regarding arms control and disarmament?
9. On what areas have agreements been reached? Why?
10. On what areas have agreements not been reached? What are the differing points of view on these disagreements?
11. Why is inspection considered by some as the crux of arms control? Why do others think that inspection is no longer the major issue in disagreements?
12. What proposals beyond the nuclear test ban treaty are now being considered for further arms control?
13. How would drastic arms control affect the American economy? What suggestions have been made for a transition to a peacetime economy?
14. What can you do about this Number One problem of the world?

BIBLIOGRAPHIES ON DISARMAMENT

"Focus on Arms Control and Disarmament." Special issue of Intercom for February-March 1962. New York: Foreign Policy Association. 72 pp.

Miller, William R. Bibliography of Books on War, Pacifism, Nonviolence and Related Studies. Nyack, N.Y.: Fellowship of Reconciliation, 1961. 37 pp.

SOME PAMPHLET MATERIALS ON DISARMAMENT

1. Arms Control and Disarmament. Washington: Government Printing Office, 1963. 38 pp. A speech by the late President Kennedy.
2. Current History. Special issues: June 1964, "Disarmament in Perspective"; July 1964, "Weapons Control Today"; and August 1964, "The U.S. and Weapons Control."
3. Duvall, Sylvanus M. War and Human Nature. New York: Public Affairs Committee, 1947. 31 pp. A statement based on the findings of psychologists.
4. Economic and Social Consequences of Disarmament. New York: United Nations, 1962. 66 pp.
5. Economic Impacts of Disarmament. Washington: Government Printing Office, 1962. 28 pp.
6. Finkelstein, Lawrence S. Arms Inspection. New York: Carnegie Endowment, 1962. 89 pp.
7. Holmes, Henry W. What About War? Medford, Mass.: Civic Education Center, 1957. 96 pp. Written for secondary school students.
8. Inglis, David R. Testing and Taming of Nuclear Weapons. New York: Public Affairs Committee, 1960. 28 pp.
9. McClelland, Charles A. Nuclear Weapons: Missiles and Future War: Problem for the Sixties. San Francisco: Chandler, 1960. 235 pp.
10. Mehlman, Seymour, ed. "Disarmament: Its Politics and Economics." Special issue of Daedalus magazine, 1962.
11. Millis, Walter, and others. A World Without War. New York: Washington Square, 1961. 182 pp. A paperback.
12. Nogee, Joseph. The Diplomacy of Disarmament. New York: Carnegie Endowment, 1960. 68 pp.
13. Spingarn, Jerome. Is Disarmament Possible? New York: Public Affairs Committee, 1956. 28 pp.
14. Watson, Mark S. The U.S. and Armaments. New York: Foreign Policy Association, 1960. 63 pp.

ADDRESSES OF ORGANIZATIONS

Since the topic of arms control or disarmament is so current, you will want to write to several organizations, such as the following, for up-to-date references.

1. American Friends Service Committee, 160 North 15th St., Philadelphia 2, Pa.
2. Arms Control and Disarmament Agency and the Department of State, Office of Media Services, U.S. Department of State, Washington 25, D.C.
3. Committee for World Development and World Disarmament, 345 East 46th St., New York 17, N.Y.
4. Government Printing Office, Washington 25, D.C.
5. Public Affairs Committee, 22 East 38th Street, New York 16, N.Y.
6. National Committee for a Sane Nuclear Policy, 17 East 45th St., New York 17, N.Y.
7. Woodrow Wilson Foundation, 45 East 65th Street, New York 21, N.Y.

Poverty as a World Problem

As social studies teachers, we try to avoid glittering generalities and sweeping generalizations—and train our students to avoid these, too. However, we do want to concentrate on some important, realistic, broad concepts or big ideas. Perhaps the most important of these on a global scale is the existence today of poverty.

Students cannot understand the world's revolutionary movements today unless they know something of today's world poverty. They cannot understand communism's appeal to many people unless they appreciate those people's despair. They cannot appreciate the hunger for education unless they recognize the hope it offers. They cannot grasp the importance of foreign aid unless they concede the importance of impoverished masses. And they can never sense the true feelings of other countries toward the United States until they relate our standard of living to standards of life abroad.

There are four levels for students to achieve in understanding poverty. An intellectual understanding of the facts of poverty is a start. An awareness of poverty's implications upon economic, social, and political affairs is another. An emotional identification with the people of the world who suffer from poverty is a third. Finally, students should find the level of personal, positive action upon which they can help fight poverty. Students may not reach the four levels in this order, but, with help, they will achieve them all. Intellectual understanding without the others is of little value; it may even be dangerous.

What, then are the major concepts about poverty that we must teach at any level in secondary schools—in every subject field in the social studies? Here are a few suggestions. You will want to assess them and see how you can implement them in your courses.

1. MOST OF THE WORLD'S PEOPLES ARE POOR. Two-thirds of the world's people live below the subsistence level of decent living. They live in mud or thatch huts, eat poor food and little of it. They have no medical care. They have little or no education. Their children have only a small chance of surviving beyond the first year of life. Their life expectancy is a little over 30 years.

    Because these people are poor, they are ill-fed, ill-housed, ill-clothed, illiterate, and ill.

2. THE RICH NATIONS ARE GETTING RICHER AND THE POOR POORER. Despite many efforts to close the gap between the rich nations of the world and the poor, the gap is widening.

3. THE DISPARITY IN INCOMES IS A MAJOR SOURCE OF UNREST IN THE WORLD. There was a time when large parts of the world either did not want much more than they had or felt that it was impossible to get it. Today, they are clamoring for a higher standard of living and more of the good things of life. Moreover, they are demanding that governments improve the basic conditions of life and are toppling those that do not. This is apparent all over the world in Asia, Africa, Europe, the Middle East, and Latin America.

4. POVERTY ARISES FROM MANY CAUSES. Consider these with students and add others.
   a. Countries are not equally endowed with resources.
   b. Some nations are controlled by persons who want the status quo. They are opposed to changes that would improve the lot of millions of their countrymen, and will resort to almost any strategem to avoid changes.
   c. Some religious and philosophical points of view have opposed the major changes that most people call "progress."
   d. Capital is lacking for industrialization, and outside capital has not helped the common man.
   e. People have not been educated well enough to bring about change and to provide the leadership needed within their countries.
   f. Colonial powers have exploited both the natural resources and the people in their possessions.
   g. Revolutions and wars have caused dislocations of people and destroyed land and property. Both of these facts have forced people to become refugees.
   h. Overpopulation in relation to food and other resources has caused much misery. Overpopulation by itself is not the chief factor.
   i. Foreign aid has been used primarily for military purposes, rather than to raise the standard of living.

5. AID IS BEING GIVEN TO IMPROVE CONDITIONS. Sources of this aid vary: private groups—from churches to lay organizations; local and national governments; the United Nations and its agencies; so-called "foreign aid"— a large amount from the United States and, in recent years, from the U.S.S.R.; groups of nations—the Colombo Plan of the Commonwealth of Nations for South and Southeast Asia, for example.

6. MUCH REMAINS TO BE DONE: WE CAN HELP. The needs are staggering, even with the aid mentioned above. What can an individual do?
   a. Examine the foreign aid program of the United States and seek to strengthen it in helping people to help themselves.
   b. Examine organizations promoting better standards of living and greater freedom. Join or assist one or more of these groups.
   c. Work with a group—a school, a church, or a club—on some relief or rehabilitation project.
   d. Be informed on the world's poverty and help inform others, avoiding preaching and fanaticism.
   e. Prepare for work with some group abroad—work camps, Peace Corps, Teachers for East Africa, Crossroads Africa, and many others.
   f. Consider some kind of work abroad as a lifetime goal.

Teaching about Poverty
as a World Problem

There are many ways in which you can help students explore the problem of poverty around the world. Here are a few of them.

1. Prepare a large chart like the one below of the annual income of persons in various parts of the world. Discuss how these people earn a living, what housing, medical help, and other necessities of life they can afford.

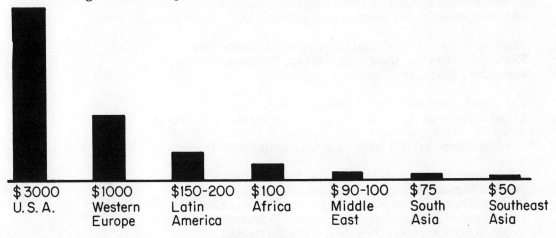

| $3000 U.S.A. | $1000 Western Europe | $150-200 Latin America | $100 Africa | $90-100 Middle East | $75 South Asia | $50 Southeast Asia |

2. Ask each student to make a budget for a family of six living in one of these areas. This is probably the best way to realize what it means to live as most of the world lives. Remind students that the figures in the chart above are annual per capita sums.

3. Relate the graph figures to the "revolution of rising expectations around the world." Where do people learn that they can live better than they have lived in the past? In what parts of the world are revolutions of this kind going on now? In what parts of the world have changes resulted from pressures on governments to improve conditions?

4. Relate this graph to the question of foreign aid. How does the United States appear to most of the world? What responsibilities do we have as a rich nation? What kinds of foreign aid are likely to help the people of a country most? What kinds of aid are likely to help them least?

5. Use the graph figures in discussing the appeals of communism. The standard of living of the people of the U.S.S.R. improved dramatically in a short span of time. How can the people of a poor country identify closely with the U.S.S.R.? How can the democracies offset this advantage of communism.

It is important to remember that a country like China or India should not be presented solely as a poverty-stricken nation. They are rich in culture, and their gifts to the world should not be overlooked.

219

PER CAPITA INCOME OF PEOPLE IN VARIOUS NATIONS

You may want to reproduce the following data on a large chart to hang in your classroom for study in a contemporary problems, world history, or world geography class. You may also want to rearrange it according to individual countries for quick reference. The figures are difficult to determine, but the general categories give an approximation of yearly, per capita income. Do not forget to point out that some persons earn far more than these amounts, and many earn far less.

United States	$3000
Canada	2000
United Kingdom, Switzerland, Sweden, Norway, Denmark, Austria	1000
Italy, West Germany, France, Belgium, Luxembourg, the Netherlands	800
U.S.S.R.	600
Argentina, Chile, Cuba, Cyprus, Israel, Panama, Puerto Rico (U.S.A.), Uruguay, Venezuela	750
Algeria, Brazil, British Guiana, Colombia, Dominican Republic, Malaysia, Hong Kong, Japan, Lebanon, Mexico, Mauritius, Portugal, Surinam	350
Cameroun, Ceylon, China (Taiwan), Congo, Ecuador, El Salvador, Gabon, Ghana, Jordan, Korea, Libya, Malagasy Republic, Morocco, Nicaragua, Paraguay, Peru, Philippine Islands, Rhodesia, Tunisia, United Arab Republic (Egypt)	100-250
Aden, Afghanistan, Angola, Bolivia, Burma, Cambodia, Central African Republic, Chad, Dahomey, Ethiopia, Gambia, Guinea, Haiti, India, Indonesia, Kenya, Laos, Liberia, Mali, Mauritania, Martinique, Mozambique, Nepal, Niger, Nigeria, Pakistan, Somalia, Sudan, Tanganyika, Thailand, Togo, Upper Volta, Viet Nam, Yemen	100 or under

Water as a World Problem

Five-sevenths of the world is water. You would think there would be enough for everyone, but ours is a thirsty world. Consider these questions about water with your class.

1. WHY IS OURS A THIRSTY WORLD? We cannot yet use salt water econom-ically. Some areas of the world lack sufficient water. There are increasing demands for water by individuals and, especially, by industries. The popula-tion of the world is increasing, so more people demand water.

2. FOR WHAT PURPOSES DO PEOPLE USE WATER? Personal uses: washing, bathing, drinking, other household uses, and as a source of home electricity. Industrial uses. Uses by society in groups—sewage disposal, recreation, etc.

3. WHAT ARE SOME EXAMPLES OF WATER AS A CAUSE OF CONFLICTS? In the United States, Pennsylvania, Delaware, and New York contest the limited water supply. Arizona, California, and Nevada have long debated the use of water in the Southwest. There are others. Use of the Jordan River in the Middle East. Conflicts between Pakistan and India over the Indus River and its five tributaries (in Kashmir).

4. WHAT ARE SOME EXAMPLES OF WORLD AREAS THAT NEED MORE WATER? Iran, Egypt, and Israel in the Middle East. Northeastern Brazil. Pakistan and India (see Point 3). Central areas of Australia. The United States (see Point 3).

5. WHAT ARE SOME OF THE MAJOR PROPOSALS FOR THE MORE EFFICIENT USE OF WATER? Keeping present bodies of water clean or purifying them. Diverting rivers—as in Australia—to desert areas. Controlling floods. Damming water for power and irrigation. Digging new and deeper wells. Re-using water—as in Los Angeles today. Increasing water supply in desert and semi-desert areas through irrigation and artificial rainmaking. Desalini-zation of sea water—"water factories," as in Kuwait. Planting fish in bodies of water and ducks in ponds.

6. WHAT GROUPS ARE POOLING IDEAS ABOUT THE USES OF WATER? Several agencies of government in the United States—cities, interstate organizations, U.S. Department of Agriculture. United Nations: UNESCO Arid Zones Project, Food and Agriculture Organization, World Meteoro-logical Organization, International Bank, and others.

7. WHERE ARE IRRIGATION AND POWER PROJECTS BEING DEVELOPED? In almost every country of the world. Many dams in the United States: TVA project, Hoover, Bonneville, etc. Scores of dams in the Soviet Union. High Aswan Dam in Egypt. Kariba Dam on Zambesi in North Rhodesia. Volta river project in Ghana. Owen Falls in East Africa. Many others.

8. WHY ARE DAMS SO IMPORTANT TO NATIONS? For recreation, irrigation, electric power, and as status symbols in today's world.

9. WHERE DO WE FIT INTO THIS PICTURE AS INDIVIDUALS? We must recognize the need for wise personal use of water. In New York City, each shower uses 30 gallons of water, each toilet flush, 3. Watering lawns, washing cars, etc., all use many more gallons.

Students should be aware of the public issues that pertain to water: taxation for water supplies and fluoridation of water for tooth protection are but two examples of citizen concern.

A SELECTED BIBLIOGRAPHY ON WATER

Obtain free copies of the Annual Reports of the U.S. Department of Agriculture and the International Bank for Reconstruction and Development.

BOOKS

1. Bauer, Helen. Water: Riches or Ruin. New York: Doubleday, 1959. 121 pp.
2. Carhart, Arthur. Water or Your Life. Philadelphia: Lippincott, 1951. 312 pp.
3. Graham, Edward H. Water for America. New York: Oxford, 1956. 111 pp.
4. Green, Ivah. Water: Our Most Valuable Natural Resource. New York: Coward-McCann, 1958. 96 pp.
5. Grosa, Leonard. "Water—The Problem That Needn't Be." Look Magazine, July 19, 1960.
6. Helfman, Elizabeth S. Water for the World. New York: Longmans, 1960. 213 pp.
7. Johnson, R. L. Water Problems of the Earth—Past and Present. New York: Geological Congress, 1960.
8. "Modern Pyramids." UNESCO Courier. August 1958. On dams. Profusely illustrated.
9. Riedman, Sarah. Water for People. New York: Schuman, 1952. 151 pp.
10. Water and the World Today: Its Use and Its Control. New York: United Nations, 1956. 32 pp. Through the U.N. bookstore.
11. White, Gilbert. Science and the Future of Arid Lands. UNESCO, 1960. 95 pp. 50¢. Through UNESCO publications.

FILMS AND FILMSTRIPS

1. "Man's Problem." Encyclopedia Britannica. 19 minutes. Color.
2. "Water." United Nations, through Center for Mass Communication of Columbia University Press. 15 minutes. Color.
3. "Water Resources: America Faces A New Problem." Current Affairs. (A filmstrip.) 35 frames. Free.

Land Tenure as a World Problem

People tend to think of disarmament, food and the population explosion, atomic energy, and other headline topics as the major problems of the world. Others are equally as important. Water, starting with clean water at the village well, is one of the world's chief worries. Land tenure is another.

Land tenure should be discussed in courses in economics, international relations, world history, and world geography, and in teaching current events in any social studies class.

The questions that follow and their accompanying notes may serve as an introduction to this topic. The bibliography is intended to help you and your students delve deeper into this basic world problem.

1. WHY IS LAND REFORM A MAJOR WORLD PROBLEM? Most of the world is still agricultural. Two-thirds of its people earn their living off the land. Parts of the world will become more industrial in the years ahead, a large segment will remain agricultural for a long time.

   Meanwhile, the population of the world is growing rapidly. Population estimates of the world in 2000 are around six billion persons. Even today, most of the world's people live on a meager and improper diet. Where will the food for the people of the future come from?

   The land of the world today is largely concentrated in the hands of a few persons. Sometimes the church owns large amounts of land. Sometimes the rulers own huge areas. Usually, a very small number of families own most of the land. In West of the Indus, William Douglas says 90 per cent of the land in the Sind area of Pakistan is owned by absentee landlords. Until recently, 94 per cent of the land in Egypt was owned in plots of five acres or less.

   The common people in many countries live much as they did in feudal times in Europe with no security of tenure. They often pay 50 to 70 per cent of the value of crops to landlords. They have no hope for the future, little or no education, no real incentives to produce more.

   Economically, present land-tenure practices are archaic; socially and politically, the situation is explosive.

2. WHY HASN'T LAND REFORM BEEN UNDERTAKEN THROUGHOUT THE WORLD? The status quo satisfies landowners. They are comfortable, see no need for change, and fear that change would be harmful to them.

   The landowners are in control politically. They intend to see that changes are not made, often allying themselves with the army to prevent radical changes.

   Too often Communists have been the only ones to demand radical reforms; therefore, anyone supporting reform is automatically communistic in the opinion of landowners and their allies.

223

3. HOW HAS LAND REFORM COME ABOUT? Many countries, including England and other European nations, began land reforms in the 18th and 19th centuries. The United States, of course, had more land available than these nations and offered it to the people at relatively low prices—through the Homestead Act, for example. Landed estates in the South were divided after the Civil War. Aid to farmers came under New Deal legislation. Today, in the United States, about three-fourths of the farms are owned in whole or in part by the persons tilling the soil.

Many other countries have recently instigated land reform. Mexico and Bolivia have programs that are among the most drastic. MacArthur began a system in Japan in 1946 that continued to be worked out in the years of American occupation.

Russia made startling changes after the 1917 Revolution. China has changed its land system under the Communists as has Formosa under Chiang Kai-shek. Egypt, Syria, Iran are examples of Middle East nations that have altered their land tenure. Kenya has consolidated fragmented land ownership and has brought about reforms in parts of the white highlands.

4. WOULDN'T LAND REFORM DEPRESS PRODUCTION AND FURTHER FRAGMENT THE LAND? Not necessarily; in Egypt, for example, it did not. Of course, land reform needs to be accompanied by agricultural education, by better seed, fertilizers, improvement of soil, etc.

Because of small plots of land, nations may need to turn to collective or cooperative farming. (To expect to have the large, individually owned farms of the United States is unrealistic.) Most countries are turning to farm cooperatives, with government assistance.

5. ISN'T GOVERNMENT INTERFERENCE UNJUST TO LANDLORDS? In current reforms, the government compensates the landlords and aids new owners with loans, both over a period of years.

A BRIEF BIBLIOGRAPHY

1. American Academy of Political and Social Science. "Agrarian Societies in Transition." The Annals, May 1958.
2. Land Reform: Defects in Agrarian Structure as Obstacles to Economic Development. New York: United Nations, 1951. 101 pp.
3. Mallory, Lester D. The Land Problem in the Americas. Washington: Government Printing Office, 1960. 17 pp. 10¢.
4. U.S. Department of State. Land Reform: A World Challenge. Washington: Government Printing Office, 1952. 81 pp. 20¢.
5. Senior, Clarence. Land Reform and Democracy. Gainesville, Fla.: University of Florida Press, 1958. 269 pp. On Latin America.
6. Gore, R. P. Land Reform in Japan. New York: Oxford University Press, 1959, 510 pp.

Illiteracy as a World Problem

Nearly half of the world's people are illiterate. Nearly half of the adults cannot read or write in any language, and nearly half of the children never attend school. There are more than 700 million men and women over 15 years of age who do not have these essential tools for living in today's world.

Figures on individual countries make these generalizations even more real. For example, here are the illiteracy figures for 1963 in six countries of Latin America.

Haiti	90%	Ecuador	44%
Peru	58%	Mexico	23%
Brazil	51%	Cuba	22%

Even more staggering figures could be presented for large parts of Africa, the Middle East, and Asia.

The chart below illustrates the world picture of illiteracy in the 1960s, taken from the statistics of UNESCO (the United Nations Educational, Scientific, and Cultural Organization):

KEY TO MAP

- 0-10% Are Unable to Read and Write
- 10-20% Are Unable to Read and Write
- 20-50% Are Unable to Read and Write
- 50-100% Are Unable to Read and Write

Source: UNESCO

Even more frightening is the fact that the number of illiterates in the world is growing from 20 to 25 million a year, despite heroic efforts of national governments, the United Nations, and scores of private organizations.

In the world of yesterday, illiteracy was not a major "crime." Today, it is. As Renee Mahieu, the Director-general of UNESCO, has pointed out, " . . . in our era of unprecedented advances in science and technology, millions of men and women are condemned to live on the fringes of modern civilization." They have to eke out their existence rather than enjoy their lives. They are the victims, in most cases, of the more powerful and, often, the more unscrupulous. They are placed, by virtue of their illiteracy, in the category of the ill-fed, ill-housed, ill-clothed, and ill.

Their nations and the international community are also cheated because illiterate individuals cannot contribute as much to the economic and social growth of the world as they would if they were educated. Economists and national planners are beginning now to see the relationship between education and national development. Denmark, Israel, and Switzerland are prime examples of nations with limited resources and educated citizens. Other nations could enjoy the higher standards of these small countries if they could develop more and better education for their people.

While students should recognize the importance of education to individuals and to nations, they should not be encouraged to believe that "illiteracy" and "ignorance" are necessarily synonymous. There are many people in the world today who cannot read and write but who, nevertheless, possess a great deal of wisdom and skill, and function with great ability in the framework of their developing nations. However, as the world continues to industrialize and develop, education becomes more and more a prerequisite for living in contemporary society.

Students should also learn of the great passion for education around the world. Seeing good schooling as a key to a better future, millions of persons on our globe are willing to make almost any sacrifice to obtain an education.

Students should understand these and allied facts and relate them to the question of foreign aid, the role of the United Nations and its specialized agencies, the number of foreign students in this country, the Peace Corps, the predominance of college and university students in movements for reform within many countries, and a host of other contemporary situations.

And students should know about some of the efforts to develop education for children and adults in almost every part of the world, as carried on by national governments, private organizations, and parts of the United Nations: UNESCO, the World Bank, and Sunfed. At the nub of the problem, one finds the lack of trained teachers all over the globe.

The following brief, inexpensive publications (obtainable from the UNESCO Publications Center, 317 East 34th Street, New York, N.Y.) should be helpful as background for you and your students:

1. Africa Calls. Paris: UNESCO, 1961. 50 pp.
2. Asia, Arab States, Africa: Education and Progress. Paris: UNESCO, 1961, 112 pp.
3. Educational Planning. Paris: UNESCO, 1965. 28 pp.
4. "Illiteracy—Challenge of Our Century." UNESCO Courier. October 1964.

Food and People as a World Problem

Will there be "standing room only" on our planet in a short time? Must a large part of the world's people starve? In stark and simplified form, these are two of the most fundamental questions that face humanity today and will be increasingly serious in the future. No high school student should complete a program in the social studies without taking a deep look at the two interrelated problems those questions pose.

Today, there are over three billion humans on this planet; by the year 2000, there will be somewhere between five and six billion if today's calculations are correct. Every day, there are nearly 175,000 more mouths to feed—each year, approximately 63,000,000 more people to provide for.

And these figures affect not only areas with large populations already, like China and India, but our own country as well.

According to the Food and Agricultural Organization of the United Nations, one-half of the world's population lives in a state of hunger from birth to death. Another one-quarter is undernourished. Stated positively, only one-quarter of today's people has enough to eat.

The daily caloric intake of various countries in a recent year follows:

3000 or over:	Canada, the United States, Denmark, Finland, Iceland, Ireland, Norway, Sweden, Switzerland, United Kingdom, Australia, and New Zealand.
2800 to 2999:	Belgium, Luxembourg, the Netherlands.
2600 to 2799:	Cuba, Argentine, Austria, France, Western Germany, Czechoslovakia, Poland, Turkey.
2400 to 2599:	Egypt, Republic of South Africa, Uruguay, Cyprus, Greece.
2200 to 2399:	Brazil, Chile, Colombia, Italy.
2000 to 2199:	Japan, Pakistan, countries of former Indochina.
Under 2000:	India, Burma, Ceylon.

You might ask your students the following questions:

1. Why is the population outstripping the food supply?
2. Why do some authorities say it is impossible to close the gap between food and population?
3. Why do other authorities say that the gap can be closed?
4. What very small changes would make a difference in the food supply?

227

5. What more basic changes would increase the foold supply?
6. What are some of the groups (governmental and nongovernmental, national and international) that are interested in these problems?
7. What are some nations and organizations doing about the control of population?
8. What difficulties do advocates of population control encounter?
9. What are some of the predictions about the sources of food in the future?
10. Why do these two problems concern people in the United States?

Students should be given some time in and out of class to read and take notes on the basis of these ten questions (or any similar list). Then they will be ready for lively discussions in depth, based on fact rather than fancy. You should guide and moderate the discussion.

To help you and your students prepare for such discussions, here is a list of pamphlets, paperbacks, and hardcover books on the subject.

BIBLIOGRAPHY ON FOOD AND PEOPLE

Some helpful material may be obtained free or inexpensively from:

Food and Agricultural Organization, 1325 C Street, S.W., Washington 25 D.C.
Population Reference Bureau, 1507 M Street, N.W., Washington 5, D.C.

PAMPHLETS AND PAPERBACKS

1. Barrett, Donald N. The Problem of Population: Moral and Theological Considerations. Notre Dame, Ind.: University of Notre Dame Press, 1964. 161 pp.
2. Bates, Marston. Expanding Population in a Shrinking World. New York: Public Affairs Committee, 1963. 32 pp.
3. Cipolla, Carlo M. The Economic History of World Population. Baltimore: Penguin, 1962. 126 pp.
4. Food for Life - Food for Thought. Dobbs Ferry, New York: Oceana, 1962. 125 pp. A study guide.
5. Hauser, Philip M., ed. The Population Dilemma. Englewood Cliffs, N.J.: 1965. 187 pp. Report of the American Assembly.
6. McLaughlin, Kathleen. The World's War on Want. Dobbs Ferry, New York: Oceana, 1961. 80 pp. A study guide.
7. Malthus, Thomas, Julian Huxley, and Fairfield Osborn. Three Essays on Population. New York: New American Library, 1960. 144 pp.
8. Osborn, Frederick. This Crowded World. New York: Public Affairs Committee, 1960. 28 pp.
9. Sax, Karl. Standing Room Only: The World's Exploding Population. Boston: Beacon, 1960. 206 pp.
10. Stewart, Maxwell S. That No Man Shall Hunger. New York: Public Affairs Committee, 1960. 20 pp.
11. The World Must Eat - Problems of Food and Population. Dobbs Ferry, New York: Oceana, 1962. 63 pp. A study guide.
12. Wrong, Dennis H. Population and Society. New York: Random House, 1961. 134 pp.

EASY BOOKS FOR STUDENTS

1. Hyde, Margaret O. This Crowded Planet. New York: Whittlesey, 1961. 160 pp. Grades 5-8.
2. Joy, Charles R. Race Between Food and People: The Challenge of a Hungry World. New York: Coward-McCann, 1961. 121 pp. Grades 6-9.
3. Orr, John B. The Wonderful World of Food. New York: Doubleday, 1958. 69 pp. Grades 6-9.

Prejudice as a World Problem

In the United States, we are faced today with many problems of prejudice, especially toward Negroes. In some respects, our country is like a volcano, long inactive but now erupting.

Without letting its universality lessen our concern over prejudice at home, we ought to see that prejudice is a persistent problem, taking different forms in different places and in different periods of history.

Here are a few examples of prejudice in the world today. Others can easily be added.

1. Restrictions in Australia against the immigration of Asians.
2. Restrictions in England against people from the West Indies, India, and Pakistan. These restrictions have been placed upon immigration only in the last few years.
3. Prejudice in Ceylon against the Tamils, recent immigrants from India. Language is one of the most obvious issues over which the Ceylonese are fighting.
4. Prejudice in India against people of lower castes, particularly the outcastes, although the antagonisms have lessened in recent years.
5. Prejudice in Korea against Koreans who have lived in Japan.
6. Prejudice in some parts of Latin America against the Indians.
7. Tensions in Canada between the English-speaking majority and the French-speaking minority.
8. Prejudice in many parts of the world (including Russia) against Jews.
9. Prejudice in Southeast Asia against the Chinese minority.
10. Tensions between tribes in many parts of Africa. As George H. T. Kimble phrased it in an article recently in the New York Times magazine section, "Racialism is an African sickness, too."

Usually prejudice militates against a minority and the phrase "minority problems" is often used in discussions of racial tension. But the prejudice may be against a majority as it is in South Africa, where the Africans, the "coloureds," and the Asians constitute a large nonwhite majority.

Sometimes prejudice is directed against people because of their religion. The outstanding example of this form of prejudice occurred in 1947 and 1948 in India and Pakistan when 15 million persons fled over the borders in the period of rioting between the Moslems, the Sikhs, and the Hindus. This is the largest mass migration in the history of the world.

Sometimes prejudice is based on socio-economic grounds and color is not always involved in these cases.

Often there is prejudice between the city and the country people of a nation or between the people of two or more regions.

You may want to explore with your classes other forms of prejudice in the world today or in the past.

This topic of prejudice could form an entire unit in classes in problems of democracy or contemporary problems. After a brief overview of the unit, individuals or groups of pupils could explore specific instances of prejudice in a given country or groups of countries.

A unit of this sort should search out the causes of prejudice. Gordon Allport's volume on The Roots of Prejudice might serve as the basis of such a study.

Some attention should also be given to the progress that has been made—as in the United States and in India.

Teachers should keep this problem in mind as it arises in various places and periods of history while teaching world geography, world history, and United States history.

A few references for teachers and good high school readers follow:

1. Allport, Gordon W. The Nature of Prejudice. Garden City, N.Y.: Doubleday, 1958. 496 pp. A paperback.
2. Barron, Milton, ed. American Minorities. New York: Knopf, 1957. 518 pp.
3. Frazer, Franklin E. Race and Culture Contacts in the Modern World. New York: Knopf, 1957. 338 pp.
4. Lind, Andrew W. Race Relations in World Perspective. Conference on Race Relations in World Perspective. Honolulu: University of Hawaii Press, 1955. 488 pp.
5. Rose, Arnold, ed. Race Prejudice and Discrimination. New York: Knopf, 1951. 605 pp.
6. Murphy, Gardner. In the Minds of Men. New York: Basic Books, 1953. 306 pp. A study of tensions between groups in India, conducted by UNESCO.
7. Wagley, Charles, and Marvin Harris. Minorities in the New World: Six Case Studies. New York: Columbia University Press, 1958. 320 pp. Discusses the Indians in Brazil and in Mexico, the Negro in Martinique and in the United States, and the French-Canadians and the Jews in the United States.
8. Wirth, Louis. "The Problem of Minority Groups," in Ralph Linton's The Science of Man in the World Crisis. New York: Columbia University Press, 1949. 532 pp.

See also the booklets in the UNESCO series on The Race Question, several of which are still available from the UNESCO Publications Center, 317 East 34th Street, New York, N.Y.

Atomic Energy for Peaceful Purposes

Most people have at least a vague idea of the destructive power of atomic energy used in atomic or nuclear bombs. This power was dramatically demonstrated when the bombs were dropped on Hiroshima and Nagasaki during World War II. Fewer people realize the tremendous possibilities of atomic energy for peaceful purposes—in agriculture, industry, medicine— especially as power.

Already the world has turned atomic energy and radio isotopes to a wide array of uses. Within a few years, this new source of energy will undoubtedly alter our world radically. Atomic energy is, therefore, an important topic for social studies classes in secondary schools.

In teaching about this phenomenon, you may want to start with the destructive power of atomic energy. Then you can pass quickly to the question of whether similar power can be and is being used for peaceful purposes.

For students who know very little about atomic energy, you (or a science-minded student) should describe, as simply as possible, the way in which atomic energy works. Show that atoms are so small that no one has ever seen one. An ordinary drop of water, for example, contains six sextillion atoms, represented by the figure:

6,000,000,000,000,000,000,000

Placing that figure on the board will certainly dramatize the size of atoms. Within such atoms are three components—protons, neutrons, and electrons, usually symbolized by these three signs:

 PROTON | NEUTRON | ELECTRON

Everything that we know in nature contains atoms, but uranium contains more protons, neutrons, and electrons than other materials and breaks into fragments more easily than other materials when a single neutron is added to the atom's center. Therefore, uranium is used as the basis for producing atomic energy. An added neutron is the "trigger" or "match" that starts fission. The process of reforming or regrouping releases tremendous power— atomic energy. The energy in one pound of uranium can produce as much electricity as 3,000,000 pounds of coal!

Students should know that the possibilities for the peaceful uses of atomic energy are more than dreams; they are present-day realities. Electricity produced by atomic energy is now being used in Boston, Chicago, New York, Pittsburgh, and other cities. Several freighters are now driven by atomic energy. An automatic weather station operates with atomic power in the Arctic. On the floor of the ocean, atomic-powered earthquake-recording devices are currently at work. Atomic energy is also being used to harden softwoods and thus to augment the dwindling supply of hardwood timber. And it is being used in experiments to desalt ocean water as a potential source of fresh water for the world.

One of the most practical uses of atomic energy is the use of isotopes as tracers and measuring devices in industry. For example, when transporting different grades of oil across the United States by pipe, the same pipelines can be used by placing an interface of a radioactive isotope between the different grades of oil. Operators on the receiving end of the pipeline can determine (with Geiger counters) when a certain type of oil has arrived at a given point.

The irradiation of foods, which will keep foods fresh for long periods of time without refrigeration, is also under way. This may revolutionize the food industry around the globe.

Atomic power is of special interest to countries that do not have adequate supplies of coal, oil, and water: India, Pakistan, and other countries in Asia. Although atomic power for homes and factories is still expensive, its costs can be reduced in the future so that they may be less than the costs of importing fossil fuels in many nations.

Industrially advanced nations are also interested in atomic power. The U.S.S.R. is intrigued with its power possibilities for the region east of the Urals, where coal is expensive because deep mining is necessary. England is vitally interested in this new source of energy and forging ahead in its use in case its oil supplies in the Middle East should be cut off.

The United States is also concerned with the power possibilities of atomic energy, and we are building many atomic energy plants. It is estimated that by the year 2000 we will need eight to ten times our present supply of electricity. Atomic energy seems to be the best possible source of that supply. Right now, we are interested primarily in "intermediate" plants called "advanced converters," which are very efficient in breeding only the fuel they can burn. Other countries are presently concerned with "breeder" plants.

In the United States, the Atomic Energy Act of 1954 established an Atomic Energy Commission, which licenses and sells materials to private plants, runs the federally owned plants, and sells materials to foreign firms and governments. This Commission oversees all our efforts regarding atomic energy.

The European Nuclear Energy Commission carries on similar activities for several countries in that part of the world.

The United Nations is also concerned with the peaceful uses of atomic power and energy and organized its own International Atomic Energy Agency in 1957.

You and your students can obtain more information on this topic by consulting the Reader's Guide to Periodical Literature for articles, and by contacting the following sources:

1. Con Edison, 4 Irving Place, New York, N.Y.
2. Department of Public Information, U.S. Atomic Energy Commission, Washington 25, D.C.
3. School Service, Westinghouse Electric Corporation, 401 Liberty Avenue, Pittsburgh 30, Pa.

Urbanization as a World Problem

Some high school students are aware of the increasing urbanization of the United States, but few of them know that this is a worldwide phenomenon of our time. In almost all parts of the world, people are moving to the cities. This is true in Africa, Asia, the Middle East, and Latin America as well as in Europe and in North America. It is true in the new or developing nations as well as in the older industrialized countries.

The most highly urbanized part of the world is Oceania (Australia and New Zealand). In Australia, at least a third of the population live in the two cities of Sydney and Melbourne; well over half of the citizens live in five major cities. In the United States today, nearly 70 per cent of our people may be classed as urban dwellers. Forty-six per cent of the population of Latin America now live in cities with 25 per cent concentrated in ten metropolitan areas that have one million or more. In Argentina, 67 per cent live in cities, in Chile 66 per cent, in Venezuela 60 per cent, and in Colombia 48 per cent. In Uruguay 40 per cent of the citizens live in the capital city of Montevideo.

A look at the 19 largest cities of the world may be surprising to some readers—and to their students. Here are those 19 metropolitan centers with their populations in 1963:

Tokyo, Japan	8,300,000	Cairo, Egypt	3,300,000
London, England	8,200,000	Tientsin, China	3,200,000
New York, U.S.A.	7,800,000	Berlin, Germany	3,200,000
Shanghai, China	7,000,000	Osaka, Japan	3,000,000
Moscow, U.S.S.R.	5,000,000	Buenos Aires,	
Mexico City,		Argentina	3,000,000
Mexico	4,800,000	Calcutta, India	2,900,000
Peking, China	4,000,000	Leningrad, U.S.S.R	2,800,000
Bombay, India	4,000,000	Paris, France	2,800,000
São Paulo, Brazil	3,700,000	Los Angeles, U.S.A.	2,500,000
Chicago, U.S.A.	3,500,000		

According to population experts, the rate of increase in our cities will accelerate in the coming years. Here are their figures for the percentage of people living in cities at 50-year intervals from 1800 until the present, with their "guesstimates" for the period between now and 2050:

	Percentage in Cities of 20,000 or over	Percentage in Cities of 100,000 or over
1800	2.4	1.7
1850	4.3	2.3
1900	9.2	5.5
1950	20.9	13.1
2000	40	25
2050	90	50

One way to introduce this topic in your classes would be to have the pupils list the ten largest cities of the world in order of size today. Then compare their ideas with the facts. This ought to develop to an interesting discussion on the world's cities. From that, you could go on to the reasons why people are moving to the cities and the problems of cities everywhere.

Or you might present your students with the statistics on cities given on the previous page asking why these cities are so big, and why almost all of them are getting bigger.

At this point, you could draw a magnet on the board to represent the cities of our planet. Ask the reasons these magnets are attracting so many people. The reasons might be grouped under two headings—those that "push" people to the cities and those that "pull" them to the cities. Among the points you may discover are these.

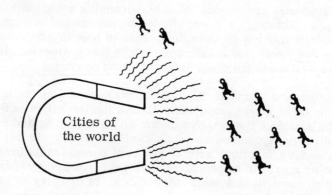

Cities of the world

"Pulling" people to the cities

1. More and varied jobs
2. Higher wages
3. Greater variety of people
4. More and better schools
5. More and better health facilities
6. More amusements and cultural facilities
7. The lure of the "bright lights"

"Pushing" people to the cities

1. Poverty
2. Less need for workers
3. Loneliness

Some problems are common to all the big metropolitan areas. You may want to discuss these:

1. Housing.
2. Transportation.
3. Government services, including health, education, parks and playgrounds, etc.
4. Water.
5. Crime.
6. Mental health, especially where changes have occured in value systems.
7. Taxation.

Your discussion should include the new cities of Brazilia in Brazil, Allahabad in Pakistan, Chandigarh in India, Tema in Ghana, and a few others. Most of these result from new governments.

New Nations and Their Problems

Since World War II, 56 nations have been formed—a fact that most people have not yet grasped. The effects of these new nations are staggering to the imagination, ranging from shifts in power inside the United Nations to changes in the world economy. Surely this is a part of recent history that needs to be studied by all students, whether in world history, world geography, problems of democracy, contemporary problems, or in other places in the curriculum.

Fourteen of the new nations are Asian: North and South Vietnam, Cambodia, Ceylon, Burma, India, Indonesia, North and South Korea, Laos, Malaysia, Pakistan, the Philippines, and Western Samoa.

Six have been established in the Middle East and Mediterranean area: Cyprus, Israel, Jordan, Kuwait, Syria, and the United Arab Republic.

Thirty-four have been formed in Africa: Algeria, Burundi, Chad, the Central Africa Republic, the Congo and the Congo Republic, Cameroun, Dahomey, Gabon, Gambia, Ghana, Guinea, Ivory Coast, Kenya, Libya, Malagasy, Mali, Mauretania, Malawi, Morocco, Niger, Nigeria, Rhodesia, Ruanda, the Somali Republic, Senegal, Sierre Leone, Sudan, Tanzania, Togo, Tunisia, Uganda, Upper Volta, and Zambia.

Two have appeared in the Caribbean: Jamaica, and Trinidad-Tobago.

Pupils will want to know <u>why</u> these new nations formed. The basic answer is that men everywhere want to be free to govern themselves as they choose. Furthermore, the idea of the white man's infallibility and innate superiority was smashed, starting around 1900. Many small nations were promised their independence in the diplomacy surrounding World War II. And, of course, the example provided by early independents—India and Ghana—encouraged other nations to pursue the same course. Perhaps you and your students will think of other factors.

Pupils will surely ask whether the new nations were ready for independence. The answer, in brief, is that no group of people is ever fully ready for independence but it must learn to be independent. In some places, the preparation for independence was better than in others: notably in the English colonies as opposed to the Dutch or Portuguese possessions. Was the United States ready for independence in 1776? Let your students ponder that question. (See Background Paper No. 63.)

In discussing the new nations, there are a number of common problems you will probably want to discuss. Among them are these.

1. Guerrilla or rebel bands within a country.
2. Inadequate transportation.
3. Inadequate communication, including the problem of a national language.
4. Poor agriculture.
5. Little industrialization.
6. Lack of capital for agriculture, industrialization, etc.

7. Determining the form of government (centralized versus decentralized) and the type of democracy.
8. Poor public health. The need for a "sanitation revolution."
9. Inadequate training of government officials.
10. Lack of education or improper type of education from days of colonialism.
11. Integration of "minority groups" or ethnic groups.
12. Care of refugees.
13. Raising the standards of living.
14. Relation of central government to tribal groups.
15. Social erosion, especially with urbanization.
16. Foreign relations.

This list, in either its present or a revised form, could be used in conjunction with the study of several of the new nations. Or it could be used as a part of an introduction to the study of new nations as a group. It should be used often enough by students as a check list to become a part of their thinking about new nations.

The literature on new nations has become extensive. It includes books and other materials on the new nations as a whole, on the new nations of a given cultural or geographical area, and on individual nations. Here are some of the general volumes on new nations as a group.

1. Alderfer, Harold F.   Local Government in Developing Countries. New York: McGraw-Hill, 1964. 251 pp.
2. Bauer, Peter T., and Basil S. Yamey.   The Economics of Under-Developed Countries. Chicago: University of Chicago Press, 1962. 261 pp.
3. Council on World Tensions.   Restless Nations: A Study of World Tensions and Developments. New York: Dodd, 1962. 204 pp.
4. Dean, Vera.   The Nature of the Non-Western World. New York: New American Library, 1963. 311 pp. A Mentor paperback.
5. Department of State.   Profiles of Newly Independent States. Washington: Government Printing Office, 1963. 26 pp. 25¢.
6. Deutsch, Karl W., and William J. Foltz.   Nation-Building. New York: Atherton, 1963. 167 pp.
7. Emerson, Rupert.   From Empire to Nation: The Rise to Self-Assertion of Asian and African Peoples. Cambridge, Mass.: Harvard University Press, 1960. 466 pp.
8. Kenworthy, Leonard S.   Leaders of New Nations. New York: Doubleday, 1959. 356 pp. The stories of the formation of 14 nations through the lives of their first heads of government. Grades 9-12.
9. Mair, Lucy.   New Nations. Chicago: University of Chicago Press, 1963. 253 pp.
10. Millikan, Max F., and Donald L. M. Blackmer. The Emerging Nations: Their Growth and United States Policy. Boston: Little, 1961. 171 pp.
11. Rossi, Mario.   The Third World. New York: Funk, 1963. 209 pp.
12. Sigmund, Paul E., Jr., ed.   The Ideologies of the Developing Nations. New York: Praeger, 1963. 326 pp. An anthology of statements of leaders.
13. Spencer, Cornelia.   Claim to Freedom: The Rise of the Afro-Asian Peoples. New York: John Day, 1962. 190 pp. For grades 9-12.
14. Theobald, Robert.   The Rich and the Poor: A Study of the Economics of Rising Expectations. New York: Potter, 1960. 196 pp. Also in a paperback.
15. Ward, Barbara.   The Rich Nations and the Poor Nations. New York: Norton, 1962. 159 pp. Very readable.

Collective Bibliographies
of World Leaders

One of the best ways to arouse student interest in social studies is with biographies. They can also enrich the study by students already interested in this broad field.

In your work as a social studies teacher, you should refer often to biographies yourself and encourage your students to read them. Sometimes the students can give brief reports to the class on the reading they have done. Often, however, no reports are needed; the students will bring their new knowledge to class discussions.

Much of the biographical material on present-day leaders must come from current magazines and newspapers. (The New York Times prints each day one brief biography of a person in the news.) Clip and file articles of this sort.

In some cases, you will want to refer to full-length biographies of famous people. There are scores of such books.

But often, you or your students will want briefer accounts for a quick background fill-in. The books listed below deal with recent and contemporary figures. They are all collective biographies.

1. Ayling, S. E. Twelve Portraits of Power. London: Harrap, 1961. 312 pp. Contains chapters on Lloyd George, Ataturk, Lenin, Gandhi, Mussolini, Hitler, Churchill, Roosevelt, Stalin, Tito, Nasser, and Mao Tse-tung.

2. Alexander, Robert J. Prophets of the Revolution: Profiles of Latin American Leaders. New York: Macmillan, 1962. 322 pp. On Ordonez, Cardenas, Alessandri, de la Torre, Betancourt, Figueras, Marin, Estenssoro and Siles, Vargas, Peròn, Castro, and a general chapter.

3. Dean, Vera M. Builders of Emerging Nations. New York: Holt, 1961. 277 pp. Very brief accounts of Krushchev, Tito, Ataturk, Ben-Gurion, Nasser, U Nu, Nehru, Ayub Khan, Sukarno, Mao Tse-tung, Magsaysay, Bourguiba, Houphouet-Boigny, Nkrumah, Nyerere, Mboya, Castro, and Betancourt.

4. Donovan, Frank. Famous Twentieth Century Leaders. New York: Dodd, Mead, 1964. 160 pp. Sections on Sun Yat-sen, Chiang Kai-shek, Mao Tse-tung, Lenin, Stalin, Khrushchev, Mussolini, Hitler, Churchill, Franklin Roosevelt, and Gandhi.

5. Greenwald, Norman D. Portraits of Power. Cambridge, Mass.: Berkshire, 1961. 112 pp. Accounts of De Gaulle, MacMillan, Adenauer, Tito, Ben-Gurion, Nehru, de Valera, Franco, Ataturk, and Abubakar of Nigeria.

6. Italiaander, Rolf. The New Leaders of Africa. New York: Prentice-Hall, 1961. 306 pp. Includes accounts of Hassan and Mohammed V, Abbas, Bourguiba, Idris, Nasser, Abbud, Selassie, Mboya, Nyere, Welensky and Banda, Verwoerd, Scott, Kasavuba and Lumumba, Youlou, Ahidjo, Abubakar and Admadu, Olympia, Nkrumah, Houphouet-Boigny, Tubman, Touré, and Senghor.

7. Kenworthy, Leonard S. <u>Leaders of New Nations</u>. New York: Doubleday, 1959. 336 pp. Each of the men described was the first leader of his country and the accounts, therefore, stress the independence movement as well as the man who led it. Chapters on Bourguiba, Mohammed V, Nkrumah of Africa; Diem, Magsaysay, Nehru, U Nu, Rahman, Senanayake, Sukarno of Asia; and Hussein, Jinnah, and Nasser of the Middle East.

8. Kenworthy, Leonard S. <u>Twelve Citizens of the World</u>. New York: Doubleday, 1953. 286 pp. Representatives of various regions of the world and of various occupations. Chapters on Ralph Bunche, Pierre Ceresole, Gandhi, Kagawa, Nansen, Orr, Eleanor Roosevelt, Sarmiento, Schweitzer, Sun Yat-sen, Toscanini, and Mathilda Wrede.

9. Segal, Ronald. <u>African Profiles</u>. Baltimore: Penguin, 1962. 406 pp. Brief biographies of 68 of Africa's contemporary leaders from all parts of that continent. Available as a paperback book.

10. Stringer, William H. <u>Summit Roundup</u>. New York: Longmans, 1959. 202 pp. Profiles of 21 world leaders. Brief accounts of Eisenhower, Khrushchev, MacMillan, De Gaulle, Adenauer, Gomulka, Tito, Bourguiba, Nasser, Nkrumah, Ben-Gurion, U Nu, Sukarno, Garcia, Rahman, Kishi, Chiang Kai-shek, Spaak, Hammarskjöld, Nehru, and Diefenbaker.

11. Webb, Robert N. <u>Leaders of Our Time</u>. New York: Watts, 1964. 150 pp. Slightly easier reading than the other references in this bibliography. Suitable for junior high school or slow readers in high schools. Accounts of Adenauer, Ben-Gurion, Castro, De Gaulle, Kennedy, Khrushchev, MacMillan, Mao Tse-tung, Nasser, Nehru, Nkrumah, and U Thant.

OTHER BOOKS I HAVE FOUND USEFUL

12.

13.

14.

The United Nations: Aims

Your aims in teaching about the United Nations will depend upon several factors: the class, its abilities and interests; the work students have had previously on the United Nations; current developments in that organization and its agencies; and the time and materials at hand or easily available.

In planning the work you will do with your classes on the United Nations, you may want to think in terms of the following possibilities:

1. ITS PURPOSES. The aims of the United Nations are stated in the Charter as four: (a) "to save succeeding generations from the scourge of war," (b) "to reaffirm faith in fundamental human rights," (c) "to establish conditions under which justice and respect for the obligations arising from treaties and and other sources of international law can be maintained," and (d) "to promote social progress and better standards of life in larger freedom." Stated simply, the United Nations was established to help build a better world. A film about it says that it was formed "because people were ashamed of their past . . . and hopeful of their future."

2. ITS POWERS. One of the commonest mistakes in thinking and talking about the United Nations is to assume that it has tremendous power, similar to the powers of national governments. Actually, it has almost no power to enforce its actions. It chiefly recommends—and nations heed its recommendations only if their national governments want to act. Exceptions have been the use of the peace-keeping function in situations like the Palestine question, Korea, and the Congo. Even in these instances all nations did not choose to cooperate. Studies of the United Nation's power should include recognition of the veto power in the Security Council and the fact that all the major powers wanted it— and still want it—in case they have to use it. The shift in power from the Security Council to the General Assembly should be included under this general information. Some classes may want to discuss the question of whether the United Nations is gaining in power or not.

3. ITS PROGRAMS AND PROGRESS. This should be the heart of any teaching in secondary schools about the United Nations. Among the many topics to be studied are the following:

   a. Its peace-keeping actions.
   b. Its work with refugees.
   c. Its aid in the liquidation of colonialism and in aid to new nations.
   d. Its promotion of more and better food, more and better health, and improvements in living standards.
   e. Its work for women and children.
   f. Its work in education.
   g. Its work in the furtherance of human rights.

4. ITS PEOPLE.   There are several ways of handling this aspect of the United Nations. One is to study the founders; another is to study the Director-generals (Lie, Hammarskjöld, and Thant); a third is to study the Presidents of the General Assembly (representing all areas of the world); still another is to select a few of the agency heads (Chisholm, Orr, Huxley, etc.). You might also want to study the work of some of the field agents of the United Nations.

5. ITS PROBLEMS.   Just as families, communities, organizations, and nations have problems, so, too, does the United Nations. It is concerned with

    a. Membership, with special reference to China.
    b. Finding the best-qualified people for the Secretariat.
    c. Financing.
    d. The influence of the ''cold war'' on its agencies.
    e. Its lack of enforcement powers.
    f. Its size now, in comparison to the early days of the organization, with attendant problems.

6. ITS POTENTIALITIES.   Discuss the future of the United Nations with some students. Whether it should be given more power would be one question to consider. Whether it should become a world government would be another. No one can forecast the future, but students should wrestle with the question as to its future and its potentialities.

7. PERSPECTIVE.   Some students should compare the United Nations and its agencies with the League of Nations, discovering the strengths and weaknesses of the two world organizations. Some will want to see the United Nations in the perspective of history, as the present-day expression of man's efforts to achieve peace and justice. In this study, students should discover that the League of Nations was built on the premise that wars arose from political troubles—that peace could be attained by better political arrangements. The United Nations is much more broadly based, with emphasis upon the economic, social, and educational aspects of peace, as well as the political. For that reason, your students should carefully examine the Economic and Social Council.

The United Nations: Methods

A variety of methods can be used in teaching about the United Nations. Several of them are suggested below. From this list, you should be able to select one or more that fit the needs and interests of your class, your own teaching style, and the aims you have decided upon.

1. THE PROBLEMS APPROACH. One of the most provocative methods to use in studying about the United Nations is to have students suggest the major problems of the world today. Write them on the left-hand side of the chalk-board, quickly and without discussion. (As the teacher, you should have a list of your own in mind to help guide the class, but you should not put your own items on the board.) Then the class can discuss what the United Nations is doing about each of the problems. Opposite the problem, indicate the name of the particular agency that is dealing with it. A discussion of this sort could easily fill two or three class periods, especially if students individually investigated one or two of the problems, by outside reading, and reported their findings back to class. A flannelboard is another good method of illustrating how the United Nation's various agencies handle world problems. The value of either presentation, of course, is that it begins with the problems of the United Nations rather than with the structure.

2. CURRENT EVENTS. You can profitably discuss current happenings of the United Nations in classes, especially if students have already studied the entire United Nations "family" previously. The advantage to this approach is that these events are currently on television and in the newspapers. The disadvantage is that it pictures the United Nations largely as a place of controversy. In spite of this drawback, current events can be used to motivate a unit of work on the United Nations.

3. UNITS ON THE UNITED NATIONS AND ITS AGENCIES. All students in the social studies should study the United Nations and its agencies in a unit of two to three weeks of work somewhere in the secondary schools. References to the United Nations and to current happenings in that organization are fine, but they do not take the place of a full study in considerable depth.

4. STUDIES OF VARIOUS AGENCIES AND COMMISSIONS. In any unit on the United Nations, emphasize the positive achievements of the several agencies. Pupils can profitably study one of them in depth and report their findings in oral and/or written form. And all students should have some idea of the major work of the agencies and commissions. The work of the commissions for various parts of the world fit especially well into world geography and cultural area courses.

5. PREPARATION OF "POSITION PAPERS." Able students can be stimulated to excellent research and writing if they prepare "position papers." Have them act as a consultant on a world problem or area and advise the Director-general of the United Nations or one of its agencies on courses of action, giving reasons for their decisions.

6. THE WORK OF THE UNITED NATIONS AND ITS AGENCIES IN COUNTRIES. Students should learn about what the United Nations is doing in selected countries, especially in the "new nations." They should find out what various agencies are doing in that particular country. This can be included in world geography courses during the study of particular countries. In these courses, one or two students might do special research on the United Nation's program in that nation, rather than having all students do this work.

7. THE HISTORY OF THE UNITED NATIONS. In some courses, special attention may be given to the history of the United Nations as a part of man's long struggle to improve the world. This seems especially appropriate in courses in world history. A time-line, developed by one or two students, would help the entire class.

8. PANELS AND DEBATES. On most issues being considered by the United Nations and its agencies, panels seem preferable to this writer because several points of view can be presented and discussed. There are, however, a few issues on which debates can be arranged. One of these is the recognition of the Chinese Peoples Republic and its admission to the United Nations. All students need not take part in these panels and/or debates. However, the entire class will enjoy the discussions most when every member has read some background material on the subjects.

9. FILMS AND FILMSTRIPS. There are several films and filmstrips suitable for use in studying the United Nations and its agencies. The ten-minute film called "Overture" is especially good as a motivating experience. It consists of music and pictures without commentary and is an emotional experience for most viewers.

10. CHORAL SPEAKING. Some teachers may want to consider the use of choral speaking in connection with their study of the United Nations family. Parts of the preamble to the Charter of the United Nations, the Constitution of UNESCO, the Charter on Human Rights, and the Charter on Children can be used effectively in this way. This is an activity that is effective for assembly programs.

11. ACTION PROJECTS. Some students may want to take part in some one of the action projects of the United Nations, such as the UNESCO book-coupon scheme or the UNICEF Halloween trick or treat program.

12. MODEL OR MOCK ASSEMBLIES. Assemblies take a great deal of time and probably cannot be done in most classes effectively. However, they do provide invaluable learning experiences for those taking part. If you are interested in this approach, see the pamphlet issued by Oceana Press (Dobbs Ferry, N.Y.: 1961. 126 pp) on How to Plan and Conduct Model U.N. Meetings.

13. ROLE PLAYING. Class discussions on the United Nations and its agencies are improved if students try to think and talk as men and women from various countries of the world, playing the roles of these persons. This helps your students adopt an international, rather than a completely American, point of view.

In all studies of the United Nations in secondary schools, some attention should be given to structure. But structure should not be the starting point, and it should be subservient to the more important considerations of world problems and international achievements.

The United Nations: Resources

SOURCES OF INFORMATION

Department of Public Information, United Nations, New York, N.Y.
United Nations Association, 345 East 46th St., New York 17, N.Y.
United States National Commission for UNESCO, Department of State, Washington 25, D.C.

TEACHING ABOUT THE UNITED NATIONS

Kenworthy, Leonard S. Telling the U.N. Story: New Approaches to Teaching about the United Nations and Its Agencies. Paris: UNESCO, 1964. 166 pp. For teachers on methods. Available from Oceana, Dobbs Ferry, N.Y.

BOOKS (for adults and good secondary school readers)

1. Claude, Inis L., Jr., Swords Into Ploughshares: The Problems and Progress of International Organization. New York: Random House, 1956. 497 pp. Very well written, although difficult.
2. Courlander, Harold. Shaping Our Times: What the United Nations Is and Does. Dobbs Ferry, N.Y.: Oceana, 1960. 242 pp.
3. Eichelberger, Clark M. The U.N.: Its First Fifteen Years. New York: Harper, 1961. 147 pp. Also available as a paperback.
4. Meigs, Cornelia. The Great Design: Men and Events in the United Nations from 1945 to 1963. Boston: Little, 1964. 319 pp.
5. Morris, James. The Road to Huddersfield: A Journey to Five Continents. New York: Pantheon, 1963. 235 pp. An extremely well-written account of the International Bank for Reconstruction and Development.
6. Munro, Sir Leslie. United Nations: Hope for a Divided World. New York: Holt, 1960. 185 pp.
7. Shuster, George N. Unesco: Assessment and Promise. New York: Harper, 1963. 130 pp.
8. Theobald, Robert, ed. The U.N. and Its Future. New York: Wilson, 1963. 190 pp. A Reference Shelf volume, with short articles by many writers.

PAMPHLETS AND PAPERBACKS (for adults and good secondary school readers)

1. Bailey, Sydney D. The United Nations: A Short Political Guide. New York: Praeger, 1963. 141 pp.
2. Beckel, Graham. Workshops of the World: The Specialized Agencies of the United Nations. New York: Abelard, 1962. 285 pp. Grades 9-12.
3. Facts About the United Nations. New York: United Nations, 1964. 54 pp.
4. Calder, Ritchie. Growing Up With Unicef. New York: Public Affairs Committee, 1962. 20 pp.
5. Coyle, David C. The United Nations and How It Works. New York: Mentor, 1960. 222 pp. A good, brief account, with an overall view of the United Nations.
6. Coyle, David C. The United Nations—What It Does. New York: Public Affairs Committee, 1961. 28 pp.

7. Coyle, David C. The United Nations—What It Is. New York: Public Affairs Committee, 1961. 28 pp.
8. Energy and Skills for Human Progress. Dobbs Ferry, N.Y.: 1963. 101 pp. A discussion guide on the United Nations and its related agencies.
9. Hamilton, Thomas J. The United Nations in Crisis. New York: Foreign Policy Association, 1961. 62 pp. A Headline book.
10. Joyce, James A. World of Promise: A Guide to the United Nations Development Decade. Dobbs Ferry, N.Y.: Oceana, 1965. 162 pp.
11. McVane, John. The House That Peace Built—The United Nations. New York: Public Affairs Committee, 1964. 28 pp.
12. World Peace and the United Nations. Dobbs Ferry, N.Y.: Oceana, 1962. 112 pp.
13. Steinberg, Samuel. The United Nations Story. New York: Oxford, 1961. 76 pp. Written as a short text for secondary school students.

CURRENT PROBLEMS OF THE UNITED NATIONS

Each year the Carnegie Endowment for International Peace (United Nations Plaza at 46th St., New York 17, N.Y.) issues a pamphlet on the issues before the current session of the United Nations, entitled "Issues Before the . . . General Assembly." This is an excellent survey of issues to be dealt with in the sessions of the current year.

BOOKS (for younger readers or slower readers)

1. Epstein, Sam and Beryl. The First Book of the World Health Organization. New York: Watts, 1962. 82 pp. Grades 5-8.
2. Griffin, Ella. Getting to Know Unesco: How U.N. Crusaders Fight Ignorance. New York: Coward-McCann, 1962. 63 pp. Grades 5-8.
3. Hershey, Burnet. Dag Hammarskjöld: Soldier of Peace. Chicago: Britannica, 1961. 191 pp. Grades 6-9.
4. Hoke, Henry. The First Book of International Mail: The Story of the Universal Postal Union. New York: Watts, 1963. 40 pp. Grades 4-7.
5. Joyce, James A. The Story of International Cooperation. New York: Watts, 1964. 258 pp. Grades 7-10.
6. Levine, I. E. Champion of World Peace: Dag Hammarskjöld. New York: Messner, 1962. 190 pp. Grades 7-10.
7. Shippen, Katherine B. The Pool of Knowledge: How the United Nations Share Their Skills. New York: Harper, 1965. 99 pp. On technical assistance programs, with chapters on several areas of the world. Grades 6-9.

Abelard-Schuman, 6 West 57th St., New York, N.Y. 10019.

Abingdon Press, 201 Eighth Ave., South, Nashville, Tenn.

The American Academy of Political and Social Science, 3937 Chestnut St., Philadelphia, Pa. 19104.

American Book Co., 55 Fifth Ave., New York, N.Y. 10003.

American Geographical Society, Broadway at 156th St., New York, N.Y. 10032.

American Heritage Publishing Co., 551 Fifth Ave., New York, N.Y.

American Historical Review, Macmillan Co., Box 2-W, Richmond, Va.

Atheneum Publishers, 162 East 38th St., New York, N.Y. 10016.

Atherton Press, 70 Fifth Ave., New York, N.Y. 10011.

Basic Books, 404 Park Ave., South, New York, N.Y. 10016.

Beacon Press, 25 Beacon St., Boston 8, Mass.

Berkshire Publishing Co., 18 Brattle St., Cambridge 38, Mass.

Bobbs-Merrill Co., 4300 West 62nd St., Indianapolis, Ind. 46206.

Canadian Institute of International Affairs, Edgar Tarr House, 230 Bloor St., West, Toronto 5, Canada.

Capricorn. (See G. P. Putnam's Sons, Inc.)

Chanticleer Press, Inc., 424 Madison Ave., New York, N.Y. 10017.

Chilton Co., East Washington Square., Philadelphia, Pa.

P. F. Collier, Inc., 640 Fifth Ave., New York, N. Y. 10019.

Columbia University Press, 2960 Broadway, New York, N.Y. 10027.

Coward-McCann, Inc., 200 Madison Ave., New York, N.Y. 10016.

Thomas V. Crowell Co., 201 Park Ave., South, New York, N.Y. 10003.

Crown Publishers, 419 Park Ave., South, New York, N.Y. 10016.

Current History Events Publishing Co., 108 Walnut St., Philadelphia 6, Pa.

John Day Co., 200 Madison Ave., New York, N.Y. 10016.

Dodd, Mead and Co., 432 Park Ave., South, New York, N.Y. 10016.

Doubleday and Co., 575 Madison Ave., New York, N.Y. 10022.

Nelson Doubleday, 501 Franklin Avenue, Garden City, N.Y.

Duell, Sloan & Pearce, Inc., 119 West 40th St., New York, N.Y. 10018.

E. P. Dutton and Co., 201 Park Ave., South, New York, N.Y. 10003.

Encyclopaedia Britannica Press, 425 North Michigan Ave., Chicago, Ill. 60611.

Fideler Co., 31 Ottowa Ave., Northwest, Grand Rapids, Mich. 49502.

Follett Publishing Co., 1010 West Washington Blvd., Chicago, Ill. 60607.

Foreign Policy Association, 345 East 46th St., New York, N.Y. 10017.

The Free Press of Glencoe, Inc., 60 Fifth Ave., New York, N.Y. 10011.

Friendly House, Publishers, 65 Suffolk St., New York, N.Y. 10002.

Funk and Wagnalls Co., 360 Lexington Ave., New York, N.Y. 10017.

Garden City Books, Garden City, N.Y.

Garrard Publishing Co., 1607 North Market St., Champaign, Ill. 61820.

Geological Society of America, 419 West 117th St., New York, N.Y. 10027.

Ginn and Co., Statler Building, Boston, Mass. 02117.

Golden Press, Inc., 850 Third Ave., New York, N.Y. 10022.

Government Printing Office, Washington 25, D.C.

Grosset and Dunlap, Inc., 1107 Broadway, New York, N.Y. 10010.

C. S. Hammond and Co., 515 Valley St., Maplewood, N.J. 07040.

Harcourt, Brace & World, 757 Third Ave., New York, N.Y. 10017.

Harper & Row, Publishers, 49 East 33rd St., New York, N.Y. 10016.

Harper's Magazine, 49 East 33rd St., New York, N.Y. 10016.

George G. Harrap and Co., Ltd., 182 High Holborn, London, W.C. 1.

Harvard University Press, 79 Garden St., Cambridge, Mass.

D. C. Heath, 285 Columbus Ave., Boston, Mass. 02116.

Heritage Printer's, Inc., 510 West 4th St., Charlotte 2, N.C.

Hill and Wang, 141 Fifth Ave., New York, N.Y. 10010.

Holiday, Independence Square, Philadelphia 5, Pa.

Holiday House, 8 West 13th St., New York, N.Y. 10011.

Holt, Rinehart and Winston, 383 Madison Ave., New York, N.Y. 10017.

Houghton Mifflin, 2 Park St., Boston 7, Mass.

The John Hopkins Press, Baltimore 18, Md.

Alfred A. Knopf, 50 Madison Ave., New York, N.Y. 10022.

Laidlaw Brothers, Inc., Thatcher and Madison Sts., River Forest, Ill.
Life Magazine, 9 Rockefeller Plaza, New York, N.Y. 10020.

Little, Brown and Co., 34 Beacon St., Boston 6, Mass.

J. B. Lippincott Co., East Washington Square, Philadelphia, Pa. 19105.

Longmans, Green and Co., Ltd., 45 Grosvenor St., London. W. 1.

Look, 488 Madison Ave., New York, N.Y. 10022.

Macmillan & Co., 10 St. Martin's St., London, W.C. 2.

The Macmillan Co., 60 Fifth Ave., New York, N.Y. 10011.

Macrae Smith Co., Lewis Tower Bldg., 2225 South 15th St., Philadelphia 2, Pa.

McGraw-Hill Book Co., 330 West 42nd St., New York, N.Y. 10036.

Melmont Publishers, Inc., Jackson Blvd. & Racine Ave., Chicago, Ill. 60607.

Mentor Books, 1310 Ave. of the Americas, New York, N.Y. 10022.

Julian Messner, Inc., 8 West 40th St., New York, N.Y. 10018.

William Morrow and Co., Inc., 425 Park Ave., New York, N.Y. 10016.

National Council for the Social Studies, 1201 16th St., N.W., Washington, D.C.

National Geographic Society, 16th and M Sts., Northwest, Washington 6, D.C.

New American Library of World Literature, 501 Madison Ave., New York, N.Y. 10022.

W. W. Norton, 55 Fifth Ave., New York, N.Y. 10011.

A. N. Nystrom, 3333 Elston Ave., Chicago 16, Ill.

Odyssey Press, 850 Third Ave., New York, N.Y. 10022.

Oxford Book Co., 71 Fifth Ave., New York, N.Y. 10003.

Oxford University Press, 417 Fifth Ave., New York, N.Y. 10003.

Pan American Union, Washington 6, D. C.

Pantheon Books, 22 East 51st St., New York, N.Y. 10022.

Penguin Books, Library of World Literature, 3300 Clipper Mill Rd., Baltimore 11, Md.

Pocket Books, 630 Fifth Ave., New York, N.Y. 10013.

Popular Library, Inc., 355 Lexington Ave., New York, N.Y. 10017.

Clarkson N. Potter, Inc., 419 Park Ave., New York, N.Y. 10021.

Frederick A. Praeger, Inc., 64 University Place, New York, N.Y. 10003.

Premier Books, Fawcett World Library, 67 West 44th St., New York, N.Y. 10036.

Prentice-Hall, Inc., Englewood Cliffs, N.J. 07631.

Princeton University Press, Princeton, N.J.

G. P. Putnam's Sons, 200 Madison Ave., New York, N.Y. 10016.

Rand McNally and Co., Box 7600, Chicago 80, Ill.

Random House, Inc., 457 Madison Ave., New York, N.Y., 10022.

Reynal and Co., 425 Park Ave., South, New York, N.Y.

Ronald Press Company, 15 East 26th St., New York, N.Y. 10010.

Row, Peterson and Company. (See Harper & Row.)

Rutgers University Press, New Brunswick, N.J.

Scholastic Publications, 50 West 44th St., New York, N.Y. 10036.

Henry Schuman, Inc. (See Abelard-Schuman.)

Science Editions. (See John Wiley.)

Science Research Associates, Inc., 259 East Erie St., Chicago, Ill. 60611.

Scott, Foresman and Co., 433 East Erie St., Chicago, Ill. 60611.

Charles Scribner's and Sons, 597 Fifth Ave., New York, N.Y. 10017.

Service Center for Teachers of History, 400 A St. Southeast, Washington 3, D.C.

Signet Key Books. (See New American Library of World Literature, Inc.)

Simon and Schuster, Inc., 630 Fifth Ave., New York, N.Y. 10020.

Social Education, 1201 Sixteenth St., Northwest, Washington 6, D.C.

St. Martin's Press, 175 Fifth Ave., New York, N.Y.

Sterling Publishing Co., Inc., 419 Park Ave., South, New York, N.Y.

Syracuse University Press, Box 8, University Station, Syracuse 10, N.Y.

Time, Inc. Books, 540 North Michigan Ave., Chicago, Ill. 60611.

United Nations Association of the United States of America, 345 East 46th St., New York, N.Y. 10017.

Unesco Publications Center, 317 East 34th St., New York, N.Y.

University of Florida Press, 15 Northwest 15th St., Gainesville, Fla.

University of Chicago Press, 5750 Ellis Avenue, Chicago, Ill. 60637.

University of Hawaii Press, Honolulu 14, Hawaii.

University of Michigan Press, 615 East University Ave., Ann Arbor, Mich.

University of North Carolina Press, Chapel Hill, N.C.

University of Oklahoma Press, Faculty Exchange, Norman, Okla.

University of Pennsylvania Press, 3436 Walnut St., Philadelphia 4, Pa.

University of Wisconsin Press, 430 Sterling St., Madison 6, Wisc.

D. Van Nostrand Co., 120 Alexander St., Princeton, N.J.

Vanguard Press, Inc., 424 Madison Ave., New York, N.Y. 10017.

The Viking Press, 625 Madison Ave., New York, N.Y. 10022.

Vintage Book, Inc., 33 West 66th St., New York, N.Y. 10023.

Wadsworth Publishing Co., Inc., Belmont, Calif. 94002.

Henry Z. Walck, Inc., 19 Union Square, West, New York, N.Y. 10003.

Franklin Watts, Inc., 575 Lexington Ave., New York, N.Y. 10022.

Whittlesey House, 330 West 42nd St., New York, N.Y. 10036.

John Wiley & Sons, Inc., 605 3rd Ave., New York, N.Y. 10016.

H. W. Wilson and Co., 950 University Ave., New York, N.Y. 10052.

World Publishing Co., 2231 West 110 St., Cleveland 2, Ohio.

Yale University Press, 149 York St., New Haven, Conn., 06511.